Praise for *The Spine of the Continent*

"Throughout, Hannibal repeats the idea that everything in an ecosystem is connected. It's a seemingly simple concept, well-backed by research, and the author discusses how, in the long run, working for the preservation of even a single species links directly to larger issues such as climate change. . . . A fine overview of wide-angle environmentalism."

—*Kirkus Reviews*

"Few California urbanites have yet to hear of the extraordinary project Mary Ellen Hannibal describes in *The Spine of the Continent*, her enthusiastic, anecdotal, on-the-scenes account of a bold concept for protecting much of this continent's remaining animal life. . . . The so-called Spine is indeed alive: Grizzly bears to the north, jaguars to the south, and the habitats of caribou, elk, beaver, fox, mink, coyote, and more—all now in trouble where they remain and all to be protected by this initiative. The Bay Area writer seems to have seen them all during her many journeys into the wilderness with their fierce human protectors . . . there's plenty of science, plenty of history, and a powerful sense of place in her tale."

—*San Francisco Chronicle*

"I have never seen a grizzly bear, wolf, lynx, or mountain lion in the wild. But Mary Ellen Hannibal's description of a plan to allow these creatures to thrive outside captivity makes me want to drop everything and head West to help."

—*Cleveland Plain Dealer*

"This book will make you want to grow up to be a wildlife conservationist (even if you're already grown-up). It dazzles with its subtlety."

—*Sacramento Bee*

When you see the right thing to do, you'd better do it.

—Paul Newman

I can't go on, I'll go on.

—Samuel Beckett

THE SPINE OF THE CONTINENT

The Race to Save America's Last, Best Wilderness

MARY ELLEN HANNIBAL

LYONS PRESS
Guilford, Connecticut
An imprint of Globe Pequot Press

Project editor: Meredith Dias
Layout: Sue Murray

ISBN 978-0-7627-8678-7

Printed in the United States of America

10 9 8 7 6 5 4 3 2 1

The Library of Congress has previously catalogued an earlier (hardcover) edition as follows:

Library of Congress Cataloging-in-Publication Data

Hannibal, Mary Ellen.
 The spine of the continent : the most ambitious wildlife conservation project ever undertaken / Mary Ellen Hannibal.
   p. cm.
 Includes bibliographical references and index.
 ISBN 978-0-7627-7214-8
 1. Wildlife conservation—North America. 2. Wildlife conservation—Rocky Mountains Region.
 3. Wilderness areas—North America. 4. Wilderness areas—Rocky Mountains Region. I. Title.
 QH77.N56H36 2012
 639.9—dc23

                                                                                    2012020223

CONTENTS

Maps vi
Introduction xiii

PART I: AMERICA'S NEXT BEST IDEA
CHAPTER 1   Bear with Me 3
CHAPTER 2   They Paved Paradise. 19
CHAPTER 3   Reptile Brain 30
CHAPTER 4   The Disappearance 41
CHAPTER 5   A Science of Love and Death. 52
CHAPTER 6   The Real Work 61
CHAPTER 7   Triple Crown 72

PART II: CORES, CARNIVORES, AND CORRIDORS ON THE SPINE
CHAPTER 8   Leave It to Beaver. 91
CHAPTER 9   Holy Cow. 118
CHAPTER 10   Not Hunting .136
CHAPTER 11   Take It from the Top 149
CHAPTER 12   Wolf Sign. 162
CHAPTER 13   Borderline. 175
CHAPTER 14   There Ought to Be a Law 195

PART III: CONGRATULATIONS, YOU'VE WON CLIMATE CHANGE
CHAPTER 15   Picka Pika. 213
CHAPTER 16   Eyes in the Sky 232
CHAPTER 17   Welcome Home. 238

Endnotes. 249
Bibliography 257
Index 264
Acknowledgments 271

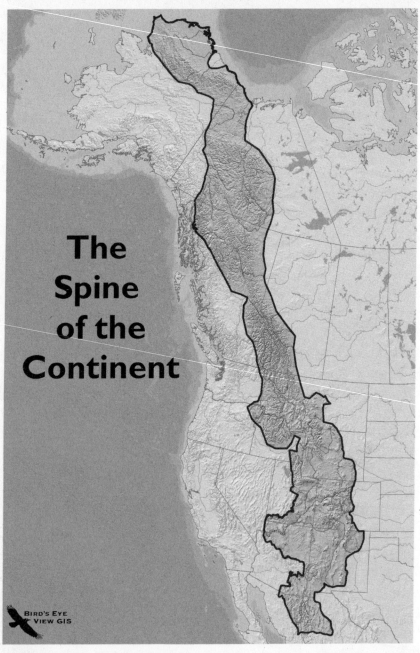

The Spine of the Continent

BIRD'S EYE VIEW GIS

A biotic conveyor belt by which both animals and humans first populated North America, the Rocky Mountains represent some of the most valuable wilderness we have left, allowing species the freedom of movement that is essential to healthy nature. This map was made by Kurt Menke, the official cartographer of the Spine of the Continent initiative. KURT MENKE, BIRDSEYEVIEW GIS. 2012.

PATH OF THE PRONGHORN

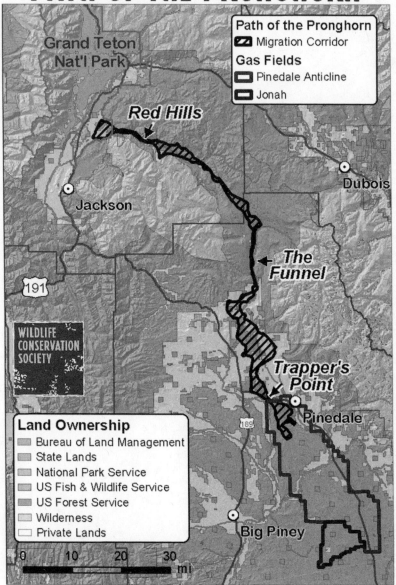

Path of the Pronghorn
- Migration Corridor

Gas Fields
- Pinedale Anticline
- Jonah

Grand Teton Nat'l Park

Red Hills

Jackson

Dubois

The Funnel

191

WILDLIFE CONSERVATION SOCIETY

Trapper's Point

Pinedale

Land Ownership
- Bureau of Land Management
- State Lands
- National Park Service
- US Fish & Wildlife Service
- US Forest Service
- Wilderness
- Private Lands

189

Big Piney

0   10   20   30
mi

The first and only protected animal movement corridor in the United States is the "Path of the Pronghorn," a migration route undertaken by a single herd of antelope for more than six thousand years. Achieved through collaboration among scientists, wildlife agency officials, grassroots organizers, and regular citizens, the Path of the Pronghorn is a model for how to move forward on connectivity protection.
BRIAN ERTZ, WESTERN WATERSHEDS PROJECT

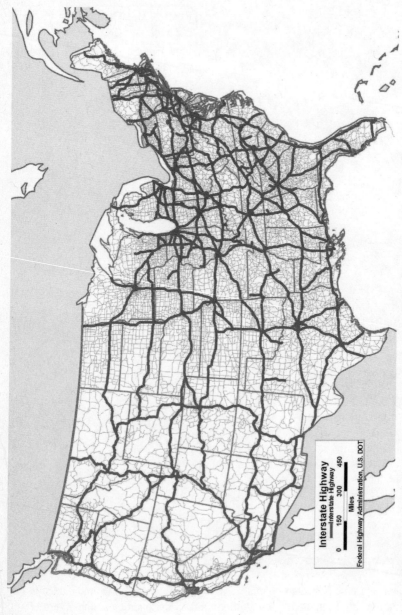

Interstate Highway
— Interstate Highway

Miles
0   150   300   450

Federal Highway Administration, U.S. DOT

The Interstate Highway System was officially initiated in 1956. The resulting network provides a means for the manifest destiny of human beings, but, when it comes to nature, our roadways are either interrupting the flow or cutting it into pieces. THE FEDERAL HIGHWAY ADMINISTRATION, US DEPARTMENT OF TRANSPORTATION

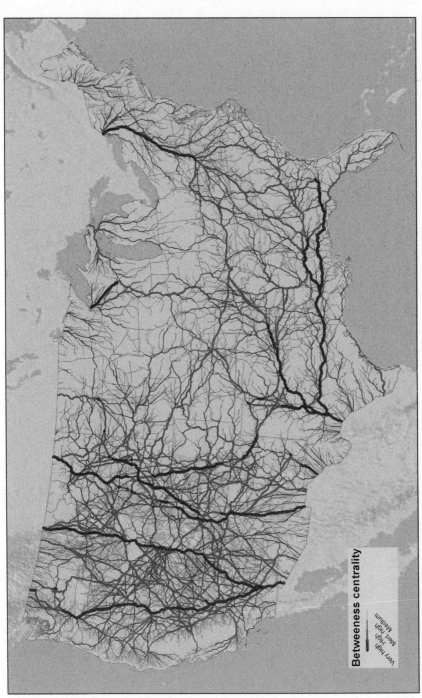

Betweeness centrality

Very high
High
Med.
Medium

By contrast, this map, which takes into account distance to roads, traffic volume, and housing density, expresses the pathways plants and animals could take on the landscape in order to renew their populations, to fulfill migrational imperatives, and to adapt to climate change. It was developed by David Theobald with Sarah Reed, Michael Soulé, and Kenyon Fields. DAVID THEOBALD, ET AL.

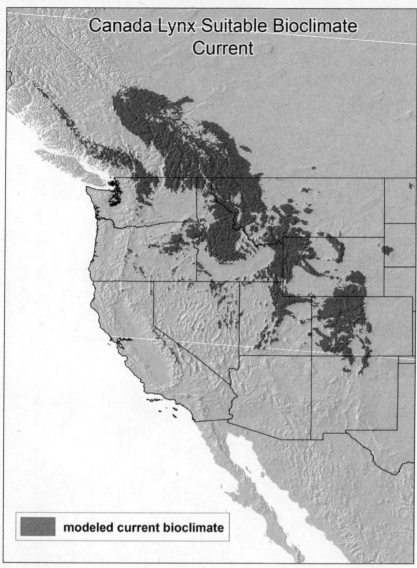

Canada Lynx Suitable Bioclimate
Current

modeled current bioclimate

To help state and federal land managers in the Rockies anticipate how to protect species into the future, Josh Pollock, conservation director of Rocky Mountain Wild, turned to Healy Hamilton. Hamilton models species distribution—or where critters live—according to temperature and precipitation envelopes that broadly indicate habitat suitability. The map above models the climate where Canada lynx could live today. HEALY HAMILTON AND STEPHANIE AUER. 2010.

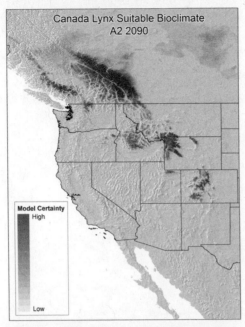

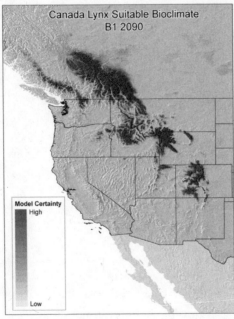

The "A" scenario projects where lynx could live in 2090 if greenhouse gas emissions continue near the present rate. The "B" scenario assumes we reduce our emissions considerably, and the future for lynx looks a lot better. In both cases, connectivity between habitat patches will be essential for these populations to sustain genetic viability. HEALY HAMILTON AND STEPHANIE AUER. 2010.

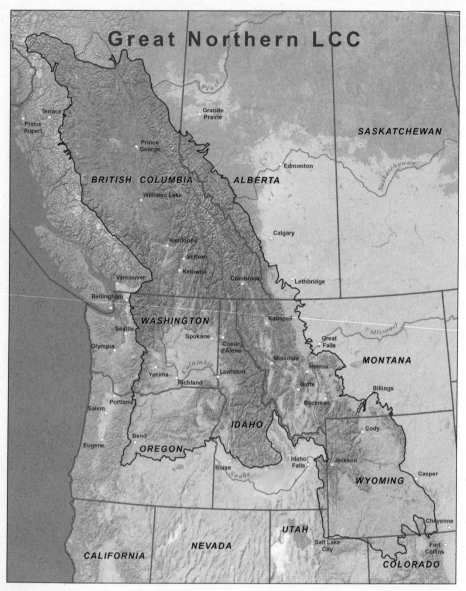

Great Northern LCC

Reflecting the scientific precept that nature does not define itself by state or sovereign boundaries, the National Fish & Wildlife Service has established 22 landscape conservation cooperatives. The LCCS are public-private networks within the U.S. and across our borders. Their outlines are based on ecoregions first defined by Robert Bailey. TARA CHESLEY-PRESTON, THE MONTANA INSTITUTE ON ECOSYSTEMS AT MONTANA STATE UNIVERSITY.

Introduction

FOR MORE THAN ONE HUNDRED YEARS, CONSERVATION HAS FUNCTIONED by drawing a boundary around a special area and limiting human impacts there; America's "best idea," as Wallace Stegner called it, has resulted in protecting jewels like Yellowstone National Park. But science today tells us this approach is failing. Nature doesn't work without connection. The web of life depends on a continuous flow of interaction within which to renew itself. Cities, highways, and agriculture have made islands out of even our largest wilderness areas. The solution is "large landscape connectivity," on an enormous scale: thus, the Spine of the Continent (SOC). E. O. Wilson calls it the most important conservation initiative in the world today. The Spine seeks to link protected landscapes along 5,000 miles of the Rocky Mountains, from Canada to Mexico. Big chunks of land we can still call wilderness along this range compose the biggest, most critical "wildway" in the United States. Protecting cores of this area and connections between them will provide nature enough room to keep its functions going, and will provide a roadway for plants and animals migrating to higher elevations as the climate changes.

The Spine is the brainchild of Michael Soulé, widely regarded as the father of conservation biology—though, now in his mid-seventies, he says "grandfather" is more like it. Soulé is a unique figure who has combined academic brilliance and moral fervor for many decades. He has disseminated the concept of landscape connectivity with great effectiveness, and in addition to steering the efforts of over twenty nonprofits with purviews along the Spine to coordinate their work in creating linkages, he has influenced federal and state agencies to incorporate connectivity in their work plans. Soulé initially conceived of the Spine to address general habitat fragmentation. But recent climate research has shown that protecting the largest possible areas of land, particularly mountainous regions, and providing scientifically selected connections between them are also our best hedges against the depredations of a warming world. Big, healthy swaths of nature are buffers. Forests and woody riparian areas hold land in place that otherwise would be washed away by flooding. Greenery absorbs heat and carbon dioxide. Species along the Spine, such as pikas, grizzly bears, wolves, Clark's nutcrackers, prairie dogs, beavers, and aspen, all do their part to keep nature functioning as the life support system we all depend on. The SOC is an adaptive strategy—helping natural systems stay healthy will in turn help human systems cope with climate change.

The Spine of the Continent sounds more literary than your usual "save the wolves" campaign, and well it might. For although the story begins in the world of science, it unfolds on the land, and that is the place of stories, culture, and history. The stories along the Spine in this book include those of regular folk such as Janay Brun, a waitress turned whistle-blower who told the truth about what happened to an incredibly rare jaguar in Arizona, and Sherri Tippie, a hairdresser who relocates beaver. There is Paul Vahldiek, a former Texas trial lawyer who is adding his own High Lonesome Ranch in Colorado to the linkages along the Spine, and with Michael Soulé's nonprofit, Wildlands Network, convening other large property owners in doing the same. Then there are the ethereal scientists, such as Rama Nemani. From command central at NASA Ames Research Center in California, Nemani applies satellite data and massive computing capacity to help land managers track the health of the national parks, and projects the impacts of climate change.

These people are inspiring. When I asked Kniffy Hamilton, the former US Forest Service supervisor who heroically got regulatory protection for the Path of the Pronghorn migration corridor—the first and only official protection of wildlife movement thus far—about what motivated her, Hamilton said, "Mary Ellen, it was the right thing to do." The Spine of the Continent is not just about a place, vast as it is; it is about the people working to restore and protect it.

In his novel *Howard's End,* E. M. Forster directed his readers to "only connect." He was talking about empathy, compassion, all that good emotional stuff. And we need to elicit all of that to save nature. "Only connect" happens to be about as succinct as you can get to describe how to save nature in the physical way as well. For a salamander in Waterton Lakes National Park, Canada, connectivity is a couple of concrete underpasses that allow him to migrate across the road during mating season without getting squashed by traffic. For a grizzly bear in the northern Rockies, connectivity means huge protected areas across mountain ranges. For a wolf, one of the most highly contested denizens of nature, connectivity means legislative protection across state boundaries. Right now a wolf living large in Yellowstone that hazards across the park's Montana boundary will find itself the object of a hunt endorsed by the governor.

Finally, the Spine of the Continent is about connecting landscapes, ecosystems, creatures, and people. It is about connecting our hearts and our heads to honor and protect this most magnificent habitat, the culmination of millions of years of evolution, where every piece has a part to play in what is officially known as Earth, the place we call home.

PART I

AMERICA'S NEXT BEST IDEA

Chapter 1

Bear with Me

I'm sticking close to Rob Watt for several reasons. For one, he's a great storyteller, and I don't want to miss a word. Watt has been a ranger for Parks Canada for more than three decades; he's also an author who has an encyclopedic knowledge of the area we are traversing, which is in the Belly River Valley of Waterton Lakes National Park, Alberta, Canada. We are checking up on the whereabouts and general situation of the wildlife that live here. It's a chilly September morning with nature's glories in high relief—the burbling onwardness of the river itself, a curious mink skittering around on the other side of it. Gesturing up and over to our left, Watt says, "There's where Albany Featherstonhaugh set up Great Britain's astronomical station," in 1874. Featherstonhaugh was measuring latitude by the guidance of Polaris, the north star, in the days before GPS, before satellites, on behalf of the British Empire. American surveyors set up their own astronomical station nearby, and the two nations thus here divided the landscape along the forty-ninth parallel after the Napoleonic wars. Watt points out more history, but my eyes are glued to signs of the present tense.

Every several feet he punctuates his narrative with the same single word: "grizzly." Watt points out overturned dead logs, shredded by bears in pursuit of grubs and insects, which they eat by the giant pawful. He elucidates huge indentations in the understory where bears, moose, or Volkswagens have evidently been at repose. Watt moves fast and it is a challenge to keep up with his practiced bushwhacking. He stops for a minute or so to touch blond, frizzy fibers entangled in a wired hair trap, used to get DNA samples from the bears with minimal interference in their daily doings. "Grizzly," he says. "The kinked hair is why they're called that." I'm starting to feel like we're trespassing on private property, in this case owned by *Ursus arctos horribilis*.

As many a grizzly-loving field biologist will tell you, these bears rule the wild. Female grizzlies weigh up to 400 pounds, and males up to 700. Yeah, they won't hurt you if you don't bother them, usually. They're incredibly smart and, as displayed in the gallant tolerance many of them showed toward Timothy Treadwell in the film *Grizzly Man*, they are not necessarily always thinking with their teeth. On the other hand, we all know what happened to Treadwell.

THE BACKBONE OF THE WORLD

I am here to research the Spine of the Continent, a landscape conservation initiative named for the entire Rocky Mountain expanse it aims to protect, 5,000 miles from the Yukon down through Mexico. I first learned about the Spine of the Continent in 2008, in the offices of Dr. Healy Hamilton at the California Academy of Sciences in San Francisco's Golden Gate Park. I was interviewing Hamilton, along with many of the other scientists at the academy, for a book about evolution, focused on selections from more than 20 million bugs, birds, snakes, diatoms, and so on, housed on temperature-controlled trays in vaults behind their offices. Following the tradition of taxonomy, these scientists begin to understand life by naming it, fixing identity down to the DNA level. They are constructing the history of relationship among organisms past and present—the ultimate family tree of all life on earth. Hamilton works on seahorses and we talked about them; then she showed me something completely different—maps on her computer screen. "Spine of the what?" I had been gazing for weeks into jars of skeletons suspended in clear liquid and had admired some impressive vertebra. But Hamilton was not talking about a gigantic specimen.

Healy Hamilton's contribution to the Spine of the Continent is called "species distribution modeling," with which she maps where species live now and where they are likely to live based on seventeen of the climate change scenarios, or "global circulation models," published by the Intergovernmental Panel on Climate Change. What distinguishes

Hamilton's efforts from other researchers' is that "we've got the macho to run all of them," which requires setting vast computer power into motion. Hamilton's maps show that as the world gets hotter, the geography that today provides the climate western biodiversity is used to will be greatly reduced. If bighorn sheep, grizzlies, wolves, elk, and aspen can't adapt to new conditions, the area they can survive in will be ever more concentrated, mostly in high, mountainous terrain. Colored splotches representing the persisting animals look like sheep huddled together, braving an inhospitable world.

If connectivity represents a fairly recent 360 in conservation thinking, climate change has added a whole new spin. "It makes no sense to only conserve species where they are now," Hamilton says, "because they are moving. We have to think entirely differently about the landscape. We have to figure out where species are going to go, where they are going to persist, and we have to protect *those* places now." It's quite a thought. What is Yellowstone, if not the bison and the aspen that inhabit it? Yet in 50, 100, 200 years, these species may be gone from the place we know as Yellowstone. While the Spine of the Continent was conceived before climate change was understood to be pressing so closely upon us, connectivity turns out to be the best strategy for dealing with it in the West. Hamilton is a passionate scientist with fire in her eyes. About the prospect of actually getting corridors protected along 5,000 miles of Rocky Mountains and environs, she says, "Those animals have to be able to get to where they need to go. We have to protect the connections. There isn't time for anything else."

THE GHOSTS OF ANIMALS PAST

The Spine of the Continent initiative is about protecting big cores of abundant nature, keeping them populated with carnivores, and connecting them to one another so that wildlife can trek from one to the next. Ergo, conservation's three C's: cores, carnivores, and corridors. We are taking this particular trek today to check on the whereabouts of some of the critters that make Waterton-Glacier International Peace Park a core. Though the place is managed, as natural parks usually are, by rangers such as Watt who sometimes conduct controlled burns to adjust the cycle of vegetative growth, and who sometimes have to interfere with big-teethed animals to prevent dustups with hikers, by most rubrics this place qualifies as wild. Almost all of the animals that historically have lived here still do. Heading farther up into Canada is the most intact ecosystem on the continent.

Watt tells us about a valley to the north where some years ago nearly intact bison bones were uncovered in an ancient graveyard. "There was no depredation on the bones," says Watt, referring to signs that wolves or grizzlies may have been responsible for the mortality. "What probably happened is the bison got snowed in one winter, and they all starved."

He notes that before the forty-ninth parallel helped drive the final achievement of Manifest Destiny, bringing white settlement, Indians used this landscape for thousands of years, and still do. Just north of us is part of the Blackfeet reservation. The original Blackfeet name for the Belly River is Mokowanis, which means stomach; this may refer to another tribe that traveled to the river to hunt bison and was called Gros Ventres by the French, or it may refer to a nearby belly-like bend in the river. We come upon a few incongruous cow patties. Although cows are not welcome in the park, "a couple of them must have strayed in here." And for tens of thousands of years before any people were here, wolves, grizzlies, bighorn sheep, and bison traveled along this route. With the exception of the bison, Watt says, "they still do."

His assertion is evidenced rather quickly by an enormous pile of grizzly scat right ahead of us on the trail. Plenty of times I have gazed on old bear poop with a sanguine eye, noting the desiccated red berry skins and twigs that have passed only partially digested through a bear's gullet. Such deposits look old and unthreatening. This is different. This looks as if ten seconds ago someone upended a compost bucket. It's 9 inches tall, green, slimy. It's still steaming.

READ MY MIND

Watt pulls his pepper spray canister from its holster and the rest of our party does the same. I know I'm supposed to release my canister, too, but

I have no confidence that I will deploy the stuff usefully. In fact, I'm quite sure that if my finger goes on that trigger I will either spray myself in the face or, worse, spray another *Homo sapiens*. If anyone among us can be trusted to do the right thing when actually confronted with a bear, it's Watt, so I stick to my plan of sticking to him.

"Hello, bear!" he says loudly. Others likewise start to make a ruckus, but calmly. The idea is that you let the bear know you are there; you don't startle him or, Lord help you, her. Mama grizzlies have quite the reputation for ferocity in defending their cubs. But I'm not entirely trusting that the group of scientists and researchers I'm with, including Watt, genuinely want to avoid the bear or bears that are clearly nearby and likely watching us. The best stories field biologists tell are of wildlife encounters. Several field assistants in the group may or may not have seen a mama bear and two cubs a couple of weeks prior. (One of them tells me, "I did not behave well. I was *terrified*." She credits a colleague with keeping cool and getting them both out of the area.) Grizzlies have been making themselves seen around here with some frequency since mid-August, and the park has closed some trails to hikers. This sort of tension, of course, heightens the spirit of scientific inquiry. Watt has met plenty a grizzly in his day, tipped his hat, and moved on. No problem. Once he came upon several wolves right around where we are now. In making a respectful exit, he was flanked on either side by the animals, which appeared to escort him out of their stomping grounds.

Just the night before John Russell, a longtime rancher, wildlife ecologist, and member of a bona fide conservation dynasty initiated by his father, famed grizzly conservationist Andy Russell, shared with me his method of communicating with the bears. "I talk to them," he said. Outside the Russell living room window, which surveys a mind-bogglingly beautiful vista of valleys and peaks including the hatchet-shaped Chief Mountain, sacred to the Blackfeet, there sits not a birdbath but a grizzly bear bath. It's very large, and reportedly in frequent use. "Oh," I had said, "do you speak in a conversational tone?" "No," he confided. "I don't say anything out loud. I talk to them in my mind. They understand. They respond." I had smiled and nodded politely.

Now behind Watt my quick dismissal of grizzly telepathy is instantly converted. As the others shout, "Hi, bear! Here we are! Not going to bother you!" I silently implore, "Please, bear, don't show yourself. I don't want to look at you!" While back home in San Francisco I could really get a lot of mileage out of a grizzly sighting, as Bartleby the Scrivener would say, "I'd prefer not to." Amid the ruckus of my companions, the bear must have heard me best. Eventually pepper spray canisters are returned to their holsters. Having looked no grizzly in the eye, we content ourselves with poring over wildlife tracks crisscrossing the gravel beds by the Belly River.

A plenitude of animals large and small have been traversing here. Tracks are like lingering shadows. Who was here? When? Populating the paw prints with visual images of their full-bodied makers conjures moose, deer, elk, fox, mink, wolves, grizzlies, coyotes, mountain lions: All these critters live in these parts and utilize this river (we did not identify prints of all of the above, but quite a few). By comparison Times Square hardly feels more diverse or crowded. We hear an occasional elk bugle but don't see many actual animals—most are on a different schedule than us daylight trekkers, and move in the crepuscular cover of dawn and dusk.

Watt tells us this is great grizzly habitat because it seasonally provides a nutritious succession of the plants, roots, and bugs that compose nearly all of the bear's diet. "Berries," Watt says, "are the key to a bear's survival, especially huckleberries." When it comes time to pig out before hibernating, the bear partakes of a veritable underworld of little mammals, which it scarfs down like hot, buttered popcorn when you haven't had lunch. There are miles of untrammeled wilderness in which to den for the winter. As for so many other species making their way to and fro along the Belly River, it's prime for seeking food and shelter, and for dispersing to other locations in pursuit of a mate or new territory.

All good for the grizzlies, until their sojourning brings them about 30 miles north of here, to Crowsnest Pass, where BC Highway 3 bifurcates their stomping grounds. Not only does BC Highway 3 pose a mortal danger to any animal trying to get across it; in the case of grizzly bears, it threatens the entire species with extinction in the lower forty-eight.

The Backbone of the World

Nobody remembers exactly where the term the "Spine of the Continent" came from. It refers to the Blackfeet people's name for the Rocky Mountains, "the backbone of the world." Today the Blackfeet live in Montana and Canada, where they have always lived; as they like to say, "We come from right here."[1] The "backbone of the world" didn't transpose into the "spine of the continent" before Wildlands Network, the nongovernmental agency (NGO) that organizes the initiative, adopted this nomenclature, but it did become "backbone of the continent" outside Blackfeet usage as far back as 1870, and maybe longer ago than that. Michael Fox, curator of history at the Museum of the Rockies, recalls gold rush slang for the region as "Uncle Sam's backbone," and finds an 1872 reference in *Croffutt's Trans-Continental Tourist* to the "backbone of the continent," which he locates in southern Wyoming.[2] Sorting out the transposition of "backbone" to "spine," the arguably harsher word brings dimension to the concept of a structural foundation, since "spine" also defines the nervous system, without which many an organism would still have shape but no animation.

And to add some more nomenclature to this picture of a vast, continuous landscape, the Belly River valley is but a divot in the amplitude of the Crown of the Continent ecoregion. The Crown of the Continent is thus called because it is command central for nature's comings and goings as abetted by the Continental Divide, the river demarcation that traverses the whole of North America alongside the Spine of the Continent. From the Crown a single point of origin sorts out the directional flow of one river system to the Pacific, another to the Atlantic. As indicated by the grand and lofty language, this water system is the lifeblood and pulse of the land.

The Earth Moved

My favorite topographical map of North America is produced by a company called Raven Maps and shows that nearly half the continent is mountains. The Rockies are mind-bogglingly big and long, yet even so are a subset of the Western Cordillera that extends to the West Coast.

Mountains are formed in several ways, but these fit into the category of those built by force of tectonic plates ramming into each other, the denser plate riding herd over the lighter one, which is subducted, or pulled under it. The compression of all this creates the uplift of the mountains, which is in constant competition with erosion, the force by which mountains are worn down, and which always wins in the end. We refer to mountains as immoveable, but they are not; mountains are coming and going just like everything else in this temporal realm, and several ranges actually predate the Rockies on the landscape, their memory lingering in the deposition of "basement rock" for this most recent main event, the Laramide Orogeny (orogeny means mountain-making), which happened 45–80 million years ago.

That the Rockies extend inland makes them unique in all the world, and people are still trying to figure that out. For hundreds of millions of years, North America would have looked like South America, with the jagged peaks hugging the shore. For 175 million more years, the mountain-building of the Rockies continued inland—as Anne Egger, a geologist at Central Washington University, puts it, "like the rumpling of a rug." The Raven map uses a forest-green color to depict land at 2,000 feet above sea level, which becomes orange as the land gets to 6,000 feet at the eastern edges of Wyoming and Colorado. It quickly shoots up to the white of more than 10,000 feet in the interior of Colorado—these are the Rockies' tallest mountains. By comparison, on the Raven map the relatively senescent Adirondack Mountains on the East Coast look as if a cool iron could take care of those wrinkles.

The Rockies are further distinguished by their jagged good looks. An early explorer, Samuel Hearne, in the late 1700s called them the "Stony Mountains." In the Pleistocene, advancing glaciers ripped down many of these mountains, stripping their surfaces bare. Erosion's complementary method to glaciation occurs by way of time and the river. John Wesley Powell, the famous one-armed explorer who founded the US Geological Survey, in the late 1800s pondered the course of the Green River through the Uinta Mountains in the Colorado Plateau. Why did it flow through the mountains and not take the path of least resistance around them?

He deduced that "the river had the right of way; in other words, it was running ere the mountains were formed. . . . The river preserved its level, but the mountains were lifted up. . . . The river was the saw which cut the mountains in two."

The Rockies also look so stony because of the general aridity of the West, which in turn influences erosion. Snowfall here is drier and that affects the rate at which it melts. Snowmelt on the Rockies is of huge interest in the context of climate change, because as temperatures rise, the snow will come down the mountains faster and evaporate faster. Snow is essentially a storage locker for water, and we are losing the capacity for meting it out. Phenology, or the schedule upon which plants green up and die, is intimately tied to snowmelt; the small mammals that depend on those plants are affected as well, and on we go down the chain of connection that is at the essence of nature.

A Biotic Conveyor Belt

Tens of thousands of years ago the ancestors of today's grizzlies, wolves, fox, lynx, badgers, beavers, and more came over the Bering Land Bridge from Russia, dispersing downward along the Spine. About 13,500 years ago, the Clovis were the first people to inhabit North America, and they came via the same route. Roughly 8,000 to 10,000 years ago a second pulse of human emigrants came. Traveling down the Rocky Mountains these Athabascan peoples made it to the American Southwest about 600 years ago and eventually became known as the Navajo and Apache. First Nations have long referred to it as "The People's Way." "American corridor"[3] is another good name for this historic conveyor belt; it is the pathway that led to our first populations of animals, people, and even plants. The water that sustains our current populations all the way down through the western United States still issues from the Crown, connecting us to a source both historic and immediate.

To this natural north–south flow of animal and human movement, BC Highway 3 takes exception. It slices across the Spine, across the Continental Divide. BC Highway 3 is a two-lane road extending more than 700 miles. On one 75-mile stretch of it, 6,000 to 9,000 vehicles traverse daily; 1,200 employees of a major coal-mining operation commute along it. More than 314 wildlife fatalities occur on a 100-mile stretch of this road per year. "It's a pinch point," says Wendy Francis, executive director of the Yellowstone to Yukon Conservation Initiative (Y2Y), an organization dedicated to restoring connectivity for grizzly bears (and the ecosystems they roam in).

Y2Y is a very big part of the Spine of the Continent initiative, more or less overseeing its work on the top end of the cordillera. Francis tells the story of Y2Y's creation,[4] as inspired by Pluie, a wolf that was radio collared in 1991 and tracked traveling more than 45,000 miles in two years, trucking over two Canadian provinces and three American states, an area more than fifteen times the size of Banff National Park. (The wolf was named by the biologist who, after several tries, finally collared her in the rain—*pluie* in French.) In 1993 she stopped transmitting, the collar later diagnosed as having been struck with a bullet. Pluie kept on keeping on for two more years and was shot, dead this time, legally, by a hunter in Canada, along with her two pups. As Francis puts it, Pluie demonstrably showed that no national park or even network of such is adequate to incorporate animal movement, and that to protect territorial and migrational trajectories, coordinated response is necessary among many stakeholders across the land. Y2Y has hundreds of partners, from private property owners to government entities, and especially in Canada, First Nations partners "who have been thinking like this about the landscape for thousands of years." While doing all kinds of work to promote connectivity, Y2Y currently focuses on grizzly bears as an umbrella species. In other words, make it okay for grizzlies to do their thing, and you've protected almost everybody else.

STOPPED IN THEIR TRACKS

Right now you and I could get out our smart phones or onto our computers, or even go to a bookstore and buy a map, and plan a road trip with the family this summer. We could decide to fly into Salt Lake City, then drive to Grand Teton National Park in Wyoming, head north to Glacier, then drive back down around and stop in Yellowstone. Or maybe give our kids a hands-on history lesson and follow part of the Lewis and Clark Trail as approximated by the National Park Service, including a stop at Great Falls, Montana, where the Corps of Discovery was confronted with spectacular walls of water that are still crashing today.

Now say you are a grizzly bear. Grizzlies once inhabited the entire north–south trajectory of the continent, from Alaska to Mexico, and from the West Coast nearly to the center of the landmass. Now their numbers are small enough to keep tabs on: There are more than 600 grizzlies in Yellowstone, and just about 900 more distributed through the northern Continental Divide, the North Cascades, the Selkirks, and the Cabinet-Yaak Mountains. The Cabinets, the Selkirks, and the North Cascades all straddle both the United States and Canada. The Bitterroots, covering central Idaho, are perfect habitat for grizzlies, but the last of their kind was shot there in the 1940s. These six areas are "recovery zones" that patched together on a map look like big watermarks over mountain ranges; they don't quite touch one another. Bears are not like wolves. While their territories are large, bears don't make such big trips looking for new grounds. Most female grizzlies live in territories that overlap their moms'. To keep the Yellowstone grizzlies genetically viable over the long haul, populations of bears need to be close enough together to intermingle all the way up through Glacier-Waterton, and then onward up to the mother lode, the still-thronging Canadian wilderness, home to more than 27,000 grizzlies. If bears in the lower forty-eight can't mix with those above, their populations will become inbred and that will be that.

CRASH

Roadkill is something we all want to turn our heads away from. Paradoxically its incidence can be seen as a boon to connectivity conservation. It takes some doing (like this whole book) to explain the gist of ecological and evolutionary connection, and it is difficult to provide real-time examples of what happens to nature when this is broken. I can tell you that bighorn sheep and grizzlies are headed toward extinction if they can't move freely enough, but it will take decades to prove my point. Roadkill, on the other hand, you can see. You can count it up, as Y2Y partner the

Miistakis Institute (*miistakis* is Blackfeet for "backbone of the world") has done in the region, with the help of a community-based monitoring project. Road Watch in the Pass enlisted the local citizenry to use an interactive mapping tool whereby sightings not just of roadkill but of wildlife movement in general were collected, then verified and tallied up.

Most important, perhaps, roadkill can be quantified. Dead animals on roadways cost money. On BC Highway 3 through Crowsnest Pass, the average cost per collision based on human fatalities and injuries, and vehicle damage, amounts to $30,760 per moose, $17,483 per elk, $6,617 per deer, and $6,617 per bighorn sheep.[5] (This perfectly anthropocentric and actuarial approach doesn't take into account any intrinsic value of the animals themselves.) Carnivore collisions are less frequent than those with ungulates (hoofed herbivores), and the animal most likely to hit your windshield is a deer. The same study assessing these damages puts the cost of building and maintaining a wildlife underpass with fencing and jump-outs (which it poetically calls "escape ramps" for wildlife) at $18,123 per annum. All these numbers help make it clear that animal movement needs to be safeguarded and that it is incumbent upon transportation authorities to do something about it.

The gold standard for wildlife overpasses and underpasses are dotted across the roadways north of here, at Banff, Canada's oldest national park. One of the criticisms leveled against all attempts at creating corridors is that the animals won't use them. But in fourteen years of monitoring (from 1996), track-pad and remote-camera data have accumulated more than 200,000 crossings by eleven species of large mammals using thirty wildlife crossing structures at Banff.

In the United States, the grizzly has been on the Endangered Species List since 1975. Dr. Chris Servheen, the grizzly bear recovery coordinator for the US Fish and Wildlife Service, advocates including crossing structures in plans for highway renovations—it's much easier and cheaper to get them built when they are planned for rather than retrofitted. In response to a question about how long it took the bears at Banff to start using the structures (reportedly a couple of years), Servheen responds, "A transboundary highway divided the population. Then they twinned the highway and built fences on either side of it. The animals lost the knowledge that there was something on the other side." Servheen remarks that in areas where bears are used to moving, there is virtually no lag in the time it takes for them to start utilizing structures made for them. Bears, remember, are smart.

BC Highway 3 is far from the only road impeding the flow of grizzly bears across the landscape. The terrain between the Purcell Mountains and Yellowstone is similarly chopped up by US Route 2, Montana Highway 200, Interstate 90, US Route 12, US Route 93, Interstate 15, and US Route 20. Wendy Francis and Y2Y have their eyes on the whole prize, which includes more than crossing structures. She describes various projects that include such prosaic goals as putting electric fencing around Dumpsters (which tempt bears too close to people) to loftier ones, such as getting a new 83,000-acre wilderness area created in Montana, as "a jigsaw puzzle. We purchase lands, we add bears from one place to another, we restore roads. We are creating a way for bears to weave their way through the landscape. What's so cool is that all these projects are interrelated. Everybody knows what everybody else is doing," says Francis. "Y2Y is the glue holding the continental vision so that everyone understands why we are doing it this way." This is a perfect summation of the goal of the Spine of the Continent, which employs similar strategies for trying to get connection all the way down into Mexico, not just for grizzlies, but for all of nature.

As for successes, "they sound like failures," says Francis. "In 2007 a grizzly was killed by a hunter just at the western edge of the Bitterroot Mountains. No one had seen a grizzly there for decades, so that was a good sign." In 2009 a rancher in Idaho, south of Interstate 90, assumed he had a black bear harassing his domestic elk, but it turned out to be a grizzly. "We're on the right track," Francis says. "It's going to take a long time."

THE CRACK-UP

What happens if we lose the grizzly bear in the lower forty-eight? Maybe not much, but we don't know. Grizzlies are at the top of the food chain and have an important place in the "guild" of big carnivores. While 90 percent of their diet is vegetation, when they do eat meat it is likely to be a moose, elk, or deer calf, or an adult carcass killed by a wolf. In preying on the young, grizzlies keep ungulate populations in check; they make wolves work harder. (Ungulate means "hoofed" in Latin; this is a general term for herbivores including moose, deer, elk, cows, sheep, and bison.) As enormous consumers of berries with seeds, grizzlies are in consort with birds and small mammals that help distribute species through their gullets, typically defecating the seeds at a location different from where they were consumed.

As Francis describes the grizzly as an umbrella species, the preservation of which is likely to ensure the protection of many other species, so it goes the other way around: Lose the grizzly and that's likely not all you'll lose. Paul Ehrlich, famous since he and his wife, Anne, published *The Population Bomb* in 1968, likens species loss to taking rivets off a plane. The plane can still function if you take out several, but at a certain point, the whole structure falls apart. And you cannot tell if a seemingly innocuous rivet might in fact be essential to the operation. David Quammen, in *The Song of the Dodo*, compares habitat fragmentation (like that experienced by the grizzlies) to cutting up a fine oriental rug.[6] Is it still beautiful? Does it still work? Can you even call it a carpet anymore?

The rivets and the rug are excellent metaphors because an airplane is a vehicle for movement, which is intrinsic to how nature works. Although it is man-made, an airplane capitalizes on aerodynamic principles that are among the amazing properties of the natural world. Quammen's oriental rug is a poignant reminder that we are losing something dense, historical, and beautiful. An oriental rug is both art and craft, emotionally expressive yet providing something to stand on. Neither metaphor quite captures the dimensionality of nature, the time and space scales along which it operates. Darwin invoked the "tangled bank." Ecologists sometimes refer to nature as a "mesh"[7]—make it an electric mesh that also has a circulatory system; liken species extinctions to taking out circuits and arteries; imagine the workings now of your house with dark, cold rooms and your body with dead zones. How long can this go on?

When an animal goes extinct, we also lose contact with a cultural history. The grizzly bear has been revered by indigenous cultures all over the world for hundreds of years, American Indian tribes among them. Plains Indians in particular honored the bear for its evident wisdom about the mysteries and potential of plants. Some tribes considered the grizzly a shaman and a healer. The Sioux holy man Black Elk attributed his gifts to bear medicine. Traditional Blackfeet place the grizzly above all other animals and call the animal "Old Grandfather." The Tinglit people reportedly considered grizzlies half human, and the Ojibwa referred to bears in general as *anijunabe*, their word for Indian.

The Native belief systems did not merely honor grizzly bears with the distinction of being almost human, but in general endowed all animal life with a more than natural status, issuing from their existence on the earth prior to people. Joseph Epes Brown writes that for Plains Indians, animals "in their anteriority and divine origin . . . have a certain proximity to the Great Spirit . . . which demands respect and veneration. . . . They are intermediaries or links between human beings and God."[8]

Should you choose to define God simply as the "as yet not known," in animals like the grizzly there is much undisclosed: for example, hibernation. While other hibernating animals wake up every couple of days to eat, drink, and eliminate, grizzlies don't. In a process tracked but incompletely understood by science, hibernating grizzlies live off the breakdown of fat, muscle, and organ tissue as a starving animal would, but then in a reversal from the trajectory that would eventually kill that animal, the bear utilizes urea to actually build new protein. As Tom McNamee puts it in *The Grizzly Bear*, "There is a phoenix inside a midwinter's bear, creating new self from the ashes of the old." Living off their own fat, hibernating bears create a unique form of bile that prevents hardening of the arteries or cholesterol gallstones. (Bear bile has the same effect on humans, and in the 1990s crystallized bear bile sold for more than $1,000 an ounce in South Korea; the black market in bear gall bladders is a major threat to black bear populations everywhere.)

The famous maternal solicitude shown by the female for her cubs begins before they are even implanted; a mama grizzly can carry a fertilized egg in her womb for many months, ready at any moment to attach to the uterine wall and begin becoming a bear, which it does not do until conditions are right. How the bear knows that she has enough body fat to support a pregnancy through hibernation, or how she knows whether there is enough forage available to support her progeny, is a mystery to us. If conditions are right for pregnancy, a bear will wake up in January long enough to deliver her cubs. She'll go back to sleep, periodically waking to minister to the cubs. For approximately three months, these little ones will not hibernate but live in a half-waking world with their slumbering dam. Talk about attachment theory. It's no wonder the mother-offspring bond in bears is so ferocious; they are more or less unified in darkness until the group emerges in spring.

From the perspective of human limitations, these natural abilities of bears are death-defying and thus amply justify the frequent Indian association of grizzlies with immortality. Even on a smaller scale of causality, however, to let the grizzly go extinct is to eliminate a repository of information about survival before we have even begun to understand it.

CHAPTER 2

They Paved Paradise

MICHAEL SOULÉ MAKES HIS WAY THROUGH A CROWD CONVENING AT THE Mt. Peale Inn in rural Utah in early 2010, and stands directly in front of me. Outside, a whirling, swirling snowstorm seems to lay a foot of snow every few minutes on the mountains around us. Inside, about twenty-five conservationists are coming in from the cold. This is a gathering of the Spine of the Continent initiative, a two-day workshop to address issues around the Colorado Plateau.

My presence among these folk is predicated on an incognito: I have been asked to suppress my identity as a journalist and participate as note-taker. Everyone is friendly and when introducing themselves asks what I'm writing about; absolutely no one is fooled by this "note-taker" business. Is it my loafers, my black pants, the look on my face? In fact, I'm about the only person here not wearing plaid flannel. "I have a theory," Soulé says, and launches right into it.

Michael Soulé is the most famous scientist you've never heard of. About thirty years ago he declared a new science, and he called it conservation biology. It was a pretty out-there thing to do. Soulé is an evolutionary geneticist, trained in the rigors of the traditional academy, where historically science is "pure." That means it is theoretical; pure science asks for the sake of the question, it likes equations, and it hangs in books, in papers, on computer screens—in the air. But in the very early stages of his career—Soulé was Paul Ehrlich's first graduate student at Stanford in the early 1960s—he began to develop the insight that habitat fragmentation is hastening extinction of species. From a genetics point of view, he saw that isolated populations of species can get only so small and only so far away from others of their kind before blinking out altogether. And basically he couldn't stand to watch it happen.

Conservation as inspired by John Muir and Theodore Roosevelt was doing its best to save nature, and it very importantly drew public attention to the necessity of doing so. But its choices were not based on much beyond evident beauty, and its method was simply to draw boundary lines on the landscape—science had yet to be brought to bear on conservation decisions. Soulé defined conservation biology to redress this disconnect. With others he conceived of this as a science that would focus on real-world issues. It would be value-laden. It would have an explicit mission: to save nature. And so the pure sciences of ecology, evolution, and genetics reached across the divide and took a page from medicine: take the pulse of the patient; diagnose; tell the rest of the world about the contagion. Among the very bright minds endorsing this endeavor were not only Soulé and Ehrlich, but also Jared Diamond, E. O. Wilson, Dan Simberloff, Tom Lovejoy, John Terborgh, Stuart Pimm, and many others who had (and still have) the highest ambitions concerning "pure" science. But they recognize that their study subject, nature, is disappearing.

THE BIG FLAW

At the Mt. Peale Inn, Soulé says to me, "We can't do it. We're too flawed. We can't escape ourselves." He has a theory. In addition to possessing first-rate scientific chops, Soulé is also an iconoclast who has been meditating for decades and even spent a stint as the director of the Zen Center of Los Angeles. He has written mostly about subjects such as inbreeding depression (in which depleted genetic materials eventually result in extinction) but has also made important contributions to what might be called moral ecology, digging with the scientist's rigor into, as he puts it, "why we can't save nature." Soulé is writing a book about the seven deadly sins. His basic working hypothesis is that the sins have a physical correlation in our brain functioning and have evolved alongside the very same mental developments that have made us so dominant. Most of the sins can be boiled down to two highly recognizable human traits: selfishness and status-seeking.

It may seem like a stretch for a scientist with strong Buddhist lean-
ings to invoke such a Judeo-Christian concept as sin,[9] but the foundation of evolutionary biology can arguably be traced to the same tradition.
The big question Darwin answered—how life begins—was first posed
by believers in a single Creator, who tried to figure out how He did it.
Scholars going back to the 1100s engaged their dialectics on the subject of origins, and the biblical story of the flood and Noah's ark focused
attention on what the natural world had to do with that. The ark, after all,
was believed to be the primary distributing mechanism whereby different
forms of life found themselves in different places. That varied life-forms
live in various places is the subject of biogeography, and it was largely
through biogeographical observations that Darwin worked out the theory of natural selection. Evolution occurs in context, and that context is
place—biogeography.

"We can't help it," Soulé adds. I confess I don't know what, exactly, to
say. It is about 8 in the morning, Mountain time, and I'm a bit jet-lagged.
Despite the uniformly good food and drink at the Mt. Peale Inn we are in
Utah after all; it's going to take a gallon of their coffee to reach my accus-
tomed caffeine threshold. My brain slowly registers: We can't save nature.
I hope he doesn't mean it.

Suddenly Soulé ceases to explain. We are the same height, about
5′5″, and he's in his mid-seventies. He has an undeniable charisma that
is not so easy to locate; he's wafer-thin, bald. So here it is, in clear blue
eyes that radiate the brain power that brought the issue of genetics
into the study of wildlife and thus drew new parameters around how
to understand what's going on outside. He has been famous among the
initiated for many decades. There is an elegance to his expression in
the mold of the academy: a point to be made, the foundations of it to
enumerate, the conclusion to be put down right here, like a stop sign.
"I talk like a scientist," he apologizes, shaking his head. "Luckily I also
cry a lot."

Having known him now for a couple of years, I wouldn't say he cries
a lot, but when he does, it's vaguely unnerving. And also impressive.
Most senior, authoritative scientists save expressive feelings for maybe

their next incarnation (which most of them don't believe in). Soulé tacks with fluidity between elucidations such as "nature relaxes to the norm," to explain why ordinary children are often born to extraordinary parents, and quoting Joni Mitchell, "they paved paradise and put up a parking lot," to explain what's happened to San Diego, the former Eden where he grew up, where he first loved nature, and the thought of which makes him choke up every time.

TREES ARE NOT ALL THEY HUG

"Mary Ellen!" In marked contrast to the contained Michael Soulé, a very large and looming man pumps my hand and envelops me in a giant embrace. "I like it when people hug right off," I say, laughing, as I am introduced to Jim Catlin. He is momentarily taken aback that I don't know who he is. "Well, we talked on the phone!" he booms.

Catlin is the executive director of the Wild Utah Project; he is a "recovering engineer" who got his PhD in ecology from Berkeley in a second chapter of his career, and has been hard at work battling especially the abuses of cattle grazing on public lands ever since. "You should write about the mail fraud perpetrated by some ranchers," he says. "It's a federal offense." Soon I meet Mary O'Brien, a regal woman in her sixties with a long braid down her back; she heads the Utah Forests program of the Grand Canyon Trust. She says, "You'll really want to write about Sherri Tippie. She's the most amazing woman. Relocated more than 1,000 beaver." O'Brien starts to massage my shoulder blades. My incognito now so completely tattered it's see-through, I begin to comprehend the general stance and emotional tenor of the very small, super-committed grassroots organizations along the Spine. They are big huggers; many of them cry easily; they feel that if only you knew, you would care, too; they love life and they can't stand to see it go.

The conservation community in the West does try to be wary of how its work is portrayed, because it often comes under assault, especially when maps are involved. Since its inception, Wildlands Network has used maps to define ecosystems and to propose protections for them; while the mapping impetus has always come straight out of science, ultra–right wing "property rights" groups seized on them as evidence the "enviros" were all about taking land from people. Flames were fanned by Wildlands' early association with so-called ecoterrorism (although it absolutely never committed any) mostly due to the history of one of its founders, Dave Foreman. In the mid-'90s groups calling themselves Wise Use and the Green Gestapo circulated fake Wildlands maps and claimed the lines drawn on them represented this enemy's incursions onto your property.

While it is hard to imagine a less threatening bunch than these gentle and quiet-voiced people gathered to save nature, the challenges they face here on the Colorado Plateau are a microcosm of what goes on south in New Mexico and Arizona and east in Colorado and north in Montana. Basically the beauties of nature share space with those who would use the ground and the resources beneath it for very different purposes. The Colorado Plateau has a wealth of mining activity, both active and potential. Utah, for example, is by and large a poor state, despite the success of the Mormons who populate especially the northern parts of it, and plenty of residents here are eager to capitalize on the resources others would save.

A GUERRILLA CELL

Warm reunions are happening all over the place in the big common room at the Mt. Peale Inn, as representatives from big outfits, such as the Sierra Club, the Wilderness Society, and the Nature Conservancy, and small ones, such as Red Rock Forests and the Tree of Life, gather. These folks are lifers. Many of them have worked together on various projects that are more like campaigns in a long, ongoing war.

There are two men in the room named Kim, both longtime Spine stalwarts. Kim Vacariu is the organizer of this and many SOC efforts. He now gently harangues the workshop facilitator about last-minute details. Tall and thin, with white hair combed straight back, he looks like he just stepped out of a Civil War daguerreotype: dignified, slightly reserved, but yes, ma'am, ready to go take that second hill. Kim Crumbo from the Grand Canyon Council is also cut in a traditionally masculine mold: black-mustached, a Vietnam vet and long-ago river guide. Crumbo is poring over a large spreadsheet in the midst of chattering folk like he's analyzing maps of enemy territory.

In the final few minutes before the workshop commences, I notice people noticing Soulé. With an index finger to his lips, Vacariu had whispered to me that "Michael might come," and is now visibly glad he did. Though Soulé is the progenitor of the Spine of the Continent, he does not attend every workshop, meeting, or conference devoted to its achievement. Nevertheless, every person in the room can trace the origin of their work to his original theories, and they know this. Many of them are scientists with degrees in the discipline he founded. The project they are undertaking today, to define a network of protection, was essentially defined by him. He likes to quote the author Edward Abbey: "Sentiment without action is the ruin of the soul." These people are often fighting an uphill battle and his single-minded focus on saving nature inspires them. Perhaps because he does look unnervingly like a bald Ian McKellen, I begin to think of Soulé's periodic appearances among the ground troops of conservation as akin to Gandalf's critically timed reunions with the defenders of Middle Earth.

PASSING THE GREEN-FIRED TORCH

And on to the rescue of the Colorado Plateau: You didn't know it needed saving. If you're an extreme-sport hellion, you've been to Moab and you know the area as pristine, the wilderness you crave when you're not mountain biking up or rappelling down its precipitous faces. If you are one of more than 4 million Americans and others who visit US national parks each year, you've likely been to the Grand Canyon, the Grand Staircase–Escalante National Monument, or maybe Dinosaur National Monument. Ticking off a life list of incredible natural places, there's Bryce Canyon National Park, Zion National Park, and more. The area, about 130,000 square miles, is situated at the four corners, over the intersection of Colorado, New Mexico, Arizona, and Utah; several mountain ranges jut up from its long expanse, including the La Sal, nearly 10,000 feet high, upon which we are currently perched.

For many of us, "plateau" evokes a place where, kale and cardio notwithstanding, a seemingly set size and shape won't budge. The Colorado

Plateau has both great width and great age. The region was first defined and given its name by scientist G. K. Gilbert. In the late 1870s Gilbert accompanied General John Wesley Powell on his famous survey of what were then western territories, the whole ambition of which encompassed about a third of the country, from eastern Colorado to California and southern Wyoming almost to Mexico. Gilbert's fastidious work and scientific insights are viable to this day. He outlined the Colorado Plateau as a region of flat-lying, mostly unshaped, mostly sedimentary rocks between highly "deformed" regions: the Uinta Mountains in the north, the Mongollon Rim in the south, the Rocky Mountains to the east, and the Basin and Range, which he also named, to the west. Gilbert saw that although the area comprises a number of smaller plateaus and basins, its consistent physiography identifies it as a single system. As have many geologists following in his footsteps, Gilbert appreciated the Colorado Plateau: "The simplicity of its structure . . . its barrenness, and wonderful natural sections exposed in its canyons." As with few other places on earth, much of the history of its formation is there visible on the Colorado Plateau, a wizened ancestor bearing witness to its own creation.

In introductory remarks, Crumbo reiterates the reasons everyone is here: to identify where conservation efforts are under way on the plateau, to join forces, to share information, and mostly to identify important areas that are as yet unaddressed. Crumbo references Theodore Roosevelt and the establishment of the national parks system. He invokes Aldo Leopold, for many the patron saint of conservation today, revered partly because he was a hunter, a game warden, and among the first to articulate a middle ground between prohibiting all human interaction on special land and rampant harvesting of its resources. In *A Sand County Almanac*, Leopold famously wrote about the apotheotic moment on a hunting trip that eventually instigated in him a new relationship with the wild, turning a blood-lusting hunter into something more:

> *We reached the old wolf in time to watch a fierce green fire dying in her eyes. I realized then, and have known ever since, that there was something new to me in those eyes—something known only*

to her and to the mountain. I was young then, and full of trigger-itch; I thought that because fewer wolves meant more deer, that no wolves would mean hunters' paradise. But after seeing the green fire die, I sensed that neither the wolf nor the mountain agreed with such a view.

This story has become a cornerstone of the Leopold legend; he published these words in 1949, decades before "green" became shorthand for "friendly to nature." At the time there was understanding that the wild world needed to be cared for, but nobody thought it was in fact under assault and in danger of being functionally extinguished, which is where we are today. Part of Leopold's appeal is his distinct framing of nature in literary terms, and whether he meant to or not, his words "green fire" have taken up a cultural counterpoint to that most famous of cultural green lights, the one at the end of Daisy Buchanan's dock, signaling "the orgastic future that year by year recedes before us."[10]

Crumbo concludes: "Leopold shot the wolf and reflected on it for twenty years; his awakening is important to our work."

WE HAVE WORK TO DO

Kim Vacariu takes over with a review of the Spine of the Continent, beginning with the founding of the Wildlands Network by Soulé and others more than twenty years ago. The Wildlands mission, to connect wildlife habitats through science-based action and networks of partners, counts among its accomplishments the concept of the aforementioned "three C's," cores, carnivores, and corridors, and the term "rewilding," which has come into general usage and describes restoring basic functioning to degraded ecosystems by returning key players, such as beavers and wolves, to them.

Nobody consulted a social scientist when it all got started, but the SOC operates to leverage what sociology calls "collective impact." Not every organization here is an official partner of the SOC effort, but they are all keenly aware that local work must be connected to other local work if it is to be ultimately effective. The workshop facilitator has people sit several rows deep in chairs around a map of the region depicted in all its topographic glory. Everyone marks up the map with what they are doing to heal or protect the landscape, and where. A concomitant list of the work is set up on an easel. Thus is the Colorado Plateau redefined, its topography of mostly sedimentary rock, the arterial waterways of the Colorado River branching through it, flanked by canyons, re-seen as a kaleidoscope of human impacts and hopeful alleviations. Crumbo pastes up numbers on the Grand Canyon; Boulder Mountain and the Aquarius Plateau; Zion Park and Desolation Canyon. Work and issues here include returning fire to the ponderosa ecosystem; moderating logging; restricting recreational vehicles in delicate places.

Big hugger Jim Catlin marks up currently roadless areas and confesses that the Paunsaugunt region, where Wild Utah is trying to do a number of things, is under the stewardship of both the Bureau of Land Management (BLM) and the Forest Service. There are groans and sighs and someone mutters, "Good luck." Every piece of land in our world is under someone's ownership or control; while 40 percent of western land (and 60 percent of Utah) is public, and under a variety of jurisdictions, each has its own set of rules and regulations and ways of doing things. There are the states themselves, there are counties, there are cities and towns; then there's the BLM and the Forest Service. Toward the end of the session someone remarks, "We could use this map as soon as possible to show where *not* to cite renewable energy—where to stay out." The consensus of the workshop participants is that the major obstacle they face in helping to heal nature is communicating the need to do so to the public.

THEN THEY PEE ON IT

Kelly Burke, executive director of the Grand Canyon Wildlands Project, tells how a good story can be worth a million acres. In the late 1990s, then secretary of the interior Bruce Babbitt had undertaken to expand the boundaries around which the Grand Canyon was protected under the Antiquities Act. "Babbitt was going to add these small lobes of protection," Burke tells me. "In designating a national monument, the idea is to capture the most scientific and historic features of a place in the smallest area. We said, 'Look at this differently.' The original proposal paralleled the canyon on the north side of the river; we said, you want to protect these long escarpments, the cliffs that are migratory corridors for birds. Those cliffs reveal the geological history of the Grand Canyon. They contain caves with great paleontological and archaeological remains. They direct raptor migration. They have long shaped human history. This is the region where Merriam came up with his life zones!" (C. Hart Merriam's 1889 life-zone concept orders living communities along elevational changes.)[11] Burke, Crumbo, and others plied Babbitt's staff with other wondrous facts about the region, pointing out historic routes where the Mormons brought down logs for their St. George temple.

"We're saying, don't just add these little blips. There's so much more here. But the staff's eyes are glazing over. Then Larry tells them about the pack rat middens," Burke continues. The Larry she refers to is Dr. Larry Stevens, a foremost expert on the area's ecology. "He tells them about these pack rats that store all sorts of stuff in the cliffs, and that some of their stores go back 50,000 years. The pack rats drag cactus spines, shiny objects, and animal bones into their middens, and when they have something new to add, they get all excited, they jump up and down, and they pee on it. And the pee crystallizes when it evaporates, sealing the nest contents." Because the Grand Canyon is so dry, these middens are preserved and now provide a wealth of information to scientists sussing out the history of climate change, among other things. "You know a lot goes on in D.C.," Burke says, admitting that maybe it wasn't just the peeing pack rats that got Babbitt's staff interested. "But you could see them pulling those maps closer as Larry was telling them about this."

A relevant dimension of Burke's story is the fluidity with which defining natural areas changes over time. The Grand Canyon was one of Theodore Roosevelt's original protected areas, but what was valuable back then was defined by artists' and photographers' views of what was pretty, from the South Rim. "Most of the Wildlands Network designs start with a mountain range and extend out to surrounding lowlands, but here in the Grand Canyon we don't have that," Burke says. "We define connectivity here along the watershed."

Among the final pledges of the Colorado Plateau workshop are resolutions to tell inspirational stories; explain conservation biology in context; celebrate successes; and develop diverse messengers (meaning, get ranchers and farmers to talk about it). Yes, all well and good and let's get at it. But if Michael Soulé had his way, if his blue eyes gazing steadily from the back of the room could bore into the intention of every man, woman, and child who has a choice to make about how to live, if he could direct those hearts and minds, he would have us institute a recovery plan for the whole world. "What we need," he says, referencing the successful US endeavor to help Western Europe get moving again after World War II, "is a Marshall Plan for nature." He came to this passion via lizards.

CHAPTER 3

Reptile Brain

FOR HIS PHD THESIS IN POPULATION BIOLOGY AND POSTDOCTORAL WORK, Soulé studied the evolution of the side-blotched lizard on the deep water islands in the Gulf of California. Lizards are fairly straightforward study subjects: They're not too smart, and compared to that of birds and mammals, their behavior is pretty simple. "They never lie to you," Soulé says fondly, and also remembers his mother let him keep lizards and snakes in the house when he was small. "These lizards are ubiquitous, and half of them in the United States have a little black blotch in their armpit, and the other half doesn't. I thought, this is a great problem, a Darwinian problem. Each island has a unique type: why?"

Both Darwin and his doppelganger, Alfred Russel Wallace, who simultaneously came up with the idea of natural selection as the means by which evolution proceeds, were profoundly influenced by what we now call biogeography, and in many ways Wallace is more responsible for its outlines than Darwin. Biogeography is like biography, only the subject is not one person, but every place on earth. The "bio" part of the term resounds both ways; it is about the life of life, a vast history of how forms have come into being and perished, how landmasses have come up and gone under, and how the twin movements of the earth itself and the creatures that live on it have evolved in tandem.

Wallace was an inveterate explorer naturalist in the same mold as Darwin, who was a big customer of the specimens Wallace brought back from his travels. While in the Amazon, Wallace observed that the river and its major tributaries separated populations of closely related species. Following this train of thought, his 1885 paper titled "On the Law Which

Has Regulated the Introduction of Species" concludes that "every species has come into existence coincident both in space and time with a closely allied species," which became known as the Sarawak Law. While he didn't posit any potential mechanism by which these "closely allied species" had become differentiated (which he would do later), Wallace set down the basic idea that speciation begins with geographical isolation.

Darwin and Wallace pondered the depths profoundly influenced by Charles Lyell's *Principles of Geology* (the first edition was published in 1830; the twelfth edition posthumously, in 1875—as if Lyell were revising from the Beyond). Lyell describes an earth in constant motion. His basic postulate is that internal heat pushes up the earth's crust into mountains that then erode down, and this ongoing process has created and is still creating the terrestrial-aquatic dynamo we call home. Wallace used the idea of a mutable earth to explain that land bridges had once connected populations of plants and animals and that their disappearance, under the seas, now separated them.

An Island Entire of Itself

Wallace tackled the cast of characters on this earth in his two-volume tome, *The Geographical Distribution of Animals* (1876), dividing the earth into six geographical regions and articulating all the factors then known to influence who lived in each one. Arguably with this book Wallace also founded the field of zoogeography. Then he turned his attention to describing the mise-en-scène, in *Island Life*. Since islands are discrete, it is easier to get a handle on what's happening on them, and it's fairly easy to figure out how old they are. Since every part of an ecosystem interacts with every other part, it's a lot easier to examine a smaller set of dynamics. To continue that metaphor, island dramas are like stark Greek plays, compared to the Proustian plenitude unfolding on continents. Islands have fewer players but like Greek drama their truths are incisive, in high relief, and it's possible to find in them microcosms of the whole of nature's working.

In *Island Life*, Wallace defined three types of islands. He divided continental islands into two categories depending on how recently they had been attached to a mainland. Continental islands start out with an assemblage of plants and animals established on the mainland—Madagascar is a famous one, and though natural selection is always working everywhere, and things have changed on Madagascar also, still continental islands present a particular temporal slice of the earth history pie. If Madagascar had never been separated from the mother ship, it's likely the abundant lemurs swinging from its trees would be far fewer if not altogether eliminated by a predator who happened not to make it onto the giant piece of landmass that got away.

Often called "de novo," volcanic islands rise up from the ocean and start out from scratch. If you've cut your feet on the lava fields of Hawaii, you know this directly. Natural erosion begins its long, steady work on volcanic islands, creating an environment in which eventually some vegetation can grow; then a sea-blown bird or rafting mammal can settle down, stay awhile, and interact with other newcomers. The Galapagos are our volcanic island poster child, and Darwin marveled over the similarities he saw between the plants and animals on these raw newcomers and those of the old Ecuadoran mainland. As in parallel universes, what had likely begun with the same materials had followed distinctly different paths. So, too, was the assemblage, or ecological community of plants and animals, similar but not the same. Isolation by water . . . similar but not the same. And thus we come to the critical role observations about geographical distribution (particularly on islands) played in Darwin and Wallace's crowning achievement, the concept of natural selection.

The entire kit and caboodle of Darwin and Wallace's thought plays out, of course, to explain how new species come into being. That was the real gobstopper they hurled into their Victorian milieu, changing the Deity's role from leading man to behind-the-scenes executive producer. They asserted that the "new" issues arose from processes already in motion, influenced by changes in the environment. Both Darwin and Wallace mulled over "An Essay on the Principle of Population," in which Thomas Malthus worried backward and forward about consequences of population growth, given that at some point, naturally, the resources sustaining a population will give out—one of life's ultimate tipping points. Darwin put the question his own way, but here is Wallace, from his autobiography, on a far-flung Ternate island (probably Gilolo) and ill with fever:

> *Why do some die and some live? And the answer was, clearly, that on the whole the best fitted live . . . and considering the amount of individual variation that my experience as a collector had shown me to exist, then it followed that all the changes necessary for the adaptation of the species to the changing conditions would be brought about. . . . In this way every part of an animal's organization could be modified exactly as required, and in the very process of this modification the unmodified would die out, and thus the definite characters and the clear isolation of each new species would be explained.*

Darwin and Wallace saw that when a population had a distinct enough assemblage of adaptations, features both anatomical and behavioral that are "modified exactly as required" to get along in the environment, it was a new species. This rather mushy line in the sand is defined mostly by the point at which species can no longer breed and produce sexually viable offspring (horses and donkeys produce mules but they're sterile). Thus biogeography, the context for geographical isolation, penetrates the history of all of life and how it came about. Ultimately the species concept gives philosophers something to argue about, too. Is life on earth one big thing with pretty permeable boundaries, or are different life-forms truly discrete, individual, separate?

Soulé did not study whether or how lizards had speciated in the Gulf of California, although later researchers showed that one population is indeed genetically distinct. He set about to figure out why different populations of lizards had different physical features; what was going on in the environment to instigate this difference; and when did that happen? The Darwinian framework is all about change.

Even as small an aperture as lizard skin markings can provide an opening into the long view of evolution. One thing that's difficult about absorbing the concept of evolution is that all sorts of different time frames are at work in it at once. When we take a class in history, it's usually defined by a limited chronology, such as "America: 1950–2000." Or in reference to an event: "The Civil War." But the history of those lizards is concerned with all kinds of time periods—populations manifested on different islands at different times. And the islands themselves have different ages.

Most of the thirty-seven islands in the Gulf of California are continental and probably had a population of lizards on them when they became distinct. But in the middle of the Gulf are deepwater islands that were never connected to the mainland—the lizards on these would have gotten out there by drifting on debris during a storm. Soulé explains that "once in a million years a branch with a lizard on it would reach an island. The lizards on the deepwater islands have been isolated for maybe more than a million years. They've had plenty of time to diverge, and they did."

ONE, TWO, THREE

"Fundamentally," Soulé says, asserting something that is more true than ever, "the evolutionary biologist is someone who counts." So he counted up how many lizards were on each island, the situation of each island relative to the mainland, what the living conditions were like for the lizards on each island, and every other little thing about those lizards. He measured things like leg length, the size of scales, and how many scales there are in a line from the back of its nose to its anus. Lizards regulate their body temperature by moving in and out of the sun. The smaller islands are cooler than the big ones, because more of their surface area is surrounded by water; as he expected, lizards on the smaller islands have smaller scales. The big islands have long, hot stretches of land between the shorelines and thus their lizard denizens have larger scales, with more surface area for reflecting back heat. Other morphological, or physical, differences between the lizards include pores on their back legs that produce a waxy substance, and there's individual variation in the number of pores on each lizard thigh, anywhere from nine to thirteen. "What I found was that the populations on the smaller islands had less variability than those on the larger islands. Why? The answer that jumps out is from population genetics."

These days a scientist studying those lizards would perhaps make as careful a catalog of the morphological differences among them as Soulé did, but he or she would also most certainly take a tissue sample back to the lab and eventually produce printouts of their genetic profiles. But in those days, as Soulé says, "there was no way to get at the genetics." This was the late 1960s and early 1970s, and although science knew that genetics provide perhaps the most definitive signature of difference between species, the technology for isolating genes or the proteins they help synthesize hadn't quite been invented.

What exactly transpired between generations and how was implied by Darwin and Wallace, but not at all proved. It is to the credit of Darwin's everlasting intuition that what he proposed as the mechanism of heredity, something he called "pangenesis," and accomplished by "gemmules" passed from mother and father to offspring, bears a rough-outline correspondence to the genetic truth. Darwin's pangenesis didn't fulfill the terms of his own best observations about reproductive patterns, because he proposed that these "gemmules" would create features "blended" from contributions from each parent. But if that were how it worked, then traits would be diluted by continued breeding with individuals with slight differences in that trait—they would get lost in the sauce.[12]

Unbeknownst to Darwin and Wallace, and working at pretty much the same time, a monk named Gregor Mendel was figuring out the exact mechanism of inheritance using pea plants. While the initial obscurity of Mendel's work is generally attributed to his humble modesty, Mendel did have a grand ambition, to develop a "generally predictable law" of heredity. He methodically crossbred pea plants, accumulating an impressive data set that Darwin might have loved. Establishing "constant numerical relationships," in sum Mendel demonstrated that traits are passed on from generation to generation, by some factor that carried information from each parent—that factor would be identified 100 years later as DNA. Mendel demonstrated that some traits are dominant and others recessive; hangers-back will show up eventually as the baton of life is passed down, or not, depending on the combination.

Mendel presented his paper in two oral sessions of the Brunn Society for the Study of Natural History in 1865, and it was published in the Brunn Society proceedings; a deafening silence ensued. In 1900 three scientists separately quoted Mendel in papers on various subjects, thus "rediscovering" Mendelism; according to horticultural historian Jules Janick, "None of the rediscoverers' papers was in the class of Mendel's paper in terms of either analysis or style." Janick says Mendel was simply ahead of his time, and points out that "one paper is not enough. The human qualities that made Mendel admirable as a person—modesty and reticence—worked against his receiving personal acclaim and fame during his lifetime." Ironically Mendel's obscurity can also be traced to the fact that he used math to explain his results, and though this is by far ecology's favorite way to do things now, in those days natural history was mostly anecdotal and narrative-based.

Since Mendel produced his pretty pea plants, genetic research has nailed down the process of heredity. Individuals get a set of genetic instructions, one from each parent; these are copied in the process of sexual reproduction. Some of the instructions are passed on exactly, and some are copied in a slightly different way due to mutation—which actually provides an individual the possibility of expression in form that the parents didn't have. This new variation is essentially what allows for adaptation, since the conditions in which we all live are constantly changing; thus the individual has a new tool for dealing with what that environment presents.

Soulé's frustration at not "getting at" the genetics shortly would find a solution. As he explains it to me, "These two geneticists at the University of Chicago, Richard Lewontin and Jack Hubby, published a paper showing you could use this technique to see how many alleles were controlling the manufacture of a specific protein." An allele is one of two or more forms of a gene that carry a trait—in pea plants, for example, an allele for tall, an allele for short. The year was 1966, and the technique was "gel electrophoresis," which opened the door into the actual physical realities of genes. "Here was a tool I could use to actually quantify genetic variation," Soulé says. The anatomical measures of variation in appearance he had been keeping track of were mirrored by the proteins in the population. "Lewontin and Hubby transformed evolutionary biology from a nineteenth- to a twentieth-century science."

Not Just the Spice of Life

Here's an example of how genetic diversity impels evolution and connects life-forms that exist today to those that came before. Going all the way back to the Cambrian era 542 million years ago, that point in time in which earth exploded into the thronging diversity of life that has continued to this day, "endless forms most beautiful," a lineage called *Cephalopoda* appeared. The word means "head feet" in Greek, maybe because many of these creatures don't seem to have much in between. Cephalopods are mollusks, marine animals with no spinal column, and an early one, the ammonite, left some really beautiful fossils; they are like stone spirals. The ammonite had one hard shell, and this was its defense against predation; along came other species with jaws, the better to crush it with, and ammonites went extinct. However, cephalopods proliferated—they branched out into other versions of themselves, including the chambered nautilus, which survived the extinction event that took out the dinosaurs. Relatives extant today include the spirula, the tiny shell of which is like a chambered nautilus in miniature, and which the animal has internalized. If you have a spirula shell in your hand, the animal is no longer there; if it was, it would look like a squid, to which it is related, and something like a cuttlefish, also related, and both of which have internalized their shell. People will argue squid, but the octopus might just win for cephalopod exemplar, with its eyesight more logically evolved than human eyesight, and its ability to change color faster than we can register it happening. Octopi and squid rule their domains using exactly the opposite sort of strategy their far-off ancestor the ammonite tried; instead of having thick armor against their enemies, they count on shape-shifting, camouflage, and quick getaways.

The ability to get along this way and the very long process of changing its bodily arrangement, outer shell to inner, all came about through evolution. Natural *selection* points to the process of generation upon generation taking from a pool of genetic options and, as Wallace put it, "the best fitted live." That gene pool has been selecting and selecting and selecting from options for all these hundreds of millions of years, and the animals have been changing and changing their strategies for survival, responding to continuously new pressures on them in the environment.

Some scientists poetically call DNA the "fingerprint of evolution," and they look to find the moment when ammonite branched into chambered nautilus; when chambered nautilus branched into its next iterations. Now they can actually pinpoint many of these moments and display them on a computer screen. They look like pretty graphs of color cubes to me, but I'll take their word for it.

DO THE MATH

Gel electrophoresis provided Soulé with a revolutionary tool for counting up genetic diversity in lizards. He could ask which populations on which islands had more "heterozygosity," or more diversity in the gene pool, and which had less, and he could be certain in his calculations. This developed alongside a contextual reboot that put the whole issue in a new framework: the legendary paper "The Theory of Island Biogeography," published by Robert MacArthur and Soulé's longtime friend and compatriot Ed Wilson, aka E. O. Wilson. I asked Soulé when he first became aware of its contents and he said, "The moment it was published."

In fact the 1963 publication of this paper was hardly noted by anyone. Maybe it made a sonic boom in Soulé's ears, but most readers of it reference the book form that came out in 1967. Even that took its sweet time in taking hold of the scientific community, years, in fact, but now the theory of island biogeography will make number two on many a biology professional's list of most influential ideas (after Darwin and Wallace). As Soulé explains it, "They brought ecology, evolution, and biogeography together in a unitary framework to understand spatial patterns in nature. It was a profound literary experience."

I don't know—a literary experience that has equations in it? I concede Pynchon, Foster Wallace . . . but they use equations as metaphors, no? But then again there is a beautiful and indeed literary elegance to the MacArthur-Wilson proposal, which sets up a dynamic balance between life and death. Taking again the island setting favored by Darwin's heirs, the authors address population from the perspective of equilibrium and posit dual forces creating that balance: immigration and extinction. Immigration brings species to an island; extinction takes them out. An island at equilibrium is the result of this ongoing process, its inhabitants coming and going and doing their thing. The changing set of species as some are replaced by others on such an island is called turnover. Right off the bat this reminds me of *The Portrait of a Lady*, by Henry James. Just think of Gilbert Osmond's world, the ever more isolated island of Old European Money, depauperate and getting close to extinction, gene pool dwindled, resources scarce. Enter the immigrant: Isabel Archer, bringing fresh American blood, and money.[13]

Michael Soulé deeply absorbed what MacArthur and Wilson had to say and applied their postulates to his own research. He established the genetic basis for the difference between lizards on smaller and larger islands, and he saw that small-island populations have less genetic variation than populations on large islands, even if you analyzed equivalent areas of land on small and large islands. Bigger islands are bigger targets for immigration, and get more newcomers. More mutations are possible within a larger overall population. And while the rate of extinction continues apace on both island sizes, on the smaller ones extinction outstrips immigration and its attendant renewal. In sum, you need a certain amount of land to sustain a certain amount of population to keep extinction and immigration holding at that balance we know from *The Lion King* as the circle of life.

Robert T. MacArthur, the coauthor of *The Theory of Island Biogeography*, was handsome (in a math nerd kind of way), bold and decisive in his thinking, and he died young, at forty-two, of cancer. To a layperson, his writing is a tantalizing mixture of unusual clarity, for a scientist, and utter incomprehensibility. In *Geographical Ecology: Patterns in the Distribution of Species*, published in 1972, the year of his death, he bracingly declares, "To do science is to search for repeated patterns, not simply to accumulate facts, and to do the science of geographical ecology is to search for patterns of plant and animal life that can be put on a map." To this, subsequent generations of evolutionary biologists, ecologists, and every other sort of -ologist have said, "Amen." Maps rule science today. And the maps he and E. O. Wilson included in their seminal work basically tell the story to anybody who can tell the difference between "more" and "less," and get worried about it.

MacArthur and Wilson illustrated their equilibrium theory with maps by John T. Curtis, a botany professor at the University of Wisconsin who had studied a single small place, 6 miles on a side, and charted this area's progression in four iterations by year: 1831, 1882, 1902, and 1950. In 1831 the Cadiz Township boasted a verdant woodland; in subsequent years the land was developed by degrees, and in 1950, that woodland was reduced to maybe a few tree stands. Now, you expect land that is developed to have its greenery reduced. But MacArthur and Wilson used Cadiz Township as a paradigm and made the observation that development was making islands out of the mainland. Since the number of species an area can support is directionally proportionate to its size, these pieces of woodland not only would start out with proportionally fewer species in them, but they also would lose them faster. MacArthur and Wilson wrote that any natural area could become an island, and so the principles of island biogeography "will apply to an accelerating extent in the future, to formerly continuous natural habitats now being broken by the encroachment of civilization."[14]

Just to give you a soupçon of where this "encroachment of civilization" has in fact come to, in "Monitoring Earth's Critical Zone,"[15] Daniel Richter and Megan Mobley point out that "more than half Earth's terrestrial surface is now plowed, pastured, fertilized, irrigated, drained, fumigated, bulldozed, compacted, eroded, reconstructed, manured, mined, logged, or converted to new uses," and they point out that all this makes changes "in the soil, root zones, and hydro- and bio-active mantles." MacArthur and Wilson predicted fragmentation on the landscape; we are also breaking up the ground itself.

CHAPTER 4

The Disappearance

IN THE 1960S AND 1970S MICHAEL SOULÉ WAS EXCITED BY THE DISCOVeries of his time, but mostly focused on the scientific ones. Of course, a lot else was going on around him, and while it's hard to imagine not being disrupted by the bucking and throwing spirit of the era, he says he was "too busy with science" to tune in or turn on. That nature was in need of defense against "civilized" onslaught was becoming widely apparent. The recently minted International Union for the Conservation of Nature and Natural Reserves published the first list of endangered species in 1958, and in 1960 followed up with a list of 135 endangered mammals. Swedish researchers called attention to acid rain in 1960. Rachel Carson published *Silent Spring* in 1962, and while her book most emphatically drew the evils of pesticides in terms of human health, she also detailed the interconnectedness of the ecosystem. Twenty-three major environmental laws were enacted during the 1970s, including the National Environmental Policy Act, the Marine Mammal Protection Act, the Endangered Species Act, and the National Forest Management Act, and that decade also brought along the first Earth Day. The Wilderness Act did pass in 1964, but most of the general social awareness about threats to the environment focused on toxins, pollutants, oil spills—the excesses of our techno-industrial charging forth. Then, as now, the health and stewardship of the land itself hadn't quite taken center stage.

Soulé's publications during the seventies have such titles as "The Variation Problem: The Gene-Flow Variation Hypothesis" (1971), which lines up phenotypic, or observable, variation, with genetic variation, and concludes that "gene flow between habitats significantly elevates variation, and isolation by distance results in a variation asymptote" ("asymptote" is a geometry term for a line and curve that come ever closer yet will never meet); and "Genetic Variation in Side-Blotched Lizards on Islands in the Gulf of California" (1973), a study whose results "appear to be consistent with the time-divergence theory of genetic variation." Gradually his body of work on the lizards was unfurling a road map and a time table for their extinction. The more isolated lizards had less genetic variation, so they were on the fast track to inbreeding depression; because they were farther away from other lizards, immigration wasn't going to work fast enough to replenish their gene pools.

By about 1977 the tenor of Soulé's article titles changes rather dramatically. There are (among many others) "Habitat Values and Endemicity in the Vanishing Rain Forests of Sri Lanka" (1977); "Benign Neglect: A Model of Faunal Collapse in the Game Reserves of East Africa" (1979); "The Breeding of Endangered Species" (1979); and "Thresholds for Survival: Criteria for Maintenance of Fitness and Evolutionary Potential" (1980). The emphasis of these queries shifted from figuring out how things are working together to observing how they are falling apart. He had turned a corner.

PARADISE LOST

MacArthur and Wilson, the pro-Earth tenor of the '70s, and the evidence of his own eyes had gotten Soulé counting up alleles not just to parse out the history of what had happened on islands, but to figure out how many of them would be necessary to keep the process of life going. "This is where being in San Diego was a big influence," he says. Soulé was a professor at the University of California–San Diego from 1967 to 1979. "When I was born there, the population was 150,000. Now it's 3 million. I was a kid naturalist and collected snakes and brought home abalone and lobster for my family. I got to love these critters. When I came back there as a faculty member at the new UC campus, the place was being devastated. Development was rampantly destroying habitats. This is what makes a lot of biologists into conservationists—the loss of places they love." In the mid-'70s, Soulé got a call from Sir Otto Frankel, an Australian wheat geneticist, who said, "I've read some of your publications on islands and lizards, and I think it relates to my work on maintaining genetic diversity."

Sir Otto Frankel was ahead of the curve, and that's why he got knighted. More than forty years ago he was advocating the saving of seeds, the preserving of different strains of plants that grow in different soil and climate zones. In 1980 Frankel and Soulé published *Conservation and Evolution*. "In this book we attempt to bring together the genetic principles for the conservation of all forms of life. . . . The unifying factor underlying survival and adaptation, in time and in space, is genetic diversity . . . the central theme of this book." One remarkable dimension of the book is the prescience of Frankel, his acceptance of an idea that every year becomes more inevitable and yet which the soul resists: that in the future, nature will not drive evolutionary choices, *Homo sapiens* will. Frankel wrote that to a certain extent man already decides which species live and which die. He wanted to remind everybody to save the raw materials for re-activating the evolutionary process: "the key to the system is the availability of the genetic building materials, the genetic resources, which alone make it possible to continue and advance the adaptive process on which evolutionary success, and indeed man's survival, depend." He was certainly right to worry that we're so dumb we would throw out the ingredients for our soup before we got around to making it. One response to this threat is the Millennium Seed Bank at Britain's Royal Botanic Gardens, Kew, where 10 percent of the world's wild plant species have been banked thus far, and plans are set to collect 25 percent by 2020.

While Frankel concentrated on the plant side of the equation, Soulé concentrated on the animals, and although both considerations have their tough spots, you can collect hundreds of seeds in a small envelope and put them in a freezer. It takes a lot longer to get a commensurate amount of genetic sampling from populations of elephants. And elephants won't just get reseeded in a greenhouse; they need enormous areas of land encompassing different types of ecosystems. You can't save elephants without saving land—and this is true of all the large mammals.

Time Bandits

With his then graduate student Bruce Wilcox, Soulé published his second textbook on the subject, *Conservation Biology: An Evolutionary-Ecological Perspective*. It also was published in 1980. In this book he articulates what's difficult about knowing what to save; fundamentally, we can't choose as well as nature does. Also, we make big assumptions. Adaptation, "the acquisition or modification of traits which 'fit' the organism more perfectly to its environment, is a process known only by inference. . . . Rarely, however, do we understand adaptation in terms of changes in gene frequency." Also, we can't be sure the choices we make will be the right ones for future environments.

In an essay in this textbook Soulé lays out the "time scale" of survival for large-bodied mammals and divides the situation into three dimensions. First you have the threat of inbreeding depression, not enough genetic material to keep the population healthy. Second you have loss of adaptability as a result. Third, the consequence of these two eventualities is that evolutionary adaptation to change in large organisms comes to a "screeching halt."

Again, what is needed to stave off the decline is landmass sufficient to sustain vibrant populations. Soulé warned that if science doesn't determine the minimum area necessary to maintain these three temporal dimensions of animal vitality, "economic and political forces [will] relentlessly encroach on the land." If conservationists don't come up with "minimal population sizes, there will be no rational way to counter these attacks, and all our efforts to salvage samples of our magnificent large plant and animal species will be wasted." And indeed, today states battle with the federal government over "minimum viable populations" of creatures on our Endangered Species List all the time.

A single black note sounded the biggest gong in both textbooks. In *Conservation and Evolution* Frankel and Soulé declare, "Nature reserves are too small to provide for speciation of higher vertebrates or plants." In *Conservation Biology: An Evolutionary-Ecological Perspective* comes Soulé's prognosis that "evolution of large, terrestrial organisms in the fragmenting tropics is all but over." One day I ask Soulé about this. "When you guys noticed what the problem was, it was already too late?" "Yes." "So there's really no hope at all that the large fauna of the tropics will be able to forge its own future, without our interference, which might help these animals survive but kind of like in a zoo?" I was referencing work he had done specifically on the tropics, and he commented that today the dominoes of large-bodied animals are falling everywhere, not just in the tropics, and that yes, speciation is over for them. "That's why us old geezers are so depressed," he says.

STOP TIME

"I should have gone into therapy instead," Soulé says. "I knew it was bullshit within the first two years, but I had uprooted my whole family. I couldn't just walk away." In 1978 Soulé, his pediatrician wife, and their three children moved into the Zen Center of Los Angeles (now called the Kuroda Institute for the Study of Buddhism and Human Values). Yes, that's right, he walked away from academia, despite having achieved a highly enviable place within its ranks. He had plenty of publications, grants, and awards, and heck, the man had tenure. And leaving a career in academia is no small gesture; doing so is frequently likened to walking through a one-way revolving door.

Soulé will simply say, and has said the same thing to journalists these thirty years past, that he was burnt out. "You look at your colleagues. Are they any happier than the Samoans or the villagers in Africa? The answer is no. They're less happy. They're driven and competitive and overworked and anxious. . . . I decided Buddhism was the way for me. I was in touch with *dukkha*, the inevitability of pain and suffering in our lives. At the time, I thought Buddhism would end my anxiety."

He traces his interest in meditation to an informal, silent meeting held by a Stanford statistics professor, Lincoln Moses, who was Quaker. He reports a "flow" experience, in which "all boundaries disappeared. It wasn't nirvana—I had a self that was watching what was going on." This occurred while he was floating in a rowboat in a bucolic lake, upon finishing *The Disappearance*, a novel by Philip Wylie. In Wylie's sci-fi tale, women disappear to men and men disappear to women. The narrative tacks between two parallel universes, each denuded of the opposite sex. "The women get near to inventing artificial parthenogenesis," or the ability that some female species have to reproduce without male assistance. "After two years of this desolation," Soulé recounts, "people learn to appreciate the other sex. They weren't called genders in those days, which is a whitewashing term anyway. It *is* about sex. When they reappear to each other, everyone is happy and ecstatic and joyful at being able to be complete as a species."

THE END OF BIRTH

While I cannot imagine oceanic bliss upon completing its narrative, *The Disappearance* is a remarkable novel. In Robert Silverberg's introduction he recounts Wylie's huge success as a science fiction writer and points out a recurring theme in his work, that of the "isolation of the superior man—the scientist, who learns to make himself invisible, seeks to gain power over others through his use of his secret and is ultimately destroyed by his own special abilities." Wylie's novel *Gladiator*, about a superman, is credited as the inspiration for the comic book character subsequently created by Joe Shuster and Jerome Siegel. Silverberg also points out that *The Disappearance* is erroneously categorized, because "true science fiction requires at least an attempt at rationalizing the fantastic event that is the mainstream of the story, and Wylie does not even try to offer an explanation" for what happens in this one.

The novel might more accurately be called an epistemological inquiry; the main protagonist, philosopher Dr. William Gaunt, muses throughout on the assumptions underlying the semantic ordering of things before this event tears the perceptive veil. Stumbling around in a world without women, Gaunt reflects that "in the demeaning of women, *man has demeaned himself*," and further determines that in defining men and women as fundamentally different, the social world has created a fallacy. "Our outward organs appear greatly different only to the mind that does not intimately know how alike they are and of what identical tissues they have been composed." This point of view he calls "ignorant." The separation at the heart of the action puts the surviving men "in a kind of autonomous extremity, a generic, perhaps animal agony over the likelihood of the ending of the entire species. It was the waking of an instinct, the innermost and the ultimate instinct of living things." Gaunt, like Michael Soulé, recognizes himself to be in the midst of an extinction crisis—one that comes about because of disconnection.

It's pretty interesting that an evolutionary biologist with an emphasis on genetics would have a near-religious experience upon reading a book in which reproduction, and thus evolution, nearly ends and then resumes. In retrospect, is it not completely understandable that a man who had in fact seen the end of evolution might on some level be traumatized by what he now knew and could never not know? "It's not death that I mind," Soulé has said on several occasions. "It's the end of birth that bothers me."

Soulé became director of the Zen Center, and he edited a volume of writings about Buddhism. In one way of seeing it, things went very badly for him there. It isn't the practice he calls "bullshit," but the politics of the center, which in their own way duplicated what he didn't like about academia. His marriage flamed out. (Today he considers his first wife, Jan Chozen Bays, one of his teachers. A practicing pediatrician, she is also co-abbot of the Great Vow Monastery in Oregon and author of *Mindful Eating*.) Of this time in his life, Soulé says, "Everything went to hell."

BATTERING RAMS

As what would soon be formally called conservation biology gestated, its development worked out partly through a big conflict among some of its leading thinkers. In 1976 Jared Diamond (who decades later published best-selling books for a popular audience, *Guns, Germs, and Steel* and *Collapse* among them) published a journal article that set off a long firestorm: "The Island Dilemma: Lessons of Modern Biogeographical Studies for the Design of Nature Preserves." Making one of the first parries to apply theoretical ecology to real life, Diamond suggested that MacArthur and Wilson's island paradigm of extinction dynamic on islands had a practical analogy to "islands" of stranded landmass, made thus by human development that severs connection to the surrounding ecosystems. Since large islands logically hold more species than small ones, and since small ones will lose species faster, he suggested reserves be large. He said they should be spaced closer together rather than farther apart.

Not so fast, said Dan Simberloff, another top-tier scientist looking at these issues. Today a prominent expert in the biology of invasives, Simberloff was another early fan of MacArthur and Wilson, going so far as to declare that their concept of dynamic equilibrium had revolutionized biogeography. But Simberloff felt Diamond had too eagerly applied a theory to the real world and accused him of glossing over details that could possibly make all the difference in how reserves actually function.

Both Diamond and Simberloff worked their hypotheses out from field work; Diamond's island reserve paper was based on his longtime work in New Guinea (on birds; he's an ornithologist), and Simberloff's on Florida mangroves. Simberloff's main *but but buts* were questions asked at a closer level of detail than what he felt Diamond had bothered with. First of all, Diamond had applied the theory as if all species were equal, when that is resolutely not the case; some species are rare, some not; some disperse well, some don't. Ergo, which species are lost first? What pattern of loss do you find regarding the whole structure of the ecosystem? Simberloff said maybe small reserves would work better to safeguard diversity of habitats. Diamond said you need large reserves to support large predators. Of course it wasn't just Simberloff squared off against Diamond; lots of voices joined in the fray. Diamond accused Simberloff of fanning flames that could impede conservation work, as opponents from industry would seize on these niggles to tank the whole enterprise to save nature.

The SLOSS (single large or several small) debate, as it was known, does productively sort a continuing tension in conservation biology today, and that is between the desire and the need to quantify nature's workings, to find inarguable patterns that can support the concrete needs of planning boards and policy makers, and the reality that nature is incredibly specific to place, untidy, and dynamic. Although conservation biology is, yes, about healing nature, fundamentally it's about understanding how nature works, period. How nature works in its entirety is not understood by science, and many say it never will be; nature is bigger than the human capacity for comprehension. We are only part of it, after all.

THE FIGURE IN THE CARPET

"Clearly there was a lot of macho at stake," I say to Mike Gilpin, in his backyard in Bozeman, Montana, on a gorgeous July afternoon, "for that dispute to go on for, what, ten years?" Mike Gilpin was about as up close and personal as anybody in the SLOSS debate; as he put it, "I was Diamond's mathematician." A warm and loquacious guy, Gilpin is retired from the University of California–San Diego, where Michael Soulé hired him back in the day. Now he devotes himself to bike racing. At the moment he's gnashing his teeth that competitors in his age bracket are beating him, despite the fact that he's in top form. Sheer physicality won't do it for him now: "How," he laments, "can I outsmart them?"

On the subject of Diamond and Simberloff, Gilpin ruefully shakes his head, but not without some wonderment in his eyes. Describing himself as a young man, Gilpin says he was a "hot shot" theoretician, someone who grasped and purposed computer modeling before anybody else even had one of the first creaking Macs. But this evident gift comes attached to a humbler self-concept. "I was a lost soul," he says, shifting emotional frequencies to tell me how he had come out of the Peace Corps not knowing what to do with himself, saw Paul Ehrlich on the *Tonight Show*, and decided to be like him. In his first few months of graduate school he went to a talk given by Francisco Ayala,[16] who had performed an experimental invalidation of the principle of competitive exclusion. Say what? Ayala had gotten two species of our favorite lab flies, drosophila, to coexist in a vial with a bit of cornstarch. I know you are as bothered and excited by this as was much of the entire scientific community at the time. "All the superstars tried to rebut him," Gilpin recalls. "But he kept arguing back. No one could explain the paradox. I heard the talk, and I realized what the mistake was. I dashed off a four-page paper to *Nature*." Barely matriculated, Gilpin launched his own career, which he calls "extremely lucky," by means of nonlinear differential equations deployed on a computer. To the credit of his character,

Ayala was pleased as punch with Gilpin and eventually helped him get hired by Michael Soulé in San Diego.

"You have to look at these two guys," Gilpin explains, about Diamond and Simberloff. "They are both highly cultured, East Coast intellectuals. Diamond has a photographic memory, and perfect pitch. He could walk around New Guinea and list the species there by the bird calls. He could do in two days what it took someone else a year to do by catching birds in nets. He was the heir to MacArthur. Based on bird patterns he inferred that extinction was the problem and he wanted to figure out what to do about it.

"Diamond is a nice guy," Gilpin continues, "but he does not like to be insulted. Simberloff basically said he was wrong and a bad scientist. Simberloff said the first thing you have to do when you see a pattern is statistically prove it could not have come about through chance—that's the null hypothesis." Gilpin says Simberloff is more or less a nice guy, too, and he got along well with him "when it was only him and me at dinner." But Simberloff would not let it go with Diamond. "Simberloff is a funny guy," Gilpin says. "In his office he had all these newspaper clippings—Jesus's face in a pizza, Jesus's face in something else—the point being you can find patterns anywhere." He adds that "Simberloff is an insect guy. Diamond is a bird guy. It's quite possible that 'several small' works for insects. Diamond's point is that it doesn't work for bigger species."

In the matter of SLOSS, Soulé is credited with deploying the Zen side of his character as the balancer of opposites, the peacekeeper. While for most of the long battle Soulé was pretty much in the Diamond camp, and his good friend Gilpin went head-to-head against Simberloff on Diamond's side, Soulé took a definitive step past the dichotomy by coauthoring a 1986 paper in *Biological Conservation* with Simberloff: "What Do Genetics and Ecology Tell Us About the Design of Nature Reserves?" Hoping "here to put the issue finally to rest," Simberloff joined with Soulé in giving preference to larger reserves, with the notable quibble that "the SLOSS question that remains unanswered is the dynamics of species extinction *after* the reserves are set up and surrounded by habitat modified by human activities."

Very poetically, for conservation biologists, Soulé and Simberloff asserted that "for a species, the nature refuge is . . . a kind of journey, though it is a journey through time rather than space. It is a journey of millennia. The destination is survival." The paper refocused attention on the fundamental necessities for keeping things going; it advocated identifying keystone or highly interactive species, "those plants or animals that might be especially crucial to maintaining the cohesion of an entire ecological community over time"—in other words, players without whom the show cannot go on for long. Nature doesn't stop entirely when an ecological community breaks down, but can slide into what is called an "alternative stable state," where it functions in some new but degraded way. This is analogous to a trauma victim who figures out a way to accommodate a terrible disturbance. The result may work on some level but isn't healthy. After you identify the key species, the next step is to determine the "minimum viable population" of those species, and then to establish the area necessary to sustain that minimum number. As to single large or several small? "When it comes to nature," Soulé says, "the answer is usually not one thing or another, but both. Another good answer is 'it depends.'"

CHAPTER 5

A Science of Love and Death

THIS COHERENCE OF NEW IDEAS AND THE EVIDENT NEED TO FIND A way to apply them instigated the establishment of a new field, and while Michael Soulé was by no means the only person responsible for this, he organized it and made it happen. With his then graduate student Bruce Wilcox (now an expert on the connection between ecology and infectious diseases), he convened the First International Conference on Conservation Biology in September 1978. All the big guys were there—Jared Diamond, Paul Ehrlich, E. O. Wilson, John Terborgh, and Thomas Lovejoy.[17] Papers from this conference were edited by Soulé and Wilcox and published as *Conservation Biology: An Evolutionary-Ecological Perspective.* The second conference took place in May 1985. Days before that meeting, committees were convened, intentions declared, and a motion to organize the Society for Conservation Biology was approved. David Ehrenfeld, whose 1970 book *Biological Conservation* was an influential precursor to all this, was the first editor of the newborn *Journal of the Society of Conservation Biology.*

In Soulé's words this new amalgam gathered tenets and techniques from a multitude of disciplines, not just from genetics and population biology, but from anthropology, landscape ecology, and sociology. It was conceived to be mission-driven, to apply pure science to the real world with the express purpose of saving it. In a retrospective paper published in 2006, and coauthored with conservation historian Curt Meine and Reed Noss, more about whom is coming up, Soulé and company described the establishment of conservation biology as a way to create a forum for "scientists concerned with extinction and how to prevent it."[18] Bringing the subject of biological diversity to the fore, this discipline reconnected this depth-focus on nature to "sources in western natural history and science to cultural traditions of respect for the natural world (within and beyond the Western experience)."

DHARMA BUM

Remembering these times, Mike Gilpin holds up his memories like a kaleidoscope. "Michael Soulé was a driven young man," he says. "When he was thirty-six he looked like he was about fifty. He's so thin, you know, he has that Gandhi ascetic look, and . . . he's grave. One day he says he had the oceanic experience. Everything is connected. I say, 'Okay, I see that. So what?' He says, 'Life is suffering.'"

Gilpin pauses with emotion. "See, I was following Ehrlich pretty closely, about too much human population, you know. I thought that's what the problem was. But Soulé was looking at extinction. He was the first to see the inbred populations in the Sea of Cortez and see that was the fate of everything, as roads and everything else are making islands all over the place. He sees that things are getting worse. He has this genetic insight that warned us about the problem."

"He was already very highly respected. He says, 'We have to have a meeting. We are going to have the First International Conference on Conservation Biology.' All the right people will be there, all the right issues, the island biogeographical stuff with Diamond and the genetics." Gilpin confesses that he was in equal parts impressed with Soulé's drive and ability to pull this off, and in the dark about what the fuss was about. "I didn't see a new science there." He says, "Michael is a great editor. He took the papers from the conference and he edited them and organized them, and he created the science. It was a really good book. Right before the book comes out, Soulé leaves."

In storytelling, Gilpin is not matched by any scientist I have ever met. M. Sanjayan, a protégé of Michael Soulé's and currently lead scientist with the Nature Conservancy, comes in a fairly close second, but Gilpin is older and has more tales to tell. As I listen to Gilpin, the sun makes a full turn in the Bozeman sky. To avoid its glare I keep adjusting my place at Gilpin's picnic table, until I make a complete circle around him.

Gilpin muses on Soulé's character. "By birth he's a French Jew but adopted by his father." (Soulé's birth father died when he was two.) "He's complex," Gilpin continues. "He has these features in his history that make him question, look deeper. He didn't know who he was." Soulé and his wife, Jan, had two boys, Aaron and Noah, and then adopted a Vietnamese orphan, Ani. "I don't know if she was the last orphan on the helicopter when the war was over or what, but she was one of the last," Gilpin says, and recounts that Soulé and Jan had a tremendously hard time helping her adjust. Ani was five when Michael and Jan adopted her, and Gilpin says it took them six years to convince her she didn't have to hide food under the bed. When the marriage broke up, Ani stayed mostly with Michael. She was rebellious, in trouble a lot, but "Michael was going to fight all the way through, he was going to see it through with this child."

Of his own character, Michael Soulé had on another occasion reminded me that like everyone else, his has "levels and levels." On the matter of the two most evident patterns in his history, his roles as paradigm breaker (chucking a full professorship, for example) and paradigm builder (acting not just as synthesizer among feuding academic colleagues, but also shaping and nourishing a new discipline and eventually hatching a plan to actually save nature), I ask him whether these two impulses might find conjunction in his ability to take a stand. "Part of it is that I've always felt like an outsider, and if that's how you feel, you rebel." He traces this self-concept to growing up Jewish in the resolutely Gentile province of San Diego. At the time he was growing up there (in the 1950s), Jews were not allowed to buy property. "My mother was out of the closet [as a Jew]," he says. "She published an article in a small magazine titled 'Gentlemen's Agreement in La Jolla.'" When Jonas Salk wanted to build his institute in the area, special dispensation had to be made so he could buy a house. On the other hand, we discuss the fact that Jewishness isn't usually a strike against individuals in academia. "Yes," he says. "When you meditate a lot you get to understand your hypocrisies—in fact, the sense of not being in the mainstream has probably helped me."

It would seem that as with biogeography, human biography is a matter of tension between the pieces and the whole. Continuing with his own trajectory Gilpin says, "I've had the most amazing career, and I've gotten to know the most extraordinary people: Francisco Ayala, Jared Diamond, and Michael Soulé. He's driven in this way. . . . He's got demons telling him to do even more all the time and he was committed to becoming enlightened. I don't know what that means. But in his way of being driven he does the most magnificent, generous things." When Soulé realized he wanted to leave the Zen Center, he went to Gilpin, who gave him a place to stay. For a few years there, Soulé was resolutely betwixt and between. "In the scientific world, however, he was famous," Gilpin recalls. Soulé's personal situation was in something of a shambles, but in terms of taking his own reins to save nature, the through-line describing most of his life, he was just getting started.

THE CHALLENGE OF THE REAL

"So Michael was doing some lecturing in my class and working on some projects," Mike Gilpin tells me, explaining that he loaned out the physical space of his lab to Soulé, who funded his work at the time exclusively through grants—he was not employed by any university. "And this call comes in. It's the national wildlife ecologist for the US Forest Service, and he wants to talk to the father of conservation biology." The man was Hal Salwasser, and he was taking very seriously an injunction in the National Forest Management Act as amended in 1976, which intoned that in protecting and improving the forest, viable populations of its vertebrate species must be maintained. Of the environmental legislation established during this time, Gilpin says, "Some very smart guys were writing this stuff." Guys with enough foresight and nuance to stipulate the word "viable," which is a pretty broad term meaning "able to live." What was a "viable population"? Soulé had previously proffered 50 as the smallest number that would prevent inbreeding depression in the short term; the number was 500 for a species' long-term survival. But what was short-term and what was long-term? Salwasser had come to Soulé with a very real-world question about all he had been cogitating. And he didn't have the answer.

"Soulé and I talked about this every day. It was the central thing we were both thinking about. You could say, well, I'm going to worry about genetics," says Gilpin. "But is that the main thing here? We have to go beyond genetics to consider individuals and populations in space and time. Genetics assumes a small population, stochastic. Looking at it from a metapopulation angle, that's all about presence-absence." "Stochastic" is from the Greek *stokhos,* for "guess, aim, mark," in the sense of shooting a target; in biology it means "random," and it is understood that random events happen in nature all the time, stuff you can't precisely determine. What happens to a single population has to be considered in the context of the metapopulation it is part of. Going back to the islands in the Gulf of California, you could say that each island has a population of lizards, and collectively, all the island populations make up a metapopulation. *Meta* is Greek for "in the midst of" and used here in the sense of community as aggregate. Metapopulation theory is similar to island biogeographical theory in exposing the vulnerability of species on nearly isolated pieces of land unless there is some possibility of movement between them. If a stochastic event such as a fire or flood takes out one population, the metapopulation may or may not be okay, depending on the possibility of renewal from nearby sources.

Lots of other influences come to bear on presence-absence, or where you find the smaller populations that together make up the metapopulation, and where you don't find them. Gilpin and Soulé hashed this all out with the aid of a workshop convened with Salwasser at Ann Arbor in 1984, at the University of Michigan, which had recently hired Soulé. The result was a book, *Viable Populations for Conservation.*

A minimum viable population (MVP) number had to take into account basically everything that affects a species—as Soulé put it in the book, it requires "a prediction based on the synthesis of all the biotic and abiotic factors in the spatial-temporal continuum." Got that? The living and the dead. Kingdom without end, amen. Or actually, with an end. MVP had been wrestled with earlier by Mark Shaffer, whose 1978 doctoral dissertation was titled "Determining Minimum Viable Population Sizes: A Case Study of the Grizzly Bear (*Ursus arctos L.*)." Shaffer divided the categories of impact into human-caused and stochastic. The big roundup of causes included recessive genes, floods, hunting, and so on. Assigning values to each contingency and calculating their effects on the overall survivability of the species (via computer) got you the MVP number. Shaffer emphasized the need for a "biological bridge" between "islands" of grizzly bear populations.

Soulé and Gilpin decided together to amp up the minimum viable population concept to better address natural dynamics. Individual risks to species would affect other risks—organisms would respond to a given pressure in a way that would have a rippling effect, and influence the efficacy or impact of another risk factor. In other words, there's not just cause and effect; there's cause and effect and effect and effect, and then another cause comes on in and effect and effect, etc.

One example of this rippling is illustrated by the plight of the black-tailed prairie dog, a once proliferative burrowing rodent, populations of which have been vastly reduced by farmers and ranchers who don't like the way they dig up and disrupt the land. In excavating their elaborate burrow system, prairie dogs change the soil chemistry, making it more porous to rain, and increasing the amount of organic materials that nourish it; they are like rototillers adding organic compost to the ground. The result is increased nitrogen content and higher populations of nematodes in the soil, which helps create richly nutritious plant life that in turn sustains herbivores. In imbuing the soil with such life, prairie dogs make what would be a two-dimensional grassland—grass and the world above it—into a three-dimensional system, with the critters in the dirt contributing indirectly to the vibrancy of those crawling, scurrying, and flying overhead. So, take out the prairie dog, and you start by losing that one species. Then add to it all the species in the soil you lose as a result, and then the impoverishment of the vegetation that results. So this is effect and effect. Invasive mesquite is known to take over areas in Texas where prairie dogs have been removed; gone are the habitat and forage for species such as ferrets, ferruginous hawks, and mountain plovers. Prairie dog colonies are associated with sustaining more than 170 other species. So eventually the ripples get very wide and deep indeed.

Working with four categories of impact: demographic, inbreeding (genetic), fragmentation, and adaptation, Soulé and Gilpin conceived each as instigating a feedback loop. When a feedback loop gets going, it makes the species more susceptible to falling into another of the feedback loops. The visual they conceived is interdependent vortices, swirling down drains of extinction processes. They called this widening and deepening of MVP population viability analysis, or PVA.

Soulé and Gilpin applied population viability analysis to another real-world question posed by the US Fish and Wildlife Service about the Concho water snake, in relation to a dam about to be built in Texas. The snake lives in small, separated habitat patches, typifying the island biogeographical situation; there was no regenerating mainland from which new genetic donations could issue. The Concho water snake was ranked as "threatened" on the Endangered Species List. (It was removed in 2011.)

The predictive power of PVA to assess the vulnerability of species to extinction has been increased by orders of magnitude since Soulé and Gilpin refined the model in the 1980s. In the first place, much more raw biological data on species has been and is being collected. Today populations are monitored annually; animals are radio collared or otherwise marked and carefully tracked to collect information about exactly where they go and when. Species' connection to the landscape is much more accurately and exhaustively analyzed now with the help of precise geographic information about land use, land cover, soils, elevation, and so on. Climate variables, such as temperature and precipitation, are likewise incorporated. And finally, computing power has exploded, making it possible as never before to process vast quantities of data, the minutiae of which nature is comprised, and to create statistical models for evaluating it. PVA today even simulates birth, death, and migration processes.

One of PVA's foremost contemporary practitioners is H. Resit Akcakaya, a professor at Stony Brook University and chair of the International Union for Conservation of Nature Red List Standards and Petitions subcommittee; Akcakaya also developed the primary PVA software tools in use today. "PVA incorporates all aspects of a species ecology," he explains. "If you look at only habitat, you won't get reproductive information. If you look at seed dispersal but don't consider how the habitat will fragment, you won't get the whole story. PVA allows you to integrate impacts and processes." When I make my mewling liberal-artsy protest that it doesn't seem likely a computer could possibly capture nature's intricacies, Akcakaya reminds me that specific, one-dimensional questions are most useful for making policy decisions about species. "The human brain can make decisions about a complex thing," he adds, "if that complex thing is based on a human experience. We use our emotions. We make an emotional judgment. But we can't think like a plant or an animal." When faced with multidimensional situations, different people bring different emotions to bear on decision-making. This is precisely the subjectivity quotient statistics and models are deployed to transcend. Ackcakaya continues. "We ask, 'How does rainfall affect the survival of this toad?' and we put that information in a modeling framework that is consistent, transparent—you always know what the results are based on."

As PVA expressly moves qualitative opinion into quantitative assertions, and with its tremendous capacity to incorporate all kinds of biological information, including earth system processes, it is a huge tool for helping understand how climate change will affect species. It does this in a relatively simple way, by measuring what temperature and precipitation levels a species lives in now, compared to what the temperature and precipitation in that particular region will be in fifty or one hundred years.

Life Lessons

Meanwhile, back at the national parks . . . Sometimes a doctoral dissertation blows everybody away, and that's what happened in 1987 when William Newmark published an article based on his, titled "A Land-Bridge Island Perspective on Mammalian Extinctions in Western North American Parks," in *Nature*. (Wouldn't "Trapped in Eden, Animals Perish" catch him a few more readers?) Looking at a map of North America, as conservation biologists are wont to do, Newmark noticed that those splotches representing national parks looked a lot like . . . islands. Testing his analogy under the mental umbrella of our favorite theory, that of island biogeography, Newmark hopped in his car. National parks keep tabs on the critters within their boundaries, so Newmark was able to talley up the number of species present in each over time. (As Michael Soulé counsels, when in doubt, count.) And thus forty-two types of native mammals from fourteen North American parks had disappeared over the previous decades. Badger and black bear from Zion, northern flying squirrel, beaver, and pronghorn from Bryce Canyon, and on and on. Kind of like a realization in a horror movie, where the besieged have battened down all the hatches only to find the zombies have vaporized through the walls . . . these lands, these animals, were protected, but it didn't do them a damn bit of good. Michael Soulé was on Newmark's doctoral committee. This thesis was proof in the conservation biology pudding: the national park system, a bust for animals. Boundaries were not the answer.

CHAPTER 6

The Real Work

IT IS ONE THING TO DECLARE A NEW SCIENCE; IT IS ANOTHER TO MAKE it stick. "These guys were mathematicians, geneticists, and they didn't fit into wildlife ecology," remembers Adina Merenlender, coauthor of *Corridor Ecology: The Science and Practice of Connectivity for Biodiversity Conservation*, and who now teaches in the Environmental Science, Policy, and Management School at the University of California–Berkeley. Merenlender was a graduate student in the audience eagerly absorbing the proceedings as the Society for Conservation Biology was founded in 1986. "They had turned their attention to species demographics, and had their own battles about that; they adapted theories from ecology, like island biogeography, and they were looking at genetic consequences of demographic populations. Hook and bullet they did not know." Here she is referring to a world more directly familiar with wildlife—those who hunt and those who fish.

While young people like Merenlender were eager for and excited by this new field of conservation biology, there was plenty of resistance and just plain befuddlement around it—conservation did not know from science, and science did not know from conservation. And the wildlife managers closest to the actual subject were accustomed to looking at problems differently than either conservationists or scientists. Scott Mills, who is today a professor at the University of Montana, and a 2008 Guggenheim fellow, remembers that when he was getting his master's degree in biology at Utah State in the mid-1980s, "if the question of how we should consider managing wildlife came up, you had to be in the closet about discussing it. You weren't a 'scientist' anymore." Mills "studied wildlife because I love wildlife," and the experience in Utah disillusioned him. "After that I interned at the National Wildlife Federation. Michael's yellow book came out and I read that sucker from cover to cover. I realized, wow, here is a person doing real science and not only is it okay to do applied conservation, there's a mandate to do it." Mills went on to do his doctoral work under Soulé.

As author David Quammen points out, Soulé's book titles have become known to "chromatically inclined insiders" by their predominant cover colors. The "yellow book" (others are brown, green, and gray) is *Conservation Biology: The Science of Scarcity and Diversity,* and this book likewise impacted M. Sanjayan. Like Mills, Sanjayan was also a biology student, also a lover of wildlife, but had grown up never imagining he might have a career directly involving it; this, his parents told him, "is not something people of my color do; it's something white people do. I see Gerald Durrell and David Attenborough on television, and indeed, they are white." Sanjayan picked up the book while getting a master's degree in biology. "Conservation—I had never heard of that word." Sanjayan didn't remember the color yellow, but rather the rhinos on the cover. He also became a doctoral student of Soulé's.

With the now explicitly quantifying tool of genetics at its disposal, conservation biology was a hammer-out-the-numbers affair (as it continues to be). "Michael held us to the highest standards of pure science. He told us, 'Be the best population biologist, be the best modeler, the best geneticist, and apply all that to conservation,'" says Mills. "I continue to tell my students they have to be able to hold credibility toe-to-toe with people who do 'pure' work." These former students of Soulé's have gone on to do important research themselves and to publish influential books. Scott Mills wrote the 2007 *Conservation of Wildlife Populations: Demography, Genetics, and Management.* Sanjayan is coauthor with another Soulé protégé, Kevin Crooks, of *Connectivity Conservation* (2006).

Through the 1980s and into the early '90s, Soulé continued to measure and analyze: alleles, numbers of species, areas they lived in. The dimension of his character that brought him to Zen Buddhism also continued to unfold. "I remember him in lotus position at Santa Cruz," says

Merenlender, laughing. "Sometimes this did not go over so well." I ask Soulé about that. "I tried to teach the students to meditate," Soulé says. "What was I thinking?"

If it was a bit of a stretch to solicit the inner peace of a bunch of twenty-something biology students at the University of California in the mid-'80s, however, the impulse to integrate values from a spiritual discipline into a quantifying system of knowledge echoes with historic precedence. Even today's number-crunching computer systems and modeling frameworks can be traced back to primary questions about the order of the universe.

LOOK AT IT THIS WAY

In pursuing both the scientific and the moral effects of the natural world, Soulé is a significant heir to the naturalists who came well before him. In "The Real Work of Systematics," a paper he published in the *Annals of the Missouri Botanical Garden* in 1990, Soulé refreshes the concept of what taxonomy is all about and he does it with quite a twist. In the first place he quotes the Victorian essayist Thomas Carlyle at the beginning of the article: "Blessed is he who has found his work; let him ask no other blessings." This may perhaps be the first and only instance of the word "blessings" in any scientific document post-Darwin. Systematics is, again, the sorting and naming of all plants, animals, fungi, and microorganisms. The idea is that by comprehending these systems we can better analyze how they work. Systematics is arguably the foundation of all biological sciences, since it lays down the grid upon which subsequent science has been articulated. You can't know what nature is up to if you don't know exactly what's there, how much of it there is, and how the parts are related.

In this piece Soulé points out the then fairly recent revelation that the earth's denizens probably don't add up to a few million species; they add up to many millions. (The counting continues today. The 2011 State of Observed Species report by the International Institute for Species Exploration at Arizona State University tallies up 19,232 new-to-science species discovered during the calendar year 2009, pushing the total close to 2 million. The report also says a safe guess is that 10 million more species could be added to that number.) This explosion in awareness was brought about by the tool of molecular genetics, and by increased exploration especially in the tropics. On the one hand we haven't discovered all life yet, not by a long shot; on the other hand, extinctions are accelerating, and many species are going extinct before we know of them.

Given this problem of "too many species and too much extinction," Soulé asks whether taxonomists should really be spending their time laboring over each and every species. Lots of the unnamed species are insects; lots more are microorganisms; and "the demise of vast numbers of bugs and worms is signaling the loss of habitat and ecosystem services . . . on which all other species, including humans, depend." He calls for new techniques for identifying species more quickly—in subsequent years, these have in fact been invented, and there is currently a robust effort under way to actually barcode the DNA of all life.[19] He adds that in "responding to these twin crises, we must look inward as well as outward," again, not verbiage you find in scientific papers, even opinion pieces like this one. He asserts that "the species problem" still exists: "Should every geographic (evolutionary) entity be elevated to species rank?" Soulé is asking one of the fundamental questions of science, the one Darwin and Alfred Russel Wallace grappled with, and the one that still instigates a great cultural divide in the United States. What is a "species"? What is the basic unit of life, how does a new one get started, and how are life-forms related? These compose the "species problem."

Back to Basics

As Soulé reminds the reader, the work of systematics "to classify all life" has a nearly 300-year-old pedigree. Aristotle and Pliny before him had described life-forms and put some categories around them, but Linnaeus established a methodology based on the now well-known binomial system of naming. Before the class, order, species, and variety hierarchy of identity, naturalists were naming things all over the place; Linnaeus established the equivalent of a spreadsheet, eventually to be reconceived into a vast family tree of all life by Darwin and Wallace, something to which new names and observations could be added according to precedent and based on similarities.

We credit indigenous cultures with imbuing the natural world with a numinous dimension, as well we should; we often forget that European traditions also reverenced the Creation (and many still do). Expressly viewing his passion for plants in the context of God, Linnaeus thought of himself as a "pastor of nature." He charged his own daily activity with helping along a sacred enterprise, to understand and revere the Creator's work. He also set himself the task of explaining the origin and distribution of life. Who, what, when, and where were points of entry through which understanding nature led directly to understanding and worshipping God. Thus, biogeography was conceived by Linnaeus as an enterprise of devotion.

There are lots and lots of different creatures and plants all over a big earth, and the more you look, the more you find. These come replete with different adaptation needs: forest, tundra, desert—the same creatures do not all live in the same sort of habitat. Linnaeus opined that the Eden of Genesis was located on the slopes of a "Paradisiacal Mountain," which he located near the equator, and he further posed his Paradisical Mountain as an island—at first the earth's only landmass. He imagined the heaving and tossing of the oceans spit up rocks and other materials to create the other big hunks of terrestrial earth, and that species heading out from the Paradisiacal Mountain hitched from there onto new pieces of land on the backs, in the beaks and feathers, and in the stomachs of other creatures. In all this, Linnaeus intuited a great deal of what subsequent scientists would show to have in fact occurred, the roiling seas, the de novo islands, the dispersing creatures.

Scientific inquiry continued to be deeply twined with spiritual matters. Linnaeus surmised that Noah's ark had landed on Mount Ararat, in Turkey, and the happy couples had headed out to new territories from there. Georges-Louis Leclerc, Comte de Buffon, pursed his lips on that one: How could those critters get across landscapes that would kill them? Rivaling the elegance of Linnaeus's title *Systemae Naturae*, Buffon published *Histoire Naturelle* (thirty-six volumes published between 1749 and 1788, and wonderfully illustrated), in which he proposed that the ark had landed farther north than Linnaeus suggested, and when the inhabitants set out for new homes, they changed as they went along, to suit the different climates they passed through and to fit into the environments where they put down stakes. Two critical concepts were thus added into the concept of biogeography: the ideas that climates and species are changeable. For this idea he is called a "transformist." Add to that his observation, subsequently called Buffon's Law and cited as the first principle of biogeography, that similar environments yet house distinct assemblages of plants and animals, and notice the long red carpet being laid out for Darwin and Wallace.

FOLLOW THE RULES

Further developments in biogeography continued to be codified in a highly categorical way, and named for the men who asserted them: In the nineteenth century, Gloger's Rule stated that among species represented in climatically diverse habitats, those in more humid surrounds are darker in color than those in drier ones. Bergmann's Rule is that warm-blooded vertebrates in warmer climates have smaller bodies than their species brethren in cooler climates. Allen's Rule is that in those same warm-blooded vertebrates, the ones living in cooler climates have shorter extremities and more compact bodies. These rules are about adaptation to climate and were establishing the basis by which we know now that species are inextricably associated with their environment. In the more-on-that department, in 1860 E. W. Hilgard showed that climate and plant life directly affect the decomposition of rock into different types of soil. Climate influences how plants decompose, which in turn influences the pH, mineral composition, and texture of soil, and that goes on to impact what plants can grow there to begin with; what plants are in a place drives the kind of animals that live there, too.

THE POWER OF PLACE

How we got from a system thought to be divine to one basically interpreted by numbers came partly by way of Alexander von Humboldt, a unique historic figure who wrote and traveled voluminously, counted among his friends and fans Thomas Jefferson (they compared their collections of mammoth teeth), and must rank high on the list of having geographical locations named after him. These include the Humboldt Current in the South Pacific, and on American soil, towns and counties from Iowa to South Dakota, Tennessee, and Nevada. The famous pot-growing center of the United States, Humboldt County in California, is named perhaps in testament to his fluid descriptions and understanding of interconnectedness, the appreciation of which its product promotes; his five-volume magnum opus is called *Cosmos*.

Humboldt hugely influenced the American transcendentalists. Ralph Waldo Emerson said he was "one of those wonders of the world . . . who appear from time to time, as if to show us the possibilities of the human mind." The Emersonian philosophy of the "transparent eyeball" through which the self is blended with nature is a Humboldtian construct. He was a great thinker but Humboldt was also a great field biologist, and he based his voluminous writings on travel all over the world. Humboldt brought natural philosophy to new heights; he also mapped a great deal of what was newly American soil (and South American). It's hard to imagine an equivalent figure today, but Humboldt was a popular hero. Even John Muir declared in a letter, "How intensely I desire to be Humboldt!"

The way Humboldt saw it, all human life is influenced by the environment, and plant assemblages are intermediaries moderating the physical and moral worlds; he did not believe in one Creator but sustained appreciation for a numinous dimension. "How powerfully have the skies of Greece acted on its inhabitants! . . . The poetry of the Greeks, and the ruder songs of the primitive northern nations owe great part of their peculiar character to the aspect of the plants and animals seen by the bard, to the mountains and valleys which surrounded him, and to the air which he breathed."[20] His emphasis on plant geography and belief that topographical patterns in nature hold clues to a more fundamental knowledge of life itself are among the characteristics that make Humboldt "an astonishingly relevant figure for the twenty-first century."[21]

BOTANICAL ARITHMETIC

To really study regions, Humboldt considered, you have to compare them to one another. Science historian Janet Browne observes that the challenge of how to do this "led naturalists into something of a quandary . . . having neither methodological conventions nor authoritative concepts to underpin their work in this particular direction." Humboldt proposed what he called "botanical arithmetic," "an elementary numerical technique that reduced absolute figures into statements of a proportional kind, which could then be arranged with others in a table." Botanists using this method could locate predominant life-forms in a region, focus on relationships thus revealed between classes and families, and sort them by geographical zone. As Humboldt's botanical arithmetic developed, it became the template for understanding distribution, and gave Darwin and his peers a way to track the principle of divergence, and thus to figure out speciation, observing adaptation, isolation, and thus, evolution. One also sees in his method the very first stirrings of what would become the statistical analysis of nature, and modeling such as PVA.

Humboldt died in 1859, the year Darwin published *On the Origin of Species,* and in some ways this moment represents a baton pass. Darwin admired and absorbed Humboldt fully, and equally promoted the concept of life on earth as a vast family tree of connection, but he leaves any internal "moral" coherence out of it. It is worth reiterating that Humboldt did not believe in a single Creator and so it was not just a God-topple that occurred here. It was more of a reframing of the subject of nature into an entirely scientific definition, science not as Humboldt practiced it, but ironically shaped by him, via his contribution of botanical arithmetic. Science today pretty much seeks to find not a moral equivalent in nature, but a numerical one. It abstracts nature to determine its mathematical correlations, and it is aided and abetted by computer power. As was Darwin, Humboldt was transfixed by unity and diversity, and he sought to help analyze the way these two expressions coincide—and now, there's probably an app for that.

Scientists still collect specimens the way Linnaeus did and have done so all these years in between; when molecular genetics came along and it became possible to identify a species with confidence using DNA, traditional taxonomy fell out of favor. Today climate change has reinvigorated the need for saving and cataloging all those physical pieces of evidence. As Healy Hamilton, who presides over massive computer modeling of species distributions, says, "They are the most verifiable record of life on earth. With them we can establish what life was like before our current climate change event, when life was 'normal.'" When Hamilton approaches a species distribution model, the first thing she does is gather all the museum records about where those animals have occurred; this tells her a species' historical range, by which she can determine its climate envelope—the range and variation in temperature and precipitation to which it is accustomed. She also knocks on the digital door of the Global Biodiversity Information Facility (GBIF), located in Copenhagen, which is attempting to convene all the digital information about the hundreds of millions of specimens in the world's collections. "Bioinformatics" describes the wrestling of biological detail into a consistent digital format so that it can be aggregated and accessed easily; inputs include traditional taxonomic identifications, DNA sequences, photographs, and distribution maps. Hamilton bewails the fact that of the 326 million records of the history of life on the GBIF (as of today—the number grows quickly!), only a small percentage are georeferenced (associated with a latitude, a longitude, a date, and a time). All of this is very much a foray into the new digital world that amplifies the categories of Humboldt's botanical arithmetic to a level he might call cosmic.

TO SPEAK OF LOVE AND BEAUTY

In his paper on systematics, Soulé suggests a few guidelines for prioritizing the taxonomic tasks, such as concentrating on representative groups of tropical insects; focusing on keystone or highly interactive species and their mutualists (the term refers to a biological interaction by which more than one species benefits). His concluding suggestion is that "education is also a high priority. . . . As teachers, systematists can profess the love of nature to students, the younger the better." Then he says, "The last of the preceding proposals brings me to my final point— it is OK for systematists to speak of love and beauty. It is even OK for systematists to express emotions in public." He paraphrases the poet Gary Snyder, with whom he has had a long friendship through the Zen

Center: "Giving succor to the earth is our final and most adult task, our real work."

In his 1974 poem "I Went into the Maverick Bar," Snyder writes about putting his hippie hair up under a cap to drink with fellow Americans "in Farmington, New Mexico." The poem concludes upon leaving the bar: "In the shadow of bluffs/I came back to myself,/To the real work, to/What is to be done." Decades later Snyder explained to Bill Moyers that "the real work is becoming native in your heart, coming to understand we really live here, that this is really the continent we're on and that our loyalties are here, to these mountains and rivers, to these plant zones, to these creatures. The real work involves developing a loyalty that goes back before the formation of any nation state, back billions of years and thousands of years into the future. The real work is accepting citizenship in the continent itself."[22]

DEEP ECOLOGY

In addition to Snyder's, another significant influence on Soulé's evolving thought can be discerned in this paper, especially in the assertion that it is "OK for systematists to express emotions in public." In keeping with his predilection for convening powwows, while Soulé was at the Zen Center he organized a symposium on Buddhism and ecology, and asked Snyder to come. "He was going out of the country but he told me the philosopher Arne Naess was in the US. He said, 'He's great, invite him.'"

On a March 2011 afternoon at his dining room table in Paonia, Colorado, Soulé's eyes fill while he recalls the Norwegian philosopher Naess, who died in 2009 (at age ninety-seven). "He was absolutely brilliant—the youngest person to ever be made professor in philosophy [age twenty-three] the University of Oslo. He was charismatic and childlike. I learned just from watching him. Whenever there was a child around, he fell to his knees at their level and played. He was totally unselfconscious. He had very few inhibitions. He was very much into simplicity like Thoreau. He was tough, a mountain man—it ran in the family. His nephew [Arne Naess Jr., who was married for a spell to Diana Ross] made more ascents of Everest than anyone but the Nepalese. I consider him my most significant mentor after graduate school."

In the 1970s Naess began to differentiate between what he saw as "shallow ecology," in which technological fixes and palliatives, such as recycling, stop short of true fundamental change, and he observed that these impulses are centered on the same consumption-based values that got us into trouble to begin with. He proposed an ethic he called "deep ecology," which penetrates to the level of fundamental change and necessitates a cultural renovation to support the ecological and cultural diversity of natural systems. Deep ecology thus receives and respects the "ecosophies" of indigenous cultures. It fundamentally critiques the wheels of industrialization, which justifies using the earth's raw materials to fuel, in the words of Naess scholar Alan Drengson, "inflated desires."[23] Deep ecology posits that the denizens of nature have a right to exist in and of themselves, regardless of their utility to *Homo sapiens*.

Soulé and Naess remained good friends over the ensuing decades. "He would visit me in Santa Cruz and we would work separately in the early mornings, then have a seminar together at around 10 a.m.," remembers Soulé. "We talked about getting down to ultimate causes. One day we asked ourselves, 'What should we do to save biodiversity in North America?' And the answer was clear. It dawned on me that we know what the problems are, primarily habitat loss and fragmentation, so once you identify the disease you can think of the therapy. It was obvious: Restore the connectivity. Basically I concluded from that discussion that we need to connect up all the wild places."

CHAPTER 7

Triple Crown

SOULÉ WAS PURELY AN ACADEMIC, ALBEIT OF A ZEN, MEDITATING, VARIETY. To follow through on nature's therapy, he had to find himself a conservation activist. He wrote a letter to Dave Foreman, whom he had met once, and who is without exaggeration a legend in the world of wilderness advocacy.

Foreman goes down in history partly as the 1980 founder of Earth First!, an often radical grassroots group born of disillusionment with trying to protect nature through approved channels. Foreman worked for the Wilderness Society beginning in 1973; he was Southwest regional representative in New Mexico and later director of Wilderness Affairs in Washington, D.C.—aka a lobbyist. Foreman is not a scientist but is widely credited with an encyclopedic knowledge and intuitive comprehension of the workings of nature and its landscapes, especially the larger ones. In Washington, he was an impassioned bureaucrat soon to understand firsthand Machiavelli's dictum that politics has no morals. Perhaps influenced somewhat by the legislative victories of the 1970s, with the Clean Air and Water Acts, and the Endangered Species Act, the Big Green environmental nonprofits increasingly plied their trade "at the table," brokering deals with the powers that be in Washington. While certain grounds were gained via this strategy, there were also significant giveaways. An example of this occurred in the late '70s, a battle royale colloquially called RARE II, for the Forest Service's Roadless Area Review and Evaluation. Instead of designating millions of acres of Forest Service land protected as wilderness, the initiative was voided; in the end 36 million acres of forest service land instead were released to logging. Foreman had worked long and hard inventorying roadless areas in the Southwest during RARE II and its predecessor, RARE I; the perceived giveaway of these pristine areas completely disillusioned him and he quit his job.

As recounted by sociologist Douglas Bevington in his 2009 book, *The Rebirth of Environmentalism,* environmental activists laid a good part of the blame for the RARE II debacle at the feet of their brethren at the big national environmental organizations. Pursuing compromise, they had given away the store; they were too full of expense account lunches to even notice how they had been had. Bevington's book is a penetrating historical look at what exactly gets done by whom in the environmental protection arena; he enumerates instance after instance in which big nationals end up giving away more than they get. That's certainly what happened in RARE II, which provoked betrayed outrage. Bevington quotes Howie Wolke, with Foreman a cofounder of Earth First!: "We played by the rules. We were moderate, reasonable, professional." But their efforts had an inverse effect to their intentions. "That's when I started thinking, 'Something's missing, here. Something isn't working.' That's what led to Earth First! More than anything else."[24]

Earth First! took a purist, outsider position: "No compromise in defense of Mother Earth" was its slogan, and it was grounded in a decentralized, grassroots sensibility. Resolutely macho in tone ("Earth First! is a warrior society"), Foreman further described its project: "The idea of wilderness . . . is the most radical in human thought. . . . Earth is not for *Homo sapiens* alone. . . . Wilderness [is] for wilderness. For bears and whales and titmice and rattlesnakes and stinkbugs. And . . . for human beings. Because it is the laboratory of human evolution and because it is home."

Foreman was famously friends with wilderness icon Edward Abbey, the author of many books, including the classics *Desert Solitaire* and *The Monkey Wrench Gang;* love him or hate him (lots of people seem to feel both ways), Abbey's writing stands alone in the nature genre for muscle and energy. The jacket blurb on my copy of Abbey's *The Monkey Wrench Gang* calls it a "classic comic gem of destructive mayhem and outrageous civil disobedience—the novel that sparked the environmental movement!" Regardless of whether Foreman and Wolke were directly influenced by it, they took to the monkey-wrenching spirit, in which they physically interfered with activities deemed environmentally detrimental. Bevington holds that while monkey-wrenching was a core identity of this fresh bloom of environmental activism, it got media attention far in excess of its actual deeds. In one notorious but not exactly harmful monkey-wrenching display, in 1981 Foreman, Abbey, and others unfurled a 300-foot black plastic "crack" down the wall of the Glen Canyon Dam, yelling, "Free the Colorado River!" Several months after Edward Abbey's death, Foreman and his wife were woken by FBI agents who arrested him. Accused of planning to blow up power lines, a plot he in fact had no part of, it later appeared the FBI had included him in their roundup based on pretty much nothing but his reputation. Nevertheless, he eventually pleaded guilty to felony conspiracy and agreed to stop advocating monkey-wrenching.

Taking a chronological look at Foreman's own contributions to environmental literature not only reflects the man's personal intellectual evolution but in some ways synopsizes developments in conservation activism at large over the same time period. From 1982 to 1988 Foreman edited the *Earth First!* journal, devoted to the nuances of what some call ecoterrorism; collected columns from this series were published in 1985 as *EcoDefense: A Field Guide to Monkeywrenching.* Following the above-mentioned *The Big Outside,* he published *Confessions of an Eco-Warrior* in 1993. With Doug Peacock he wrote a novel, *The Lobo Outback Funeral Home* (2004).[25] In 1991, Foreman and another Wildlands founder, John Davis, began editing the *Wild Earth* journal, a publication beloved until its demise in 2004.

Foreman's 2004 *Rewilding North America* is dedicated to Michael Soulé, and it is deeply influenced by the precepts codified by conservation biology; Foreman credits Soulé with coining the term "rewilding" to describe restoring not just the players in an ecosystem but also processes, to restore healthy functioning. *Manswarm and the Killing of Wildlife* is Foreman's 2011 book, in which he tacks full-circle back to Paul Ehrlich. "The population bomb did not fizzle. It blew up. It is still blowing up."

These days Foreman, who left the Wildlands Network in the early 2000s, is somewhat reclusive, though he continues to publish, does some occasional public speaking, and with his wife leads wilderness expeditions. On the website for his Rewilding Institute he posts "Around the Campfire with Uncle Dave Foreman," which picks up in spirit where *Wild Earth* journal left off.

SELF-WILLED

Kim Vacariu, the Wildlands Network leader of the Colorado Plateau workshop, is one among many who wish the old Dave was back on center stage in the conservation movement. "He's an incredible, galvanizing speaker," says Vacariu, telling me about a talk Foreman gave at the University of Arizona in the mid-1990s. "I'm there with my table set up, you know, with information to give out about our little nonprofit. Dave is giving a speech to a huge auditorium packed with students. I'm waiting for him to finish, hoping to sign up a dozen people or so in support of Wildlands. At the end of the speech, Dave howls. The kids howl back. Then they storm the stage. I'm holding on to my brochures for dear life!"

I got a taste of Foreman's oratorical power myself at a 2010 wilderness conference in Berkeley, California. This being Berkeley, the conference attracted not just academics and nongovernmental organization (NGO) professionals but also people who looked to have been wilderness activists for quite some time, people of a certain age, the same demographic I had stood among several months prior at a Patti Smith concert in San Francisco—that is, gray-haired and resolutely hippie. Rocking on in wheelchairs and with walkers. Interspersed with these avid greensters was a handful of nicely turned-out young people who don't use the word "wilderness" so much as they do "biodiversity." The language shift expresses how much science has penetrated the working definition of nature. It could also reflect a diminution in wilderness to the point that it doesn't rank being named.

Foreman closed the three-day conference, and it seemed by their rapt attention, their half-smiling faces turned eagerly toward him as he took the stage, that Foreman is what these aging hipsters had come for. An otherwise unprepossessing man, tall and somewhat stiffened by various physical ailments, Foreman has a tone that is measured and deep, and has music in it, which he expertly controls. He began by quoting the first line of Aldo Leopold's *A Sand County Almanac:* "There are some who can live without wild things, and some who cannot." To Michael Soulé's three C's—cores, carnivores, and corridors—Foreman added "three W's: wilderness, wildways, and my favorite word in the English language, wildeor, which is Middle English and means 'self-willed animal.' The ancient people who saw animals as self-willed and the land as self-willed had respect for the earth."

Foreman's voice rumbled on. He did an expert literary job, combining his pro-wilderness exhortation with a natural history of select bird species, finding in their qualities parallels with the best traits of conservationists. The western scrubjay has vision, intelligence, and farsightedness. They like to hide peanuts from each other and can remember where 10,000 peanuts are; there's nothing smarter than a corvid. The curried bill thrasher is dominant and not afraid. The ladder-backed woodpecker works harder than everybody else. And so on.

In conclusion he said, "Always keep the vision of what conservation is all about. It's where the wild things are. They are beings, for their own sake, living their own lives. Untamed life is wildlife. Here's where it starts: Life is good. Manifold tangled life is better. Not under the heel of man is best. Untrammeled. The beating heart behind all conservation is that. We have great hearts full of wildlife. Life is a self-willed process. That is evolution. Our kinship extends to all living things. That's the genius of Darwin. Every earthling is related. We need to bring evolution out more in conservation. To preserve the stream, the flow, the process of life. The big view of time and space all over the earth. I'm going to close with a Zen koan: What is the sound of evolution?"

Faces, bodies craned forward, including mine. We were transfixed, about to hear evolution. Foreman asked again, louder, "What is the sound of evolution?" And then he howled. A big, long, loud wolf howl. The crowd had been waiting for this. It howled back.

CONNECT THE DOTS

As conservation biologists worried over genetic resilience and habitat fragmentation, a logical palliative was proposed: create corridors to connect separated habitat. E. O. Wilson himself was among the first to articulate this idea,[26] and Dan Simberloff again took the critical lead. Through the '80s the very idea of corridors was questioned: Were they worth what they would cost, would animals use them, how could they possibly be designed for multiple species, wouldn't invasive species use them as revolving doors, and wouldn't hunters and poachers similarly use them as access points to quarry? Reed Noss, now professor at the University of Central Florida, was (and is) a stalwart proponent of corridors—and unlike most of his fellow scientists, he had actually designed and implemented them. One of his parries: "The goal in this debate—conservation of biodiversity—might be served best if all parties, whenever possible, refrain from arguments based on theory and analogy, and devote their efforts to solving concrete problems in real-world landscapes."[27]

Noss has long reminded conservation biology that it's one thing to argue positions on paper, and another thing to deal with the real world. He is sensitive to the fact that "connectivity," while codified by science, has long been intuitively understood by those with hands-on experience outside. "Wildlife managers had been discussing connectivity and managing corridors for decades, at least since the 1930s," Noss tells me. "People working on the landscapes knew squirrels used wooded fence rows to travel woodlots, and so on. By the mid-1940s, some people were suggesting multispecies pathways between reserves, for example, using rivers and riparian corridors. One of the first people thinking about this was Victor Shelford." Shelford was an eminent ecologist, the first president of the Ecological Society of America, in 1916, within which he established two committees. One of these was defined as "pure science" and charged with identifying high-quality examples of American ecosystems. The other had an advocacy function and was charged with getting those ecosystems protected. Aldo Leopold served on those committees and presciently wrote about protecting large carnivores everywhere on the continent. Shelford was eventually seen as too radical and driven out of the Ecological Society; his students and younger colleagues formed a new group, the Ecologists' Union, defined by activism aimed at protecting land. This group later became the Nature Conservancy.[28] Noss also points out that the first sentence of the first article in the first issue of the professional journal of the Wildlife Society in 1935 begins, "In this new and growing field of conservation biology . . ."

Noss is particularly poised to remind us that there is nothing new under the sun and that what academic researchers were busy translating into equations scrolling across the page, close observers of wildlife had known all along. "I was much more familiar with the pragmatic side of all this and how it might be applied by NGOs." Noss is an important link between academia, conservation professionals, and policy makers, because he worked at the intersections of all three before too many other people saw they needed to be connected. At the University of Florida, he worked with Larry Harris, author of *The Fragmented Forest*, one of the first books to ponder just what was happening to species in fragmented habitats. Harris had started mapping specific corridors, and in 1985 Noss proposed a regional network of preserves incorporating 60 percent of Florida.

"I made a pretty simple map of Florida," Noss explains. "We took a wall map at a 500,000 scale [that is, 1 centimeter on the map corresponded to 500,000 kilometers on the ground]; we had aerial photos and satellite images; and we had heritage program data on rare species and habitat information about the Florida black bear and the Florida panther—we knew they had to roam long distances. We didn't have GPS in 1985. GIS was in use by the early '80s but I didn't know anyone using it; we used Mylar overlays and Magic Markers to draw corridors."

Noss and Harris (with others and led by Bill Partington), convened a corridor conference. It was attended by a candidate for governor, and so the newspapers covered it. "My map appeared everywhere. At first there was some backlash: this is some crazy, radical idea. But within a couple of years the state agencies in charge of acquiring land for conservation started using and refining my map. In 1991 there was a workshop of state agencies, with Audubon and the Nature Conservancy; they put together a habitat priority map." Noss notes that "the people of Florida really wanted their bears and their panthers."

With much refinement, Noss's map is still in use today. While it started out as an attempt to define a particular corridor, it has morphed into something bigger; despite the fact that it is outlined by the state of Florida, the map reflects the idea of defining the world "bioregionally"; it conceptualizes the land and its physical workings within a regional framework, and entails planning across the whole ecosystem.

At the time he was first scratching it out, other attempts to conceptualize nature in ways that reflect the realities of ecology included Norman Myers's "hot spot" idea, which advocated picking areas around the world with the highest levels of biodiversity and saving those first; the National Heritage Network had been established in 1974 and began to inventory biodiversity state by state, a process that continues to this day, its information available through NatureServe.[29] Mike Scott pioneered "gap analysis" when he realized that Hawaii's most threatened birds lived outside the state's protected areas. You can just feel these people grasping at the precious features of life under siege and trying to find some way to contain the hemorrhaging. While elements from many strategies find application today, none has found as much usefulness or ubiquity as the map. Reed Noss's map of Florida was the foundation of what would become the Wildlands Project (and eventually Wildlands Network).

ACROSS SPACE AND TIME

Michael Soulé was not the only person inspired by Arne Naess to actually make a physical difference in the world; in 1989 Doug Tompkins, who famously founded both the North Face and Esprit clothing companies with his then wife, Susie, established the Foundation for Deep Ecology based on Naess's formulations. In 1991, when Soulé wrote to Foreman, he and Noss had a meeting planned at Tompkins's house in San Francisco, where they intended to devise a land conservation strategy. Foreman invited Soulé. And the Wildlands Project was born.[30]

Soulé, Noss, Foreman, and a handful of others set off to re-create if not the ultimate unified creation, then at least enormous swathes of it that could be expected to function as wholes. The premise of the Wildlands Project, based on the tenants of conservation biology, was that national parks and wilderness areas are by themselves incomplete; a new understanding of the regional landscapes and ecosystems had to incorporate connectivity. Soulé declared, "The movement has not been bold enough. Implementation of strategic, visionary, continental conservation plans must occur on a temporal scale of decades to centuries." He quoted Arne Naess: "The key is thinking *big*, both in time and in space."

Wildlands members set themselves the task of establishing a continental system of reserves, or cores, surrounded by buffers and connected to each other. This approach would represent all native ecosystem types in all their successional phases; support viable populations of native species; and do nothing less than maintain ecological and evolutionary processes, including fire and predation. The result would be managed to adapt to changes that come down the pike as species and relationships among them evolve. The "cores, carnivores, corridors" paradigm was codified in a 1999 book, *Continental Conservation: Scientific Foundations of Regional Reserve Networks* (edited with John Terborgh). In their introduction, Soulé and Terborgh write, "Perhaps the most sublime moments in intellectual life are when old frameworks dissolve and new ones take form. This appears to be happening to this trilogy." While encouraging conservation at the community level, the book calls for thinking and planning on "grander geographic scales"—as their title declaims, on a continental scale.

VISION QUEST

The Wildlands Project got its work under way through what it called "vision mapping." As a vision implies a formulation in the back of one's mind that is yet to be made manifest, so the Wildlands vision mapping was a bit of a grapple at the outset. Michael Soulé wanted to produce a symbolic national vision map that other conservation groups would support and help implement. But where to begin and where to end? In its first few years Wildlands convened meetings all around North America, proposing areas to connect everywhere from Alberta, Canada, to the Great Lakes, from Alaska to the Gulf Coast. Soulé and Reed Noss pressed for scientific rigor, so that all maps would be standardized and coordinated, their governing principles replicable. Since the map or maps Wildlands wanted to produce would include the literal grounds of evolutionary processes, thus uniting past, present, and future, and would also incorporate ecology, or how every living thing constantly relates to every other living thing, and since the traveling routes of animals and plants also would be referenced . . . one imagines James Joyce confronted by similar ambition the day he sat down to write *Ulysses*. The vision mapping got only so far before some radical reorganization of priorities had to occur. Eventually Wildlands' regional mapping efforts cohered around the Spine of the Continent, with more localized efforts, such as that at the Colorado Plateau, intended to link up with similar efforts from the Yukon to Mexico.

AN IDEA WHOSE TIME HAS COME

"When you really dig into the real world and try to work out the mechanism by which large landscape protection can happen," says Keiran Suckling, the longtime executive director and founder of the Center for Biological Diversity, who worked for the Wildlands Project in its early days, "the value of these large-scale visions is to provide inspiration and goals. While very lofty, they help direct the smaller scale actions that are really the ones that can make this happen. It's those tens of thousands of actions every year by hundreds of groups that added together really achieve the vision."

Partly because Wildlands Network has such a gargantuan ambition and stretches its arms all down the continent, the actual acres of land it has succeeded in protecting don't come anywhere near what might satisfy Michael Soulé. (In addition to the Spine of the Continent, Wildlands includes efforts to create connectivity along the East Coast as well.) At the same time, this tiny nonprofit has had an outsize influence on conservation, and that is in first of all defining connectivity as the fundamental priority in land protection and in providing a network model for how this can actually get done.

Currently "connectivity" is on the front burner of federal and state agencies, including the National Park Services, NASA, the US Fish & Wildlife Service, the Forest Service, and so on. The Western Governors' Association (WGA) is spearheading an effort to coordinate connectivity among nineteen states. Interior Secretary Kenneth Salazar established Landscape Conservation Cooperatives all over the country to address fragmentation as much by joining hands across jurisdictions as by providing easements around new housing developments. Among other sources, both the WGA and the cooperatives are using various wildland network designs that originated from the Spine of the Continent. One of Wildlands Network's most robust current enterprises is the Connectivity Policy Coalition convened by Strategy Director Kenyon Fields, and made up of representatives from NGOs large and small. This group tracks opportunities to influence policy makers to include connectivity in, for example, President Barack Obama's America's Great Outdoors, and revisions to Forest Service rules.

SALVATION BIOLOGY

In the summer of 2010 Scott Mills called Michael Soulé and said he was planning to pass through Soulé's hometown of Paonia, Colorado, and would like to stop by for a visit. Of course Soulé would be glad to see one of his former protégés. "So I rang his doorbell," says Mills, chuckling as he tells me, "and ten minutes later, the doorbell rang again, and it was Sanjayan." This would be M. Sanjayan, lead scientist for the Nature Conservancy—probably the doctoral student of Soulé's who disagrees with him the most but may love him the best. Fifteen minutes later, the doorbell rang again, and there appeared Kevin Crooks, who had helped Soulé conduct mesopredator studies of coyotes in canyons, and continued the work on his own. Crooks has been described to me by Sanjayan as the one of the three of them who has followed most closely in Soulé's footsteps.

"So we talked for three days," Mills tells me. "Twenty years after starting out with Michael, our question was: What is conservation biology today, is it going the right way?" When Soulé studied with Paul Ehrlich, the department was simply "biology." These days you practically need a PhD to even get through the categories of academic discipline on offer from the country's leading centers of conservation biology and environmental sciences. As Mills says, "You've got ecosystem services, human dimensions, conservation genomics, landscape mapping, or connectivity—there are all these subdisciplines. Is this a good thing, or have we lost our vision and we don't know what conservation biology is about anymore?"

I know what Soulé's response to the question is without having to ask, and indeed Mills says that of the four of them, the elder statesman is the most pessimistic and disappointed. On the one hand, Soulé is simply assessing the cultural and physical landscape, and obviously the human drive for consuming its natural heritage has not abated since science first told us all what we are losing. But on the other hand, Soulé is not giving himself and the discipline he founded enough credit. Not only has a sophisticated concept, "connectivity," made its way into the bureaucratic mind-set as well as into the academy, it is actually being applied. Yes, in a preliminary way, but still. Crooks tells me that in preparation to repeat this four-way discussion at a conference in November 2011 at Montana State University, he reviewed Soulé's early textbooks. "Until 1993 they were the only books about conservation biology," he says, "and they were primarily focused on the viability or extinction rates in small populations." The purview of conservation biology has exponentially expanded since then (partly due to Soulé and others' subsequent emphasis on continental conservation). And Crooks tells me he hesitates to even bring up the philosophical divide between conservation as a "pure" or an "applied" science with his students, because they just don't see the dichotomy. "If you are a conservation biologist now, you are embracing a value-based mission," he says. Scott Mills further observes that as an active professor, it is hard to be too discouraged about the fate of nature. "Every year a new crop of fresh faces are sitting there in my classes," he says. "They've all come to the discipline because they want to help."

"We're idiots to think someone should listen to us just because we did the science," says Sanjayan, making his own assessment that conservation biology has not connected with the world outside itself. Sanjayan is nearly as critical of today's state of affairs as Soulé: "If you read the journals, you don't see the big ideas; you see increased depth in small ideas. Nothing is translating into changing what's going on out there." Sanjayan is one of the most affable, entertaining, and outgoing of contemporary scientists; you can check out documentaries he's narrated, his *Huffington Post* blogs, and even his appearance on *The Daily Show* on the Nature Conservancy's website.[31] Enthusiasm bubbles through his critical stance. Even while he warns me that nature is mostly degraded already, Sanjayan also tells me connectivity on a continental scale is "still quite possible on the Spine of the Continent."

Sanjayan credits Soulé with bringing the human voice into conservation. In graduate school, "we were surrounded by this notion of critical thinking; Michael also emphasized kindness and compassion. He still does. He uses the word 'love.' I use the word 'empathy' to describe what's missing from the conservation community, which is to be able to listen to someone who doesn't share your point of view. It's hard to do, but science without a social fabric is mute."

Sanjayan says that Soulé's humanism "dominates how I view conservation and the Nature Conservancy (TNC). He actually disagrees with me." Sanjayan is here referring to a shift in TNC's outreach strategy to emphasize people, what nature does for *us,* rather than advocating for nature for its own sake. "TNC is much more anthropocentric now. I'm one of the people responsible for the pervasiveness of that view." He notes that Soulé has always tolerated and even appreciated passionate disagreement. "He was more radical than his students, which is a cool place to find your adviser. And he has never sold out, which is brilliant."

What We Talk about When We Talk about Nature

Soulé was more opposed to anthropocentric framing in the past than he is now. When the Wildlands Network was the Wildlands Project, it hewed much closer to Arne Naess's deep ecology and Dave Forman's "wildeor," or self-willed animal and plant life, both of which advocate nature for its own sake. Soulé's focus on the seven deadly sins is part of a realization he came to through his lifelong "search for the ultimate cause of the extinction crisis. It's not nature but human nature that is the problem." Though he also concedes that "it's all one system." Today he is more keen on soliciting the human-focused motivation for saving nature. The private lands initiative is part of this. "The scales fell from my eyes," he tells me, describing how he had thought of public lands in Wallace Stegner's terminology: as "the geography of hope." Today he sees more hope in private property owners who steward nature in part out of their own self-interest. Maybe this evident "sinfulness" will be our salvation in the end.

Soulé's progress from pondering lizards to tracing the origins of sin marks an instructive stopover in "The Social Siege of Nature," his 1995 essay responding to a cultural studies conference on "Reinventing Nature." The earnest academics convening this conference were led by singular environmental historian William Cronon, notably author of *Changes in the Land: Indians, Colonists, and the Ecology of New England,* arguably the first and probably the best-written synthesis of how American history has intersected with degradation of the very ground being claimed. In my mind, there is no doubt everyone at that conference had nature's best interests in mind, but the way cultural historians talk clearly fell on Soulé's ears as a strange and distorted language. "When I discovered that social critics were deconstructing both nature and wilderness, even questioning their existence and essential reality, I wondered how and why."

Soulé turns the taxonomist's eye onto sorting and categorizing the ways people view nature. "Most scientific concepts exist side by side with the most pagan," he writes, "even in the mind of a single person." In a direct precursor to his current investigation of brain science and its correlations with the development of sin, he lists "nine distinct cognitive formations," including "Magna Mater" from the hunter-gatherer era of human history, where he finds a "pagan sense of divine oneness"; there's the "wild kingdom" formation, "the venue of trophy, camcorder, and life list," and finally "biodiversity: the living nature of the contemporary Western biologist." Soulé goes on to organize nature into four processes that he explains: physical, evolutionary, ecological, and anthropogenic. We are still in the realm of category, explication, analysis—all what you expect from a traditional scientist.

And then the essay takes a big turn. "Living nature is under siege," he writes, from cultural and social directions. He focuses on the critics who slice and dice "meanings" of nature. Their predilection for treating nature as a concept and not as a physical thing is anathema to Soulé; under the terms of this sort of discussion, he writes, "nature is no longer natural." Where "science is a way of gradually increasing our knowledge of living nature," the deconstructionist alternative "is to deny that nature is real or to insist that if there is anything 'out there' we can't know it." He supposes that social critics deny the existence of a "real" nature because they are suffering from "sensory deprivation" and experiencing a "solipsist hallucination that the world is illusory." In this essay he starts to address the "cultural filters" that separate the observer of nature from nature—what he later identifies as sins.

BANISHED FROM PARADISE, REDUX

Sin meets science in the brain but the two were perhaps first acquainted in the Garden of Eden. In the traditional Christian way of looking at it, the seven deadly sins are but a subset of the cataclysm that first pushed Paradise into an alternative stable state. That would be original sin, and it signifies human separation from God. Eden, of course, was a place where death was not known, and the animals therein did not hunt and eat one another. Sin brought about predation and death. In an evolutionary biological way of looking at it, sin also brought about life, since death and decomposition are important parts of the carbon cycle, and in a more balanced state of affairs than we have now, extinction is necessary to make way for new life-forms.

Bringing his moral and intellectual quest back to the concept of sin is full-circle back to the origins of conservation biology, rooted in biogeography and its religious impetus. "Conservation" means to save, to guard, to keep. It might as well be called "salvation biology," or, to keep digging at the Latin roots of the words, "to save life." Yes, conservation biology is trying to go back, to put things back in order. Perhaps here science and religion have found a mutual cause. Religion is from Latin, "re," back, and "ligio," to bind; ergo, "to bind back." And science tells us "only connect."

The Garden of the World and Its Gardeners

In the late nineteenth century push to Manifest Destiny, William Gilpin implored settlement by invoking divinity: "The American realizes that 'Progress is God.'" As a historical figure Gilpin is the shadow counterpart of the heroic John Wesley Powell. Gilpin was a land speculator and used every means possible to push his agenda. He is responsible for the assertion that "rain follows the plow," a bizarre climatic theory claiming that if you start farming land, rain will follow, so no worries about trying to farm arid lands. As Americans will, they bought his dream of the West as the "garden of the world."[32] God and the Garden therefore make another appearance in the trajectory of how we got here and what we should do about it.

Perhaps the best connotation of the world "garden" is the implication that someone must take care of it. Today the West is indeed a wild garden, full of biodiversity, a magnificent expanse of land in parts of which big-teethed beasts still roam. It is an arid garden, however. And our caretaking task has changed; rather than convert the land even to agricultural purposes, conservation biology gives us the crystal-clear direction to preserve what is still wild, connect the wild places with each other such that plants and animals are free to move from one to the other, and in the case where development proceeds, be mindful of the other creatures that utilize the landscape.

The next part of this book focuses on various conservation issues and work along the Spine. I have not been comprehensive—that would take 900 pages, at least. Nor have I stuck to profiling only the work of NGOs that are official Spine partners. I've chosen people, places, and creatures that reflect on the historical trajectory, or how we got here. I have also attempted to choose subjects that build on one another, to help illustrate how the fate of beavers, cows, aspen, and wolves (and us, of course), to name a few, are intertwined. The whole story most of these individual ones tell together has a theme. In addition to habitat loss and fragmentation, much of the ecological devastation wreaked on our landscape can be traced to extirpating top-tier predators—grizzlies, wolves, and jaguar. Our precursors thought, and some people still think, that all these animals do is kill. Now science tells us that their killing is fundamental in keeping ecosystems healthy. If this is sin, we need more of it.

The folks in these pages are all heroes. None of them do what they do for money or personal aggrandizement—because in the field of conservation, there really isn't any available. These are citizens helping restore natural processes on our land so that it will function better. The very good news is that nature does bounce back, or still has the potential to in most places, at this moment in time. Which of course, is running out. Let's get to work!

Part II

Cores, Carnivores, and Corridors on the Spine

CHAPTER 8

Leave It to Beaver

ONE FIVE-STAR GENERAL IN THE CAMPAIGN TO SAVE NATURE IS MARY O'Brien, and she has a thing for beaver, the championing of which she has completely converted me to. In the first place, the quest for beaver has arguably had more impact on American history than the pursuit of any other single natural resource, its influence lasting well over 200 years. There's a reason Canada flies a beaver flag: This lowly rodent likewise has a similar history up North.

The story of how the United States was settled rarely includes full acknowledgment of the main vehicle by which it occurred: the fur trade. In his recent *Fur, Fortune, and Empire,* Eric Jay Nolin notices that the colony at Plymouth Rock would have expired within a few years if its members hadn't learned from the local Indians how and where to hunt beaver. He then traces the ensuing centuries of conflict between the British, French, Dutch, Indians, and eventually what would be Americans through the story of the fur trade. In large measure, territorial grabs were motivated by what was the natural resource to exploit du jour, and more and more land had to be ventured onto as beaver were systematically extirpated from region after region.

While contemporary historians are awakening to the ecological impact of American settlement on these shores, there is still no comprehensive account of the damage wrought by the extirpation of beaver and the subsequent insertion of cattle onto the land, and what this has cost and continues to cost us. Even as comprehensive a book as Marc Reisner's *Cadillac Desert: The American West and Its Disappearing Water* begins its sorry trajectory in the late 1800s, with John Wesley Powell's cautions about the dangers of rampant settlement on such parched land. By that time the beaver had already been decimated. The operations of western waterways were already degraded. Donald Worster's *Rivers of Empire* is all about the hubris and sheer manipulation of waterways to establish the West. But we need an ecological historian to actually document how much water was stored by beaver dams, and how the pace of its flow, the rate of its evaporation, the wealth of the fish and bird species it supported, and the rate of erosion and flooding of its banks compared to what is going on now.

This blindness to the fact that ecosystem services are provided by the plants and animals that live on the land and in the water is hardly a thing of the past. It's not just that we have amnesia: We have never realized what was going on here, under our feet. It's as if the 60 million or so beaver that populated North America before 1600 were just sitting in ponds all across the continent, just waiting for us to trap them, and that our doing so would not have repercussions. Wrong.

The extermination of beaver from North America arguably marks the point at which our landscapes began to buckle and slide down the ruinous course we find them on now. There are other milestones to count up: the decimation of the bison for one, the ubiquity of cattle for another. But especially in the West, where water has always been an enormous issue and will become more important as climate change affects it, there is a real imperative to put beaver back on the waterways. They aren't always easy to live with, but in most cases, that is fairly easily remedied.

HAIL MARY

As Utah Forests project manager for the Grand Canyon Trust, O'Brien directs the Three Forests Coalition, which puts her in charge of stewardship issues around the Dixie, the Fishlake, and the Manti–La Sal National Forests of southern Utah. On a map, these forests compose core chunks of the state, which in turn are at the core of the Colorado Plateau and the western United States. In contrast to the wildness of the Waterton-Glacier region, which can be called intact, the operations of nature here are much diminished. The Grand Canyon Trust would like to restore the area with native plants and thereby restabilize the soil; provide sage grouse with the cover of tall grasses and provide pollinators with flowers; protect cottonwood, aspen, and willow from overbrowsing by cattle, elk, and deer; and restore beaver to the waterways. Fundamental to the Spine of the Continent is not just preserving such core wilderness areas from development, but in helping make them work again.

In October 2010 I joined O'Brien and a cadre of volunteers to assess various swaths of the Fishlake, to measure the presence and health of aspen and willow trees alongside several creeks that run through it. "These locations all had active beaver sites on them, so we want to see what kinds of conditions they're dealing with—where they're choosing to go. We're measuring how close aspen is, how dense it is, how many old remnants are extant. Same with willow." (There is not much cottonwood in the area.) "I want to go where there is beaver, because if that habitat is similar, it's pretty clear you can reintroduce them to those other sites and have success."

At sixty-five, O'Brien has a regal bearing; bone thin and straight as a rod, she has a beautiful salt-and-pepper braid down her back, and a deeply tanned, somewhat wizened demeanor. Her high cheekbones, bright brown eyes, and big, strong teeth give her a Native American look; in fact she's Scotch Irish. O'Brien's father was a Presbyterian minister. Her PhD is in botany from Claremont College, "though I always knew I'd work for a conservation-oriented NGO." Her dissertation work involved wasps. "I loved the Pavement Plains of San Bernardino National Forest and wanted to do my research there, whatever it was!" She studied pollination patterns in two species of buckwheat. "A plant wants to get its pollen to another of its species—otherwise the pollen is wasted. Native bees are the king pollinators. They're specialists. Wasps are considered promiscuous and will go to any bloom, so they aren't so useful to flowers. But I glued little numbers to their butts. I'd knock 'em out with dry ice and get pollen off their butts." The two smallest species of a particular wasp in fact went only to the smaller of two buckwheats, and the larger species went to the other. The medium-size wasps went to both. "I found that although wasps in general deserve their rap, the individuals were constant and always went to the same flower." This redemption story puts one in mind of the religious context of her youth. And if it might at first seem like a reach for a botanist to eventually find her way to advocating beaver on riparian systems, O'Brien's mania for detail and precision has clearly always been in evidence.

WHAT YOU SEE

The twelve or so volunteers for this trip, who have come from all over the country, convene in a little town called Loa, from where we caravan to the spot where we will camp for five nights. Fishlake National Forest is lush, the air temperate and sweet; veils of autumnal yellow aspen leaves flutter against low hills that are both green and rocky. O'Brien has us all pull over to observe a couple of spots along the way. The first is a long spillage of rock issuing from some bare jutting promontories about a half mile from the road. "This is a glacial moraine," she says. "These rocks are about a million years old. You can tell by the amount of lichen on them, which in this climate grows about an inch a century." Farther on we stop again, where the road intersects a forest of aspen that stretches as far as the eye can see. Our group clusters and looks up, our visual field now blanketed with those famously quivering leaves. The shuddering of aspen leaves both prevents the leaves from tearing in the wind and keeps insects darting and dashing after a moving target with elusive margins.

"This is the Pando Clone," O'Brien says. "It may be the largest living organism in the world, though a giant fungus in eastern Oregon might be bigger." Pando is Latin for "I spread," and a declarative statement has rarely been so emphatically evidenced. A US postage stamp recently honored the clone as one of the forty Wonders of America; as journalist John Hollenhorst notes, this "may have set some sort of a record for making something very small out of something very big." Not all aspen grow this way, but the Pando has extended its girth by sending underground shoots out from one original seed, which have sprouted to become over 40,000 genetically identical stems that we see as trees. Pando is male, and depending on your metrics, he may be 80,000 years old; other accounts put him at a million years old. And not only is Pando perhaps the oldest living organism in the world, he may be the heaviest, at approximately 13 million pounds.[33]

We are all fairly hushed and then hear a couple of gunshots. It's an impressive sound, and standing there in the quiet of this very large area it's almost as if we can hear the wind whooshing behind the bullets as they fly. Shots heard on city streets are more jarring, but of much shorter duration. Whatever else hunting is, it certainly deals with the immediacy of a moment. In the context of lichen growing an inch a century, of a single tree growing over 106 acres of land, the sound of the present being torn by gunfire induces a sort of psychedelic disorientation. It feels impossible to truly grasp the long time frame in evidence all around us. William Burroughs described "a frozen moment when everyone sees what is on the end of every fork" as "Naked Lunch." O'Brien, pointing out a few things about Pando, now serves ours up.

"Look at the size and height of Pando's trunks," she says. "They're all about the same. It's like you've walked into a village where there are only very old people, nobody middle-aged, nobody young." She points out signs of stress on nearby trunks, splotches of disease, bark splitting into ugly cankers. "Pando is dying," she says. And thus we are introduced to the theme of the next several days, which is the Molotov cocktail, as far as nature in the West is concerned, of cattle-grazing, super-abundant elk and deer (the hunters notwithstanding), and the steady encroachment of changing temperature and precipitation patterns brought on by human activities—aka climate change. The aspen are all the same age here because rampant deer, elk and cattle chew the new sprouts to the ground before they can mature. Pando isn't allowed to have the thousand or so generations of Methuselah that he deserves. And the mature trees that are beyond the reach of the ungulates are stressed by lack of water and buffeting temperature changes.

INTO THE WOODS

Aspen, the most widespread tree in North America, are what is called a "foundational" species, their structural diversity providing nourishment, protection, and homes for thronging biodiversity. More than 100 vertebrate and invertebrate herbivores hang out in aspen forests, and more plant and butterfly species than other forest habitats. Birds love 'em.

Only nerds would call them "primary cavity nesters," but woodpeckers get that title because they actually carve out a space in aspen trunks for their nests. When they are done with the nests, "secondary cavity nesters" who couldn't whittle a toothpick move in, violet green swallows and purple martins among them. The racket in the forest is coming from the aspen stands. Elk and deer largely prefer aspen (grass is at the top of the elk menu), and so do cows. The elk and deer feed after the cows, which means that with all three ungulates on the landscape, you've got very long open-for-browsing hours.

Is SAD an apt acronym or what? It stands for "sudden aspen decline." In 2004, it seemed like total disaster had struck aspen across the West, and they were all dying. The thinking now is that the alarming death of whole canopies can be attributed to the climate events that occurred in 2002. A very meager snowpack that winter was followed by the hottest summer temperatures on record in Colorado. Aspen meet their water requirements from snowpack melting through June; summer storms make a big fuss but don't actually yield that much water. Between the lack of moisture and heat stress, many aspen were toast. Aspen stand in the richest soils, and those that were not over-browsed withstood the lack of moisture and heat stress; so did trees younger than twenty years old. But many other trees were set upon by pathogens and insects at a rate heretofore unseen, and their roots died first. Two or three years after that, people noticed the dead over-stories. SAD is a visceral warning of what may lie ahead when future climate and precipitation trends likely bring hotter summers more frequently. It's even more complicated with snowmelt, because even if precipitation increases, hotter temperatures will melt it faster and harder. The life cycles of plants and animals depend on more or less routine responses to seasonal changes in temperature and precipitation. Intermountain wildflowers are on a strict schedule and blossom in mid-June. If the snow melt has already run its course, the flowers wake up thirsty and perish quickly.

There is a whole host of environmental bromides that are nearly impossible to resist trotting out yet again. Gazing at Pando in wonder, our group registers an awesome testimony of nature's glory. The next minute it turns ugly. Remember that drawing of a young woman's profile that, if you look at it in a slightly different way, becomes a hag? The quote, from Aldo Leopold: "One of the penalties of an ecological education is living alone in a world of wounds."[34] The "living alone" part means he sees what the untrained eye glosses over; just because a stand of trees looks impressive doesn't mean it's healthy. Thanks to O'Brien we all join Aldo Leopold in witnessing this particular wound—at least he is no longer alone.

But what we are *not* seeing in the Fishlake National Forest or indeed nearly anywhere in the entire lower forty-eight is what the country looked like 200 years ago—not just because there were no great malls of America dotting the landscape back then, no office towers, no ranchettes, no Desert Mirages, no McMansions. The entire green and brown purview of even the wilderness areas that have remained relatively pristine through our civilizing assault is fundamentally different than it used to be. Before John Deere and Webcor began to alter the landscape, our friend the beaver was doing the job. As O'Brien says, "Restoration of the beaver is a restoration of a landscape to which we don't have a cultural connection."

ON THEIR BACKS

If not for the beaver, in fact, we might not be here at all. We handily remember that the Pilgrims who came over on the *Mayflower* were dissenting from the strictures of the Church of England, but forget that everything, including religious freedom, has a price tag. The spiritual quest of the Pilgrims was underwritten by an outfit called the Merchant Adventurers (a saucy moniker reflecting the spirit of the times, as "venture capitalist" does today), and they expected to make a profit from the deal. The Merchant Adventurers furnished the Pilgrims with the *Mayflower* and a store of supplies, and everyone aboard the ship was slated to work to pay off their debt over time. Far from a clear shot across the ocean hence to create the destiny of America, the Pilgrim voyage was beset by delays; half its provisions were consumed before the expedition was truly launched. Samuel de Champlain's maps from fifteen years before the voyage showed plentiful French and Native American settlements on these shores; but the Pilgrims, their own population bifurcated by disease en route, confronted a practically empty landscape upon arrival. The Indians who lived in the vicinity had likewise been vastly reduced by an epidemic. Initially the Pilgrims not only found zilch on offer to provide a means for paying off their debt, but they also were confronted with likely starvation.

As babes in the woods, they struggled from their arrival in November till March 16, when a "tall confident Indian walked 'boldly' into the midst of Plymouth." This was Samoset, and he heralded not just his own presence but introduced the Pilgrims to Massasoit, the "great sachem of the nearby Pokanoket," who taught them a thing or two about cultivating the earth and harvesting the waters of fish. Massasoit also introduced them to the beauties of the beaver, which was roughly akin to offering pre-IPO stock options on a company that would thrive and profit for 300 years. Like a savvy stockbroker, Massasoit also benefited from sharing his trade secret.

The beaver has a starring role in many Indian cosmologies—alongside other species and the elements, of course. Northern Algonquin peoples put the beaver at the very center of Creation. In their story, the earth was originally enveloped by water; enormous beavers, otters, and muskrats dove down into it and retrieved mud that was then shaped into landscapes by the Great Spirit Manitou. There were in fact gigantic beavers roaming over North America once upon a time. Beavers do physically create landscapes, and digging up mud is an integral part of the process. All Creation tales bridge the literal and the symbolic; that's their job. This one integrates ecological history, animal behavior, and the dynamics of earth's physical forces—and in it the human story takes a respectfully supporting role. One legend had it that beaver had once been able to speak, but the Great Spirit took this power away because in the context of the animal's other awesome abilities, beavers were headed toward a level of understanding that would supersede mankind's. I bet the Great Spirit regrets that move. Talking beavers would likely have engineered a better future than the one our boiling, toasting earth is facing today—although it must be admitted that beaver brains are the smallest of any mammal's relative to body weight.

From the very beginning, Indians were central to the fur trade, and in fact it could not have gone on without them. Historical synopsis paints our indigenous culture as being pretty much steamrolled, the land so associated with Natives stolen out from under its original inhabitants. That happened—but mostly much later. At Plymouth, the Pilgrims were happy to join with the tribes and the feeling was mutual. For a decade, the beaver trade facilitated by the Indians gave the Pilgrims a way forward in their new world and helped them get out of debt to their old one. The Indians also benefited. While they did sometimes trap them on land or set nets for them in the water, the Indians the Pilgrims met also sent their dogs after beaver and otherwise rousted them from their homes. One practice was to damage the beavers' dam, wait for the animal driven by its instincts to commence repairing it, and then best the beaver with spears or arrows. Sometimes the lodge was destroyed to force beavers into the water; when they came up for breath: death. When the water was frozen, Indians tested the ice for shallow spots in which they cut a hole; again when a beaver came near it for air, it was scooped out of the water with a curved blade on a stick and flung out on the ice with enough force to smash its skull.

Intricate alliances and rivalries between various tribes weighted the struggle between the Dutch, the British, and the French. While fur trading depended on European markets, for a very long time the indigenous peoples were arguably a dominating force determining who else got what piece of the trade. The way in which the Native culture came largely undone reflects on what happened to nature in America over the same time period. Yes, the Indians had a deep and involved bond with nature, and breaking that particular connection helped bring down not only the Indians but also the health of our natural landscape. Two incredibly dense and beautiful systems were simultaneously diminished if not entirely destroyed.

The market economy and the devil's goods were joined with other nefarious forces: one explicitly so, in the form of terrible exterminations due to disease; the other was clothed in the frock of God—the Jesuits, and their relentless push to dismantle Native spiritual beliefs and replace them with those of the church. Say what you will about Christianity, revering animals doesn't have much to do with it. (In the matter of the beaver, the medieval church allowed eating this animal on fast days, along with muskrat, because they live mostly in the water and so are "cool," as opposed to "hot" and sinful.)

But if disease was a huge demoralizing factor, as well as a physical instrument of thinning the ranks, and if the missionaries busily snipped away at the ties that bound Native Americans to a reverence for the natural world, the fur trade made this sorry transaction literal and complete. Consider that by the 1700s, beaver was not a proxy for money. Beaver *was* money. For 150 years, the standard of currency in the fur trade was not cash but beaver skins. A prime quality skin from an adult animal, a so-called made beaver, was the unit of barter; from records of a tally taken by the Hudson's Bay Company post at Albany Fort in 1733: "1 for 1 made Beaver; Gun-Powder, 1 ½ pounds for 1 Made Beaver; Brandy, 1 Gallon for 1 Made Beaver," and so on. Thus, value itself was definitively transferred from the animal to its proxy ability to turn into something else, something man-made, and Indians as well as whites abided by the terms of this transaction. Indians once hunted according to sacred rituals in which the animal's spirit was gravely honored; once the beaver was explicitly equivalent to money, the numinous was gone.

Indian taste for European goods increased over time. Francis Parson's 1762 portrait of Cherokee Chief Cunne Shote portrays a clearly dominant male, erect knife blade in hand, gazing with calm assurance at the viewer. He's wearing a lot of bling: an ample metal necklace with multiple strings of beads, medals at his throat, silver wristband and armband. His white dress shirt is totally European. His red cloak, made of fine English wool, is draped over his left shoulder like George Washington might have done. But the knife in his hand and the feather on his head say Indian warrior-leader. The portrait is a vertiginous hybrid, as is R. J. Curtis's of Osceola, the Black Drink, who led the Indians in the Seminole Wars. His costume is more a colorful mélange of variously printed sashes and scarves; his turban-with-feather headdress looks like that of a Renaissance page. The Black Drink's white name was Billy Powell; he had more white blood than Native and his demeanor reflects the straddling of worlds.

If the signs of status among Indians were increasingly reflected in European goods mostly obtained by trading beaver skins, a different sort of escalation and enumeration of status was driving the trade from across the Atlantic. For centuries, all kinds of fur were staple commodities in Europe, which led to the near extirpation there of animals including the beaver. Of course this was a chilly time—nobody had central heating. In the thirteenth and fourteenth centuries, squirrel was the skin of choice; the next century it was marten. Royalty all over the world draped themselves with furs—it's hard to imagine, but Henry IV of England had a robe made of 12,000 squirrel skins trimmed with 80 ermine—was he able to move in this sea of fur? Going back into history, Agamemnon wore a lion skin and Paris a leopard; these sorts of choices reflected an identification with the essence of the animal. What was displayed on the body was possessed internally by the wearer, or so it was believed.

The popularity of beaver spiked up in the late 1700s and stayed that way, though, not to keep anybody warm, but due to a mania for beaver felt hats, the styles of which were finely keyed to levels of social rank. Beaver fur felts exceptionally well. The undercoat of the beaver pelt is covered with tiny barbs that cleave together tightly and make a soft, durable felt easily manipulated into elaborate shapes. The best beaver for felting came from cloaks that had been worn by Indians for some time, the use wearing down the coarse guard hairs of the pelts (which otherwise had to be laboriously removed), and human body oils adding lubrication. Umbrellas hadn't been invented yet, so beaver hats did have some utility, but they weren't particularly warm, and that wasn't what the whole thing was about anyway.

It was about fashion, pure and simple, though of course fashion is anything but. An outward expression of shifting regimes, and overall social organization, the styles of beaver hats changed according to who was sitting on the various thrones of Europe, or who the military brass were at a given time. Plenty of natural resources were being plundered at the time to help females rank one another (whale bones for corsets, for example), but the beaver hat was primarily a male accoutrement.

Samuel Pepys bragged about paying eighty-five shillings for his beaver hat. Michael Soulé's observation that we are helpless to stop decimating nature because we are as immature as high school students dissing each other in the hall finds a very long historical antecedent.

Read My Lips (Get Me Fur)

It is a bizarre feature of the human psyche that we will go on depleting resources until they are completely gone and then expect to find some new sustenance just around the corner. In the matter of beaver, the routine was for trappers and traders to decimate a beaver population, and then move west to find more. Thomas Jefferson famously sent Meriwether Lewis and William Clark to "open" the West, looking in particular for an all-water route from the Missouri to the Pacific, which would be used primarily to expedite the fur trade. Such a straight shot was not found—a few hills called the Rocky Mountains happened to be in the way—but the good news communicated back to Jefferson by the Corps of Discovery was that the western lands of North America were indeed teeming with populations of big, fat beaver.

Where previous chapters of the fur trade were characterized by jockeying among the British, the French, the Dutch, and the Indians to control various territories for exploitation, by the time Jefferson became third president of our freshly hatched country, the American hand was well defined. Manifest Destiny, while not a term put into play quite yet, was nevertheless a wheel set in motion—inexorable motion. In 1803 Jefferson asked Congress for $2,500 to fund an expedition up the Missouri, to go for the fur. The lands Lewis and Clark were to traverse were claimed by the British and the French, and to placate these empires Jefferson called the planned trip a "literary pursuit" in the service of advancing geographical and scientific knowledge of the continent, all of which did truly interest him. Needless to say, nobody was terribly deceived by this literary stuff. The famous journals of the expedition always keep their eyes on the prize, which was the West's commercial potential, defined at the time by furs. Lewis suggested to Jefferson that the 340 miles between the Missouri and Columbia Rivers, while enormously difficult to traverse, would eventually provide "passage across the continent," expediting the harvesting of more furbearers than "than any other streams on earth." Lewis added, "I am fully convinced that we shall shortly derive the benefits of a most lucrative trade from this source, and in the course of 10 or 12 years a tour across the continent by this route will be undertaken with as little concern as a voyage across the Atlantic is at present." This would be much faster than sending a ship around Cape Horn to deliver Western goods back East.

The fur trade got a big shot of adrenaline from Lewis and Clark's reports. While more corporate operatives, such as John Jacob Astor, participated in pressing west,[35] consolidating trading practices and jockeying for control of the market, a new sort of player entered the fray: the trapper, or mountain man. By the time trappers and fur merchants got to Utah, in the mid-1800s, their methods for trapping and killing beaver were honed and efficient. Populations were so reduced in so short a period of time that by 1899 it was illegal to kill them. Beaver are a pretty hardy species and their numbers did rebound; at the same time, the onrush of human development got beaver in its crosshairs. By 1912, trapping of beaver resumed.

WHAT ARE YOU WEARING?

In almost equal measure as their fur, beaver were pursued for castoreum, secreted by sacs both sexes harbor in the anal region. Castoreum was widely used, going back to Solomon and Hippocrates, as a practical cure-all; Pliny said it calmed the hysteric; and it also has been credited with killing fleas, stopping hiccups, curing headaches, and reducing fever. In fact castoreum contains acetyl salicylic acid—which is what makes aspirin work. Castoreum was widely used in perfumes (including Chanel No. 19) to establish a "leathery" note. While synthetics now replace the animal's secretion in a lot of them, purists of course argue for the supremacy of the original.

Beavers use their castoreum to construct scent mounds that define their territories, and individual animals have their own signature smells. Smell telegraphs an ovulating female, and also differentiates a close relative from a stranger, all the better to procreate with, to avoid inbreeding. But chemical signaling goes far into the very cells of the natural world and into the dense web of interaction that is called coevolution, or two species developing traits in relation to each other. Plants contain compounds that defend against being eaten by those who would nosh (including beaver but also insects). Beaver are generalist herbivores and can make do among a pretty wide range of vegetation. Part of their evolutionary success undoubtedly has to do with their ability to sequester potentially deleterious plant compounds and repurpose them as castoreum. The concept of coevolution is credited to Paul Ehrlich and Peter Raven, the latter for many years director of the Missouri Botanical Gardens. It's worth considering that if you ever did, in fact, dab a bit of Chanel No. 19 on your wrists before the company went synthetic, your olfactory pleasure was the result partly of an animal's ancient standoff with the willow, aspen, or cottonwood trees that are its favorite dinner.

BABY, IT'S COLD OUTSIDE

Mary O'Brien is supported on our trip by Joshua Porter, a young environmentalist who says "all right" a lot, like an outdoorsy Lou Reed, if such a thing can be imagined, and frequently quotes Wendell Berry. Earlier O'Brien and Porter picked out a campsite for us in a meadow by a creek, the other side of which is dense with evergreens. We are under a low rise on which sits the road, and in the distance are picturesque mountains. Everyone sets about erecting shelters. The volunteers on this trip are young and old and all are practiced campers. Several couples have big, substantial-looking tents, but most of the rest of us have brave little singletons, which in the quickly darkening October evening look negligible. I kind of feel like it's time to go *inside* somewhere.

Our routine for the next several days is quickly established. Porter sets up a kitchen under a big tarp, replete with metal tables for his *mise en place,* and burners to get big pots of delicious things bubbling, the raw materials of which are stored in a phalanx of large coolers. The rest of us help as needed. We eat, we chat, we praise Porter for his cooking. *"All right,"* he says. As the night gets dark and cold fast, we eat (really good) tamale pie, made in a Dutch oven on the open fire, a bunch of total strangers now gravitating closer together around the proverbial camp fire.

As with each day on the trip, I emerge from my nylon blip of a tent at about 6:30, in the deep, dark, freezing October morn, and stumble over to the kitchen tent where Porter has already been at work for at least a half hour, and where one of two recent college grads on the trip is always already helping. Porter asks me if I was warm enough in the night. "No," I admit; the cold had kept waking me up. Porter counsels me on staying warm, telling me to not resist the urge to get up and pee. In fact, not wanting to stumble into the pitch of freezing night, an occasional coyote howl punctuating the faraway whoosh of wind on its eternal course, I had studiously avoided all liquid intake after 4 p.m. the day before.

"Your body uses an amazing amount of energy keeping the urine in your body sterile," he explains. "If you just get rid of it, all those calories can go to work keeping you warm." He tells me that you can actually wear too many clothes to bed (I am also guilty of this). "You want your body heat circulating in your sleeping bag," he says. "If you're wearing really efficient layers they keep the heat too close to the area they're covering." That night I wrap my vest and coat loosely around myself. Instead of my flap hat I use the head space in my sleeping bag. When I stumble out of the tent, the night sky greets me in silent explosion. To think I could have missed this! "Thank you," I whisper to those burning communiqués from afar. "You are *stellar*."[36]

UNTIL THE COWS COME HOME

On our first day of fieldwork we all drive to Tasha Creek, where O'Brien shows us an extensive series of inactive beaver dams, which have sectioned this part of the creek into a terraced cascade. "See what a peaceful environment they create for themselves?" she observes. The water glistens around elaborately intertwined sticks, all traces of the mud the beaver would have originally used as cement having long been washed away. An active beaver dam gets incessantly touched up, and the mud sprouts all kinds of greenery. By comparison, these dams look like skeletons.

O'Brien's question, the one the gang of us have convened here in Fishlake National Forest to help her ask, is: Can beavers coexist with cattle grazing, and if so, how? Beaver will eat a lot of things but prefer willow, cottonwood, and aspen. Cattle will eat even more things and they will keep on eating and eating until . . . In Utah and on much of the vast western lands grazed by cattle, the cows never go home. Or hardly ever.

The jurisdictions in charge of managing wildlife in any given state are byzantine and often work at cross purposes; clarity on what actions to take on behalf of any given species comes (or does not) through a murky filter of confused objectives. In Utah, for example, the Forest Service, a federal agency, is responsible for maintaining habitat for wildlife, but not the wildlife itself. So if the Forest Service surmises that there are too many elk on the land, they can't easily do anything about it. "For all intents and purposes, the state agencies manage wildlife. And there's a bad funding mechanism at play," O'Brien says. "They get much of their money from hunting tags. They want as many elk and deer out there as possible so they can sell more tags." The way state and federal governments divide up their tasks does not reflect current knowledge of how nature works. As Jim Catlin of the Wild Utah Project puts it, "The fact that water and wildlife are managed by the states, while the federal government manages habitat and watersheds, adds up to generally dysfunctional ecosystem management."

Still Water Runs Deep

Beavers are rodents and sport the specialized choppers that distinguish the order (*rodere*—to gnaw). Their teeth are bright orange and look like something you would buy in the hardware store. If another sort of mammal tried to use its teeth to the same tree-razing purpose, it would quickly need dentures, but beaver teeth never stop growing—what gets worn away is perpetually replaced. If a beaver stopped wearing them down, its continuously growing teeth would pierce its brain pan. Talk about a treadmill—keep chewing or die.

Everything is different when beaver are around. Here's what happens: Beaver move into an area along a stream or a creek, part of the freshwater system that ultimately connects over the continent in a vast network like human veins and arteries.

A beaver sometimes cuts down a whole tree working alone (depending on the diameter, it can do this in an hour); sometimes several work together on either side of the trunk. They start to make lumber from it at the top where the branches are small, though many beaver dams evince big fat logs sawed out of pretty thick parts of the trunk. Depending on the depth of the water in which they're working, beavers first construct a base, in a large stream using sticks up to 6 feet long, propped against the bank pointed upstream at a 30-degree angle. They weight down the sticks with stones secured with wads of grass and mud. The beavers float sticks down through the pond, hauling their plump and industrious little selves up on the dam and adding the new timber to the pile. They align the sticks with the flow of the water. Contrary to cartoon depictions, beaver do not use their tails to pat mud onto their work, but mostly use their front paws, which are rather uncannily similar-looking to human hands.

Within a matter of days upon moving into a new neighborhood, beavers will usually erect an elaborate lodge for themselves and progress handily on constructing a longitudinal span of mud-cemented twigs, sticks, and logs to still the water behind it. Heading both upstream and downstream there is often a progression of dams stilling pond after pond, depending on how many beaver the area is supporting and the topography of the river or creek. Systems of up to eighteen active dams have been observed in a single colony, each creating a pond with a different water level. At other sites, one big dam does the trick. Beaver dams can stay active for decades, if the food source for the animal is renewed at a sustainable pace, and even when beaver leave a site for whatever reason, the dams they leave behind can persist for decades, even centuries. Beaver dams never totally stop the water; there is some flow-through, and most fish migrations make it across their barriers. A breached beaver dam triggers a whole other set of effects, flooding the surrounding land and creating a beaver meadow, which can likewise persist for centuries.

THE TANGLED BANK

I once had a poetry professor who described romanticism thusly: "It's flow, it's creativity, it's beauty, it's completion, it's process, it's wholeness.

It's what you want." The same could be said about beaver ponds. Of course biologists like to say things like, "Network-scale diversity of macro-invertebrates (McDowell and Naiman 1986) and riparian herbs (Wright et al. 2002) increases when all three segment types are present in a network where beavers are native." (Got that?) "The inclusion of beavers in a network can also increase the presence of rare species that depend on transient habitat (Bartel et al. 2010)."[37]

What these earnest people mean is that there are more kinds of fish, more kinds of birds, amphibians, insects, and microbes, better dirt, more small mammals, more of everything good, in beaver ponds. And they are hospitable stopovers for critters passing through.

One of the most profound effects of beaver-made wetlands is on the water itself. The very smallest inhabitants of them, bacteria, fungi, and phytoplankton, feed on impurities and clean the water as it flows through. In her excellent book *Water: A Natural History*, Alice Outwater points out that a generation after the Clean Water Act was passed, a full one-third of streams and lakes in the United States are still impure; while industry has stopped polluting, waterways stripped of beavers may no longer be able to clean themselves naturally. "By dredging, by damming, by channeling, by tampering with (and sometimes eliminating) the ecological niches where water cleans itself, we have simplified the pathways that water takes through the American landscape; and we have ended up with dirty water."

Trapped behind beaver dams, sediment that would otherwise be carried along by the free-flowing water is a rich source of nitrogen on which microbes feed. From there we move up the food chain. There are more bugs in that dirt because there's more nutrition there; frogs and other amphibians come around to eat the bugs. Birds who like to eat bugs come on by, too, and also those bigger ones that eat frogs. Small mammals such as muskrat join the fray, and otter, fox, coyotes, and so on, the teeth and claws generally getting sharper and bigger as we go.

And each class of organism brings its own ripple effect of more and more interaction. Birds not only find an ample food source at beaver ponds but also utilize the wetland vegetation as cover for breeding and nesting; migrating birds use beaver ponds as motel–cum–recreation centers; cavity nesters find hidden little places and construct their hide-aways. Beaver lodges are often repurposed by muskrats and otters, which use them as shelter and avail themselves of the ample food source in the fish-enriched water. Predation feeds the beast but also keeps populations in healthy balance. More small mammals bring carnivorous reptiles, birds, and larger mammals. Beaver ponds with vibrant vegetation over-hanging the banks provide cover for spawning fish and those that would avoid becoming the lunch of something bigger. The presence of beaver on the whole brings in a more diverse bunch of fish than would other-wise live there. And then those that want to eat the fish bring their own suite of behaviors and habits, including mink, kingfishers, and heron—it goes on and on.

In that they affect whole cascades of other interaction, beavers are known as a "keystone" species, though some scientists prefer the term "highly interactive species." They function as multiconnectors. Wolves are also keystone species, but where they dominate a hierarchy of effect, bea-vers create bridges between the terrestrial and aquatic worlds. Befitting their ability to pass between these two elements, beavers have fishlike qualities; underwater, they use their tails as rudders; they have valves that close off their nostrils and ears; a membrane makes "diving goggles" that protect their eyes; and they can even close their lips behind their teeth so they can gnaw while submerged. The beaver's sense organs are aligned in a row like those of hippos and alligators, also semi-aquatic creatures, so that nostrils, eyes, and ears can glide above the waterline while the rest of the animal is below.

As my Romantic poetry professor would have said, "This is good." Having lots of different players taking lots of different parts creates the very stuff of life. Birds and bees and beetles pollinate flowers; others eat seeds and disperse them elsewhere; all of this helps keep habitat some-where else vibrant and active as well. I contain multitudes, said Walt Whitman, and so do beaver ponds.

Beaver activity doesn't just jazz up the immediate neighborhood but also creates suburbs. They not only rejigger the ecosystem, but also affect the lay of the land itself. Cutting down trees on the edge of the streams opens up the area, creating new ponds, swamps, and meadows. They actually store a supply of water that can be released in the event of drought. This slowing, spreading, and layering of water is precisely what makes them pests in some areas—you may not want your backyard flooded, for example. But there is no downside to letting beaver help the miles and miles of wild land creeks in a place like Fishlake National Forest attain better resilience, especially confronting climate change.

YOU EAT LIKE A COW

O'Brien has led volunteer trips to measure willow and aspen browse in these forests since 2008, providing the data to the Forest Service. "I'm showing them where the cattle or elk are making it inhospitable to beaver," she says, "and they agree with me that beaver should be back on the land." Despite the fact that everybody can see it with their own eyes, you can't just say, "Too many cattle spend too much time here," and expect anything to be done about it. You have to measure the stuff growing out of the caked dirt at the water's edge, spiky little remnants of . . . well, to figure that out, you have to look closely. We set out to document and measure two types of willow that grow here on Tasha Creek: *Salix boothii* (Booth's willow) and *Salix geyeriana* (Geyer's willow). You can tell the difference by the glaucous coating on the Geyer's branches, underneath which the plant has a purplish hue. As with Pando's younger sprouts, most of the willow we measure has been browsed below the leader, which means the plant cannot grow tall enough to produce catkins, by which it reproduces. Some of the plants are in fact mature, perhaps even ten years old, but have on them not a single leaf. In other locations we will see these species growing as shrubby trees up to 12 feet high and 6 feet wide; here the negligible stubs can be measured in single digits. And that's exactly what we will do as the day proceeds. At the outset of every measured transect a photograph and a GPS record is made: proof of where we were and what we did. In pairs of two we measure, call out to each other, and take note. Then we move on, 2 feet at a time. Yup, folks, this is the life of a field biologist, part of the time, anyway.

Born to Run

The next day we head out to UM Creek in a couple of cars; the day is bright but about to change its mind. At a certain point we consolidate into two trucks that can ford a nearly roaring stream. The "E-Street Station" is playing on satellite radio; this is Bruce Springsteen 24/7, and currently we're listening to a live concert in Copenhagen.

We drive along into Right Fork Pasture and then we meet . . . cows. Hundreds of them. The truck O'Brien is driving ahead of us stops. We stop, too, and get out and look at the cows. They aren't supposed to be here. Every year the Forest Service determines a pasture schedule for how many cows can graze on what stretches of land for how long; it's called "annual operating instructions." "I used to have to make FOIA requests for them," O'Brien has told me, "but finally they said, 'Heck, Mary's going to ask for these every year, we might as well post them on the web.'"[38] Right Fork Pasture has ten different permittees running 1,630 cows. This year's instructions have directed that these cows were to be gone by August 18; it is now October 3.

O'Brien is stricken. She looks stiffly at the cows. The rest of us wait for a pin to drop. It is not that cows on land is in itself a bad thing; it's the way they are managed, or in effect, not managed, that does the damage. Say an 8,000-acre allotment has 300 cows on it, and they are left to their own devices month after month. Those 300 cows could graze on just several acres in healthy farmland, and then they could be moved to another site so that the land could recover. But often that's not how it goes.

Cows like to linger at the edge of waterways. At 1,000 pounds apiece they place an enormous pressure on the banks just by standing there. Eating up the native plants and grasses, which have deep roots that help hold the river's edge in place, they pave the way for invasives like Kentucky bluegrass to come in; these are shallow-rooted, and rhizomatous, which means the roots all interlock and prevent anything else from sharing the space. When floods come it's all ripped out, and with it go the banks of the creek or stream. Overgrazing takes out the dense diversity of grasses and flowers that in turn feed the pollinators: butterflies, bumblebees, moths. To reiterate our theme, poorly managed cows devour the willow and aspen that beaver feed on and so usurp the dense ecology instigated by my favorite rodent. Have you ever walked head-on into a herd of cows coming down a lane? They do not brook your presence; you'd better get out of the way. That's how they are on the land.

The cows stare back at us. They are mostly black and rather beautiful in that bovine way. Their brand looks like an I Ching symbol, a large "O" with a line under it. I imagine it translates into something like "mindless destruction." Cow after cow after cow with the same symbol: mindless destruction after mindless destruction after mindless destruction. For the next few hours we count the cows, take their pictures, and get GPS readings for their exact location. We pick up littered beer cans. I ride with O'Brien for about an hour to a hillside that has an antenna sticking out of it; she can get Internet access here. The persistence of the cows is respectfully reported. The Boss is still playing Copenhagen.

DAM IT

On our fourth day in Fishlake, we convene early and O'Brien divides us into two groups destined for two different locations. I know what we're all thinking, which is, "Please send me to the direction where there are no deep, dark rain clouds," because the sky is now bifurcated. As it turns out, we all get soaked that day.

I'm paired with Shirl McMayon, an arborist and a wealth of interesting information. For example, when aspen leaves so beautifully shed this mortal coil, the unpoetic term for it is "abscise." As a tree lover, McMayon once bore ill will toward beaver—"the little loggers!"—but education about the whole system they promote has made her a fan. She even dresses up like a beaver to help educate schoolkids about their doings. O'Brien charges the two of us with taking GPS readings, photographs, and measurements of a series of beaver dams on a creek while she and others do willow transects. When we park at the top of a hill looking down, we can see the major initiating dam, and a series of subsequent constructions, each looking from here somewhat smaller than the one before it. This area is lush with tall, broad willows. They are like giant shrubs, bearing not much resemblance to the weeping willow variety immortalized in storybooks (but notice the next time that the illustrated willow is almost always next to a creek, as it depends on water just as much as its less picturesque brethren).

Near the ginormous initial dam is the beaver lodge—we sight a few smaller ones at various locations downstream. Beaver lodges look like hills made of sticks; if they had chimneys and geraniums out front you might be tempted to knock for Frodo or Bilbo Baggins. Inside there are breathing chimneys, exits, storage areas for food, and living quarters; beavers know at which level to place their beds vis-à-vis the eventual ice level of a frozen pond. Dams can routinely measure up to 6 feet high and 18 feet wide but can also get much, much bigger. You can check out one such staggering structure online (it's also visible from space): a 2,790-foot beaver dam in Wood Buffalo Park, Alberta, Canada.[39] Surmised to have been under construction for more than thirty years, this dam is the work of multiple beaver families, and some offspring have set up major shops nearby. Wood Buffalo Park is pristine, the last breeding ground in the world for whooping cranes, and home to an endangered bison species that still goes hoof to throat, so to speak, with wolves.

McMayon and I set to photographing and measuring dams, and I am entrusted with the GPS. In the lush, dense willows, and walking across long stretches of dams, we are soon isolated from the others. O'Brien has done us a favor by giving us this job; we are cataloging a healthy ecosystem. She surmises that there are probably twelve dams here; McMayon and I traverse one after the other, marveling at the dense industry in evidence, the stillness of the water. The lengths of the successive dams get shorter and shorter, holding smaller bodies of water within their bounds; some are split by patches of land, covered with dense willows, and we creep through these on the lookout for the next dam. It is like entering into an ever more refined maze, but a more apt analogy would be to the circulatory system, starting with a major organ and branching out into smaller and smaller capillaries. The beaver's system of regulating water flow works in a similar way. I keep taking erroneous GPS points, which I later find out is common and easily corrected, but at the moment I trade the device with McMayon and take over with the tape measure.

A fit of cold rain makes it impossible to document the dams without my pen dissolving the paper I'm writing on. At one interval McMayon and I huddle together under my rain poncho and emerge to measure again when the sky is merely spitting at us. On my various treks along the Spine of the Continent I have gleaned some practical wisdom, in addition to Porter's guidelines for staying warm, and here is the sum: Make field notes in pencil—it doesn't run in the rain. While you may get very lucky with a cup of Peet's coffee provided by a particularly civilized researcher, carry your own Starbucks instant—you will be happy. Bring enough to share—you will make others happy as well. Carry iodine pills, because then you will be able to drink the water. Don't worry about mild discomfort like McMayon and I experience this day—difficulty amplifies the experience of discovery. A headlamp is a girl's best friend. And finally, find a way to leash yourself to the GPS you are entrusted with.

We walk across a small dam and start to document it, and McMayon suddenly can't. "I lost it!" she croaks. The transistor radio–sized GPS device has somehow slipped from her grip. I look around at uniformly dense bushes, indiscriminately small bodies of water divided by bewilderingly similar patches of earth. We can't tell exactly what direction we came from. McMayon takes off, presumably to retrace our steps but I'm not at all sure she's going the right way. We both wander around, losing each other, shouting out to each other, finding each other again. It begins to get dark, and big splotches of rain start to bully us. I timorously suggest we come back tomorrow, with more people; the area is not so large that we couldn't canvas it efficiently. "Tell Mary I lost the GPS?" says McMayon, in agony. She disappears again into the willows.

Yes, we have actually lost the device by which one fixes location with all certainty, and moreover, we keep losing each other. Today we get an "F" in field biology. After a while I figure if I keep wandering around I really will get lost, so coming to a fairly open expanse, I look for a place to sit down. Instead I spot an alarmingly fresh pile of scat, which I know is not cow dung. I stare at it: mountain lion, coyote? No wolves in these parts, and bear poop is bigger. Because there is hair in it I surmise it is coyote; mountain lions don't like to eat fur but coyotes don't care. While

I'm not exactly worried that this creature is going to want to make a snack of me or McMayon, this evidence of the food web in action puts me on the alert. I'm probably being watched. From where? The entire panorama seems to have, if not eyes, then some sensate responsiveness, every part of the scene tuning in to every other part. Not too much later McMayon and I are calling to each other and pushing through the thickets toward each other's voices—I catch sight of her long, swinging dark hair—McMayon looks at me, then looks down, and there is the GPS.

SHOW ME THE MONEY

Part of Mary O'Brien's work is coordinating other NGO and agency efforts to quantify the value of beaver on the landscape. We live in a dollar-and-cents world, after all, and money is our arbiter. With funds from the Walton Foundation (an NGO branch of the family operations that bring us Walmart), O'Brien contracted a consulting firm to analyze the flow, storage, and transformation of materials and energy within the Escalante Basin, which covers about 2,000 miles, with and without beaver on it. In sum, the report says that if beaver were restored along the 400 miles of creeks and streams that form and feed the Escalante River, their dams could change the flow patterns of up to 500,000 acre-feet a year and recharge (or replenish) the aquifers. (An acre-foot of water is the amount required to cover one acre to a depth of one foot.) Stored water would be valued at $1.4 million to $4.2 million a year. Add to that the value of increased riparian habitat and that's an additional $175 million to $470 million per year. Then there's the avoided cost of having to restore the waterways to reduce water temperatures, a metric enforced by state regulations. The beaver would throw this in as part of their deal and save up to $411,000 per square mile. Mark Buckley, the senior economist and lead author of the paper, tells me all these estimates are extremely conservative and don't include the voluminous benefits provided by a healthy ecosystem, including carbon sequestration and cleaner air. "I'm putting this document in front of as many eyes as I can," O'Brien says. "People have just got to get it."[40]

One set of data O'Brien might show around to ranchers and those who regulate them comes from an unexpected source—the Newmont

Mining Corporation, one of the world's largest gold companies—and in an unexpected place, Nevada. Newmont has been mining in the north-central part of the state for more than thirty years, and about twenty years ago acquired a cattle ranch abutting its property. "We thought we could manage the ranch better than it had been," says Paul Pettit, an environmental manager who routinely troubles himself with questions about how mining activity impacts water quality and water flows—and works to meet regulatory standards around those. The impetus for actually ranching the land came from a desire to participate in the community life of rural Nevada. "Sometimes it seems like mining companies come into ranching communities and change the way of life there, buy up the land, get rid of the cowboys. We didn't want to do that."

Nobody was thinking about beavers when the customary ranching style of leaving cows to their own devices was reshaped on the TS Ranch. But once the cows were enjoined from endlessly eating at the creeksides, the vegetation began to flourish there. "We've always had some beaver here," says Pettit. "The mountain men used to trap in Nevada. But there weren't many. Now they're everywhere."

Scale It Up

Beavers on the landscape here have effects beyond their beneficence to the TS Ranch, basically through the efforts of Carol Evans and Pat Coffin, two longtime fisheries riparian biologists with the Bureau of Land Management. Evans and Coffin have been documenting changes on 900 miles of streams here since 1977. Yes, that means they have *numbers* that prove many streams have improved and are providing better habitat conditions for the return of beavers. "We've been blown away by how many beaver moved in here after the cattle grazing was revised," says Evans, "and at how quickly the system has healed. The changes have been rapid and dramatic." Willow, sedges, and rush have blossomed and the usual host of critters that love them have followed. The water levels have increased. With monitoring help from the Nevada Department of Wildlife and Trout Unlimited,[41] Evans and Coffin have even identified three new small populations of cutthroat trout—a threatened species—in these streams.

The TS Ranch and others in the vicinity have adopted something called "rotational" or "prescriptive" grazing. The cows are allowed to graze an area heavily, but then they are moved off of it for a long enough time such that the grass can regenerate. This method does not just prevent degradation, it increases the richness of the forage. It does necessitate some upfront investment in moveable fencing to control the cows, and requires more manpower to actually move the fences. Evans is optimistic that if more ranchers knew what having a healthy riparian area looked like, with beaver helping retain and clean water, they would line up to make the change.

CHAPTER 9

Holy Cow

AMERICAN VISITORS TO INDIA OFTEN COME BACK DUMBFOUNDED THAT in streets filled with dire human poverty, cows are given pride of place. Such a sight is the very picture of a deep cultural construct that seems to not make any sense. Guess what: We are not so different here. Cattle grazing on public lands is heavily subsidized by the federal government, so yes, all of us taxpayers are helping to pay for tremendous environmental degradation. Poor cattle grazing practices denude the soil, and if you think that isn't such a big deal, remember the Dust Bowl. Impoverished soil is vulnerable to invasive plants that do their own part to wreck the land and its ecosystems, until it becomes devoid of nutrients and loses its fertility. Polluting the waterways where they hang out, cattle destroy habitat, not just for beaver, but for everybody who comes with beaver and more besides. That mesh of life is here reduced to a few threads.

It was all bad enough before climate change reared its stormy head, but now the landscape's ability to hold together under the onslaught of flood and drought is paramount. The historic impetus that endorsed eradication of predators to protect livestock may never have made real sense, but now it is not just counterintuitive, it is downright destructive. Moreover, carbon emissions from burning fossil fuels may pose the biggest threat to our environmental health right now, but pollution from agriculture is a close second. You would think it might be easier to reform some cow policies than it would be to quell the beast of global industrialization, especially since so much of the depredation occurs on public lands, but you would be wrong.

The present-day hold the ranching community has over the health of more than 260 million acres of public land is based on the history of how it got onto the land in the first place. The Forest Service and the Bureau of Land Management, the two federal agencies charged with stewarding public lands, coevolved with the ranching industry. State and federal wildlife agencies that are charged with protecting the denizens of our biodiversity are bound by tradition to give preference to the livestock industry's concerns over all else. There is nothing unilateral about the agencies, of course, and there are many people working within them who are doing the right thing, and many more who would like to, but the fact remains that not nearly enough is being done about bad grazing on public lands.

HOME ON THE RANGE

The beaver is how our forebears got out West. Pursuit of the beaver reached its endgame in the mid-1800s, by which time there was hardly a set of choppers left anywhere on the landscape. The removal of one animal to make a nation was quickly replaced by the massive insertion of another one to help make that nation stick: cattle. As an agrarian, place-based activity, ranching provided a great anchor for giving the "westward ho" influx of people a means to stay put. "Manifest" destiny was not just a clarion call to inhabit the continental landmass; "manifest" also means struck by hand, and implies an action resulting in substance and consequence.

But if the removal of the beaver pervasively devastated the health of western watersheds, so the arrival of cows in number has had an even more consequential level of impact on the land. In the service of making way for more cows, first of all came the decimation of bison. Bison were the dominating herbivore in North America for thousands of years, having arrived on the continent in the mid-Pleistocene Era (130,000 to 300,000 years ago); various counts put them at 20 million to 60 million animals roaming together on the land prior to European settlement. One observer, Colonel R. Dodge, on his way from Fort Zarah to Fort Larned on the Arkansas River in 1871, encountered a "dark blanket" of buffalo; from the top of a hill his analysis of a solid mass of the animals, which he surmised extended for 25 miles, put a rough estimate of their number—right there, right then—between 2.7 million and 8 million.[42]

Ranging over ecosystems as diverse as boreal forest in the north and the desert southwest, and over such a very long time, bison get that famous "keystone" designation, because their interactions influenced how the landscape developed and was maintained. As beaver engineered the waterways, so bison were responsible for the density and diversity of vegetation types, particularly grass, all across America. Bison were not the only species in abundance all over the West; virtually all the animals and birds we might be thrilled to get a brief sighting of now were present in profusion.

We're so acculturated to a landscape vastly reduced in numbers of wildlife that the scenes reported by John James Audubon, traveling up the Missouri River in 1843, sound like they are from some other planet. On an American Fur Company steamboat taking hunters and trappers into the wild, Audubon was in pursuit of specimens for *Viviparous Quadrupeds of North America*—this was his folio of paintings depicting mammals ("viviparous" means "live birth"). On June 3 he catalogued:

> one Goose with a gosling, several Coots, Grebes, Blue Herons, Doves, Magpies, Red-shafted Woodpeckers, etc. On a sand-bar Bell counted ten Wolves feeding on some carcass. We also saw three young whelps. This morning we saw a large number of Black-headed Gulls feeding on a dead Buffalo with some Ravens; the Gulls probably were feeding on the worms. . . . We saw four Elks, and large gang of Buffaloes.

The scene Audubon describes is one of thronging life. Unfortunately for them, bison of course competed with cattle for forage. While fairly impervious to the predators it had met with for millennia before Europeans came along, bison were pretty much as easy to kill by men with guns as beaver had proved to be before them. The railroad provided additional techno power to dispatch them quickly and en masse (shooting bison from moving trains was part of the sport). Where it took European expansion several hundred years to decimate beaver, bison were reduced within decades. The killing of bison reached its fever pitch in the 1870s, when hundreds of bison-hunting parties moved across the prairies, hunters shooting animal after animal after animal, without the others in the herd quite noticing until it was too late for them. The downed animals were skinned (bison hides were fashionable in the same fevered way that burned through so much beaver) and their carcasses were left to rot on the land. By the mid-1870s, there were no more bison in Colorado and Kansas; moving south, hunters depleted Texas of its bison by 1878.

Bison hides were the easy dollar ticket, but there were sociopolitical reasons for speeding the wipeout. Bison were integral to Indian societies and political strategists saw getting rid of the bison as a good inroad into subduing native hegemony on the land. As cattle ranching took hold of the West, the British invested in some of the operations; in 1877 one such Brit, William Blackmore, decried the slaughter and the coeval "extermination" of some Native American tribes, in the introduction to *The Great Plains of the West and their Inhabitants* by Richard Irving Dodge, but he reasoned, "The countless herds of buffalo, which formerly fanged the plains, will be superseded by treble the number of improved American cattle; the sparse herds of the smooth-haired antelope will be replaced by countless flocks of woolly sheep; and the barren prairies, now covered with the short buffalo grass, yellow sunflower, and prickly cactus . . . will under cultivation teem with yellow harvests of wheat and corn, providing food for millions." He added that the "only reminiscence of the Red Men" will be the cities, counties, and states named after them. In large measure, he got his utopia. He also happened to describe an ecological wasteland.[43]

The West of course was the ground for other convulsive grabs after natural capital, most prominently gold, silver, and lead mining, but activity (and wealth) having to do with extraction came and went, as ore was struck, removed, and exhausted. (Mining continues in the West today, dominated by big corporate entities.) Cattle ranching would appear to be more renewable; there seemed to be endless acres to graze cows on. A massive system of dams answered the nagging question of water in the West, to solve by a feat of human ingenuity the one impoverished feature standing in the way of a whole new world of wealth and well-being for a young nation's fresh population.

Perhaps most important, though, ranching was a stabilizing, community-oriented business, and lent itself to the formation of a strong culture, both familial and institutional, that pertains to this day. According to an interview with Michael Robinson, author of *Predatory Bureaucracy*, the political power of the ranching community has its seeds in the relative powerlessness of ranchers when the industry was born:

> Ranchers came out West as one of the first waves of settlements right after the trappers and the hide hunters, and they were followed quickly by the railroads. Ranchers were horribly vulnerable to droughts, storms, to wolves, to their cows wandering across boundaries, and to train companies. The railroads offered an incredible convenience, and ranching grew as a result of easy transport, but they could, and did, charge ranchers what they wanted for their services.

"Cattle production as a part of a self-sufficient community had problems at the outset," remarks Jim Catlin of the Wild Utah Project. "But when the train arrived in the West, it became an export crop. The explosion of numbers that have decimated the West is tied to the arrival of the rail." Individual ranchers were vulnerable to the dominance of the railroad companies, and Michael Robinson says they organized in self-defense. Through mutual cooperation and by forging strong government ties, ranchers protected their stock, formed a base for battling market forces, and established an intricate irrigation system of canals, diversion ditches, and dams across the West to provide cattle with water. What we would now call an environmental disaster was well under way by the late 1800s, as western forests were denuded of trees, their timber harvested in the service of building and fueling mining operations, to build houses and to heat them. Any individual or timber company could cut down trees anywhere; timber companies took possession of millions of acres of land, and harvested them as beaver had been harvested: methodically, relentlessly, with no thought of sustaining a core population or any sort of regeneration. Mountainsides relieved of their trees began to erode, and downstream flooding created big problems for the tenuous communities below them.

This was the era of John Muir, who founded the Sierra Club in 1892. He famously advocated saving forests for their ineffable value, both an intrinsic and a transcendent quality that he connected with spirituality. But it was a far more utilitarian impetus that led to protecting the forests, the recognition that in order for the wheels of the West to keep turning, some forests had to persist. The national forest system was instigated in 1891, through a law granting presidential power to set aside "forest reserves"; this laid the groundwork for what would become the US Forest Service in 1905. The forest reserve set-aside was an exemption from land laws established to encourage western settlement, and plenty of westerners opposed such an exemption. There was widespread sentiment against any restrictions whatsoever on homesteading, grazing, or timber cutting. Right here is the opposition the West has since maintained against the federal government. Thus, the conflicts we face today were laid out in their dichotomous glory before the turn of the twentieth century.

WOLF AT THE DOOR

Not just rampant harvesting of timber was threatening the health of the West—cattle and sheep were already at it. Ranchers were accustomed to letting their cattle graze absolutely anywhere. In an effort to contain them, Gifford Pinchot, the first head of the Forest Service, imposed a grazing fee; Pinchot did his due diligence and had gotten many ranchers to see that permitting was a move in their favor, as it "would ensure that no more than one person's cattle would be allowed on any given tract of land." However, many ranchers were enraged by it, and complained that it was unfair of the government to collect a fee to allow grazing on land that was "heavily infested with wolves." The ranchers wanted quid pro quo: protection from predators. Thus, in the very first year of its existence, the Forest Service provided leghold traps to its rangers. So the killing began.

Wolves were dispatched with alacrity by those who raised livestock. As human encroachment spread across the former wilderness, the natural prey of wolves was of course depleted, and they naturally turned to those hefty beauties hanging out forever by the rivers and creeks as replacement food. Cows bred as livestock evolved from wild bovine from Southeast Asia; they need water (bison, on the other hand, did not evolve with abundant water and are naturally better adapted to the West). Cows have to be spread across mile upon mile of stream, making it very difficult to protect them against predation; neither do they have the nimble wariness of their fellow ungulate the elk. Perhaps more than any other animal, wolves compete with humans for prey. The mindlessness with which both beaver and bison were virtually eliminated now fell into full swing in the matter of erasing wolves from the landscape, and a fervent, moral outrage was added to the onslaught. It was righteous to kill wolves.

Michael Soulé points out that evil really gets under way when it is institutionalized, and, alas, the institutions that truly mechanized and streamlined the killing of wolves and other predators were civic ones. Federal, state, and county organizations all chipped in; a bounty system was implemented and then found to be inadequate (and corrupt). The Bureau of Biological Survey started providing poison tabs to the Forest Service and the Parks Service for distribution to their ranchers: the State of Colorado received 17,000 poison tabs in 1919. By the early 1920s, most of the wolves were gone; coyotes stepped up to their ecological niche and began killing the larger animals that were once the province of wolves, and so, coyotes became the major antipredator focus and object of the hunt.

The understanding that killing successive species on down the food chain might not be such a good idea began to slowly dawn on some people, notably Aldo Leopold. Leopold was brought up a hunter and he enjoyed it. One of the reasons his legacy is so relevant today is that while his heart did turn, it didn't change all at once. Leopold helped establish the New Mexico Game Protective Association, affiliated with the American Game Protective Association, and these were funded by gun manufacturers. Devoted to keeping healthy populations of prey running around to dodge their bullets, these companies wanted predators out of the woods and fields as much as ranchers did; at one point Leopold advocated increasing congressional monies to fund the Biological Survey's predator eradication program. His more delicate definition of "control" was posed in light of supporting the activities of people who were out and about in nature: students, farmers, sportsmen.

In 1933 he published *Game Management*, thus formally establishing the discipline, and in which he considered the ecological relationships between predator, prey, and habitat, but it was still a few years before he really got that for an ecosystem to be healthy, the predator had to be in the picture. Writing about a 1936 hunting trip to the Sierra Madre, he described the terrain as what the American mountains were like before the "juggernaut" of cattle grazing: "To my mind, these pine-clad mesas spangled with flowers, these lazy trout streams burbling along under great sycamores and cottonwoods, come near to being the cream of creation. But on our side of the line the grama [pasture] is mostly gone, the mesas are spangled with snakeweed, the trout streams are now cobble-bars." He noted that the Sierra Madre still supported mountain lions and wolves and wondered whether "the presence of a normal complement of predators is not, at least in part, accountable for the absence of irruption."[44]

There were early inklings from scientists and wildlife professionals that wholesale extermination of predators was not a good idea. Dr. Joseph Grinnell, who founded the Museum of Vertebrate Zoology at the University of California–Berkeley, advocated for allowing predators "to retain their primitive relation to the rest of the fauna, even though this may entail a considerable annual levy on the animals forming their prey."[45] Grinnell was one of ten committee members on the new American Society of Mammologists, at the first meeting of which in 1918 several academics hazarded a criticism of the Biological Survey's extermination policy. Arguments against it included the general one on behalf of studying how life works: Since science does not have full knowledge of all species, and since the effects of species operate in concert, it is not a good idea to take out any piece of the puzzle. There was also what is essentially a genetic argument, that predators cull prey populations of weak and sick animals.

Bolstering these apostasies came an object lesson in what are now called "trophic cascades" on the Kaibab Plateau, part of the Colorado Plateau, and which President Theodore Roosevelt made a game preserve in 1906. At that point there were an estimated 4,000 deer on the Kaibab, and this low number was attributed in the longer term to cattle grazing, which had since been largely removed from the area, and in the shorter term, to overhunting. Wolves and other predators weren't blamed for this one, because they were long gone. Given its new designation, hunting was prohibited on the Kaibab. Now relieved of every competitor and check on its population, the deer population boomed. And kept booming. By 1924 there were 100,000 deer, and they began to starve. Hunters were actually brought in to kill the deer and stem their misery, but the entire landscape was decimated in the process. Because this event had not been scientifically measured and documented, the lessons of the Kaibab remain anecdotal but did provoke advocacy against predator eradication.

Still, the state and federal agencies kept up their work, handing out poison and facilitating every other way of killing predators. The tension between those advocating removal of predators and those against it continues in full force to this day, made much more complex by the antipredator sentiment within the very foundation of the governmental agencies charged with protecting wildlife. While the Forest Service and the BLM are today chock-full of scientists who know full well that the so-called balance of nature requires tolerance of predators, and while most of them have pursued their careers because they love wildlife, there is yet deep institutional history connected with advocating for the interests of livestock over the interests of predators. The short-term thinking, of course, puts the dollar value on the head of cattle—that's why it has to be protected. But the wolf also has a dollar value, in performing an integral service in keeping nature going—this has not sunk in to affect policy whatsoever.

ROOTS

That today's ranching community is fundamentally conservative and resistant to change can be traced to the initial difficulty of establishing itself on arid lands, and also to the fact that many ranching families trace their origins to before there was a United States. One Forest Service study aimed at better understanding the attitudes of permittees in northern New Mexico toward the government and about their land and their work reveals that often the practice, and the permits, has been handed down through generations.[46] Of sixty-two permittees interviewed, twenty are the fourth generation on their land, dating family length of residence on the ranch to their great-grandparents; nine are fifth generation; and nine more are sixth generation. Five date their family's arrival to the 1600s; one, an American Indian, makes no generational count because the number is essentially limitless. Only nine of the sixty-two are third generation or more recent. Since US "conquest," as Raish and McSweeney put it, of the region during the Mexican-American War dates only to 1848, this puts a healthy percentage of these ranchers on the land before it was American soil. It wasn't until 1891 that land leases were offered to be claimed. There are layers of history and resentment built into these facts. People who were on the land before it became American had to petition to claim what had been theirs for a long time. This was often an expensive proposition and not everybody could afford it; people lost land. Additionally, dubious and essentially illegal maneuvering delivered much of the land into hands other than those that had worked it for so many years. Commercial ranching and timber operations frequently laid waste to the landscape, after which much of it was sold to the government; thus, the Forest Service manages a lot of land in the area that was not originally public. The Treaty of Guadalupe Hidalgo, by which this conquest occurred, is not at all forgotten by this group of permittees. These are not obscure historical details. To many ranchers, these wounds feel fresh.

Family Values

The study does not approach the actual grazing practices by these permittees or discuss the health of their land. Rather, it addresses the quandary of struggling landowners tempted by development to sell out. The study finds, however, that "keeping land in the family and upholding traditional values are regarded more highly than material possessions or monetary gain." Most of those interviewed declare their commitment to keeping the land in the family, and teaching their children to work it. The authors conclude that "the tremendous social, cultural, and economic importance of these operations argues for future research designed to move the study of these types of agricultural enterprises out of the realm of purely economic study into disciplines that can assess the full range of their contributions." What this means is that the focus on continuance maintained by these people has many valuable social effects, which need to be acknowledged and valued as we cast our cold eye on the shortcomings of the public ranching system. Michael Robinson observes that "the value of continuance is something ranchers hold on to dearly. Right here in my local newspaper [in Pinos Altos, New Mexico, August 2011], there's a notice for a 4-H competition." The 4-H is a youth-focused organization, in Robinson's terms, an "agricultural pedagogy thing, to get kids interested in agriculture," and among the awards offered are ones for public speaking and parliamentary procedure. "These people are teaching their children how to be engaged with civic life. They have transmitted this necessity from generation to generation." The 4-H was established in 1904. The four H's that make up the organization's emblem stand for head, heart, hands, and health. This four-leaf clover is trademarked and copyrighted, and protected by the federal code that also safeguards the signifiers of the US presidential seal, the Red Cross, and Smokey Bear. This is an American brand. Robinson says, "The ranching community functions as a grassroots organization that works effectively to promote its interests." The conservation community would do well to take a page from the strategies of the ranching community in building grassroots support. (Jim Catlin points out that this continuance has a chimerical aspect. "Ranchers displaced Native Americans," he says. "Many a time I have been to a meeting where a local rancher talks about five generations of history. However, when someone says they have twenty generations on the land, they are ignored.")

Ranchers on public lands have also garnered benefits over the decades that they are quite loathe to have modified. The grazing fee is based on what are called animal unit months (AUMs), an administrative approximation of the value of forage necessary to feed one cow and calf for one month. In 2011 permittees paid $1.35 per AUM to graze public lands. Yes, this is a paltry amount. Moreover, controls in place protect ranchers from the vicissitudes of the marketplace: When the value of beef goes down, so does the AUM. A 2005 Government Accountability Office analysis of the situation reported that the Forest Service and BLM took in $21 million in grazing fees, against which they spent $140 million to subsidize the operations. Jim Catlin reminds us that many other uses of public lands are subsidized, including recreation, hunting, camping, and so forth. "I would be happy to subsidize ranching," he says, "if it left the land at its ecological potential. To subsidize ranching practices that cause significant harm to the land is bad policy."

Neither do these dollar amounts take into account the indirect costs of analyzing and addressing degraded stream qualities, removing invasive species, or stabilizing soil—damages resulting directly from grazing, all of which are routinely paid for by the Natural Resources Conservation Service and the Environmental Protection Agency, government entities (i.e., you and I pay for them).

All those jobs, though, right? No. There is a really sad irony in the grazing-on-public-lands story, which is that many permittees struggle to get by. Twenty-six percent of ranchers on public lands are corporate entities, and these do make money. So on the one hand, subsidies don't do enough for many ranchers and give too much money to corporations that don't need it. In all, we are talking about a very small group of people. Mark Salvo of Wild Earth Guardians notes that Nevada, which is composed of more federal land than any state other than Alaska, provides 1,228 ranching jobs, to which he compares the 37,000 people employed by a single casino.[47]

UNTO DUST

Damage to habitat from poor cattle grazing on public lands is associated with driving many species onto the Endangered Species List, including sage grouse, native trout, cutthroat trout, prairie dogs, the northern Aplomado falcon, the Sonoran desert tortoise, and of course, the gray wolf and the Mexican wolf. Overgrazing doesn't just destroy plant life and thus degrade riparian areas and wipe out habitat for nature's myriads. It also strips the soil of its nutrients. The grass is chowed down so hard it can't establish healthy roots. And a healthy root system is what makes good soil, rich in microbes and all sorts of animal life—full of nutrients, and able to hold water. There are big human health issues contingent upon soil vibrancy. For example, it is possible to eat an orange that has no vitamin C in it. Soil with no roots, no ability to hold water, stripped of its biotic components down to its bare minerals, is also soil that erodes come the first rain.

MOVING ON

Soil is another resource decimated as the pioneers moved west over the continent. When Columbus first arrived, between 4 million and 10 million people already inhabited North America, and many were at least partially sustained by agricultural or landscape management practices (including what we now call prescribed or controlled burns). But the Indians tended to work a piece of land and then move on from it; the colonists practiced a more sedentary style of agriculture, using the same plots over and over again. As tobacco began to help the colonies as they strained against the British stranglehold, so did the degradation of these fertile soils proceed apace. Tobacco is notoriously hard on dirt, taking out ten times the nitrogen and more than thirty times the phosphorus than food crops. After five years, land used to grow tobacco was dead. It was easy enough for farmers to just go plow up some new ground; there was always new land for the taking.

Despite their differing ideologies, both George Washington and Thomas Jefferson decried the bass-ackward way the colonials farmed. In a 1796 letter to Alexander Hamilton, Washington wrote, "A few more years of increased sterility will drive the Inhabitants of the Atlantic States westward for support; whereas if they were taught how to improve the old, instead of going in pursuit of new and productive soils, they would make these acres which now scarcely yield them anything, turn out beneficial to themselves." Thomas Jefferson did not offer so generous an explanation: "It is from our having such quantities of land to waste as we please . . . [and] we can buy an acre of new land cheaper than we can manure an old one." Jefferson became an advocate of contour plowing, which protected farmed hillsides from erosion, and some European farmers, notably the German and the Dutch, "treated dirt like gold" and prospered accordingly. But the drumbeat went on. No less a student of denuded rock than Charles Lyell, whose *Principles of Geology* so instigated Darwin's thought, was impressed by vertiginous gullies carved into Alabama and Georgia by erosion's quick work. Visiting in the 1840s, Lyell encountered families abandoning their farms and moving to Texas or Arkansas. As many rural permittees today suffer the same predicament, so these folks were economically hog-tied, unable to take the time or care to manure their land or give it a rest, despoiling the source of their livelihood to stay in business.

Arguably nobody really understood what kind of ecological havoc was being sanctioned as beaver, bison, and wolves were eradicated from the landscape and cows inserted in their place, but there is no such excuse when it comes to soil degradation. Even Plato made the connection between healthy soil and healthy populations. And soil loss is associated with the demise of civilizations around the world. See: the Greeks, the Romans, the Mayans. Each culture lasting about 1,000 years.

And we keep doing it today, despite a rather stark object lesson called the Dust Bowl. This was the 1930s debacle in which overgrazing and farming without crop rotation denuded over 100 million acres of Oklahoma, Texas, New Mexico, Colorado, and Kansas. Exacerbated by drought, what in a healthy formation would have been dense soil secured to the earth by deep roots instead turned to dust. Huge wind storms kicked that dust up and some of it reportedly fell as far as Washington, D.C. The Dust Bowl is memorialized in *The Grapes of Wrath*, in which John Steinbeck follows the displaced as they do what historically every overuser of an exhausted landscape has done on American soil: Head west.

BREAK IT DOWN

As with water, there is nothing so fundamental as dirt. Mix the two together, and you have the history of life. Many of us who visualize "core" wilderness as a green and brambly place with stilled ponds and hurtling creeks, swooping raptors and chirping songbirds, small mammals scurrying and big-teethed predators pouncing, miss the point that the core of the core is dirt. Soil, that is, wherein lives perhaps more biodiversity than all other abodes containing it combined. Much of the restoration work in the West usually gets billed by the NGOs and scientists who do it as "riparian," or river repair efforts. Other restoration work involves removing invasive plant species so native species can grow where they're supposed to. Both prongs of the problem come together in the dirt; healthy soil around creeks means healthy water. Healthy soil is not being sucked dry or commandeered by plants that thrive with abandon because they left the constraining features of their homelands back home.

We spend a lot of time worrying about the atmospheric carbon cycle, as well we should; that's the arena of greenhouse gases. But the atmospheric carbon cycle has a consort—the geological carbon cycle—and through it is created the ground we stand on. As with biology, geology starts with weather. Rain pounding down and seeping through rock began to break it apart, releasing minerals that formed into clays. More water percolating through redistributed those clays and thus was formed the first soil. Fossil soil dates as far back as 350 million years, giving it the same birthday as the first plants. David Montgomery, author of *Dirt: The Erosion of Civilizations,* puts it poetically: Soil, he says, is "the frontier between geology and biology," the place where what is not living (rock) comes alive (soil). Soil is where the rest of life is instigated from, in constant interplay with sun and water.

Water breaking apart rock rearranges its elements and invites a whole host of newcomers to come join the party. Microbes, willing night or day to get it on, add their own je ne sais quoi to the chemical composition, helping create just the stage for plant life to come and root itself right in the middle of everything. Decaying plant materials further enrich the dirt, aided and abetted by the thronging masses that live in it—over 95 percent of terrestrial diversity is in the soil. Let's focus on worms for a moment because Darwin did, in his final work, *The Formation of Vegetable Mould Through the Action of Worms* (are you intrigued?), observing that the lowly squirmers not only grind up leaves but actually break down small rocks, their stomach acids rivaling plant roots in the power to dissolve.

Not only do worms help make soil, they move it, with every bit as much consequence as do earthquakes, but over much longer and more gradual periods. Darwin observed worms plowing up soil by digging up their burrows; the soil moves downhill an average of 2 inches a year. He calculated that together English and Scottish worms moved almost half a billion tons of earth per annum, and considered them a major geologic force influencing the shape of land formations over millions of years. "It may be doubted whether there are many other animals which have played so important a part in the history of the world."

Clever chap, but Darwin didn't know that the process by which those worms moved earth on the surface of the earth is part of a bigger cycle triggered by erosion and comparable to what happens as an iceberg melts. Like icebergs, most continental landmass is hanging out below sea level; as erosion lessens the above-water load, what's underneath comes pushing up to compensate for the difference. (This is called isostasy, from the Greek, *iso*—equal; *stasis*—setting, weighing; thus, weighing the same.) In addition to recycling nutrients from dead stuff in the soil, worms contribute to the downward-moving trends of weathering and dissolution of rocks that are perpetually engaged with upward-moving trends that make mountains both slowly and, in volcanic pique, quickly.

CARBON COPY

That *carbon is the building block of life* is not exactly the formulation the Indians had in mind when they conceived Creation stories that involve beaver and muskrat bringing up mud from deep waters with which to build the earth. Nor was it on the minds of the Hebraic authors of the Old Testament who named the first man Adam (in Hebrew, "earth" or "soil") and woman Eve (Hebrew for "living"), the union of which created mankind, called by the Latin *homo,* from "humus," living soil. But the stories colorfully tell the tale otherwise recounted in terms of DNA and dirt. Some scientists propose that in the journey from rock to soil, clay minerals provided the stage on which the first organic molecules cohered into living organisms. The fossil record dates the earliest marine life to about the same time as the oldest soil. Guanine and cytosine, two of DNA's four bases, form in clay-rich solutions. A hospitable ground for complex life was certainly established regardless of whether the spark of Creation ignited right there in the dirt.

Meanwhile, back at the ranch . . . The immediate concerns of ranchers are by necessity those related to reducing feed bills, increasing the productivity of forage, mitigating the damage erosion does to their water source, and in general, doing anything that will help them stay in business. Scientists want them to see that mob grazing is not just a quick palliative—for most ranchers, it would entail more man-hours herding the cows, and the out-of-pocket expense of moveable fencing, costs that are more than offset by increased productivity. It is a way forward, to the head of the class in fact, on mitigating climate change and potentially representing an income stream by way of carbon trading, which I heard one scientist at a conference joke is a good thing as long it's underground. Healthy root systems sequester carbon. By some process that is not quite understood, mycorrhizal fungi around healthy roots create a "microbial bridge" that siphons carbon out of the atmospheric carbon pool, where some of it becomes carbon in the soil. The process helps create humus, the good stuff that in turn promotes soil structure and plant growth. In exchange for carbon from the roots, the mycorrhizal fungi trade phosphorus, zinc, nitrogen, and more to the plant. While the forage aboveground is improved within a season or two as a result of mob grazing, the root system needs a few years to get going on this ability to sequester carbon.

The Marin Carbon Project, a ranch in Marin County, California, is working with a phalanx of brainiacs to develop and quantify its carbon sequestration with the goal of developing soil system management practices that enhance the climate, and eventually establishing a market base for the service. John Wick, whose quizzical expression makes him look like he stepped out of a Monty Python movie where everything is silly but makes perfect sense, describes how he came to the carbon table. In 1998 he and his wife bought 540 acres next to the gorgeous national seashore at Point Reyes. "We were environmentalists and 'leave it alone' wilderness people. The first thing we did was put a fence around our land to keep our neighbor's cattle out. We watched our land turn into a weed-infested mess." Jeff Creque, an agricultural and rangeland consultant, told him he had perennial native grasses on the land and suggested he needed to graze it. After some rough starts, they started rotationally grazing cows.

Eventually this turned into a big success, and with Creque and Dr. Whendee Silver, professor of ecosystem ecology at UC Berkeley, Wick began to get the idea that they could actually ranch carbon as well as cows. And of all places, Marin County ought to be able to establish a carbon economy. The question is how to measure it in order to market it. Silver says, "Unfortunately, we can't measure soil everywhere," and proffers the "Century Soil Organic Matter Model" as a tool for broad use. The Marin Carbon Project team is experimenting with soil amendment routines (composting) for enhanced carbon sequestration, as well as scrutinizing the daily schedule of the cows. Currently they are working with the EPA, the California Air Resources Board, the Bay Area Air Quality Management Board, and others to implement an on-site soil system management program prototype in Marin. It is expected to offset 500 metric tons of greenhouse gases. Ultimately they would like to establish protocols that can be broadly replicated and applied.

It should be noted that not everybody is so keen on rotational grazing. Dr. Boone Kauffman, a Forest Service scientist who frequently consults on watershed restoration, laughed and groaned at the same time when I mentioned my enthusiasm for the subject. "I feel like I'm getting old," he said (he's probably in his mid-forties). "Like I just want to say, 'Not that old mob-grazing stuff again!'" Kauffman explains that such a management strategy might be good on landscapes that are better adapted to cows to begin with but that there should really be no grazing whatsoever in the desert Southwest, where there simply is not enough water to sustain it.

CHAPTER 10

Not Hunting

I SEEMS THAT EVERY REPORTER WHO COVERED A POTENTIAL WOLF recolonization in Colorado in 2010 had to mention Cristina Eisenberg's dimensions: 5 feet 2, about 100 pounds. Are small women so rare? But when I meet the woman I understand the impulse. Eisenberg is the science adviser to the High Lonesome Ranch near Grand Junction, Colorado; the author of *The Wolf's Tooth*, about trophic cascades; and as of this writing on the cusp of a newly minted PhD—this is her second if not third career, and she's going gangbusters at it. Eisenberg has Mexican ancestry and there is something of the *Mater Dolorosa* in her physiognomy. Her presence far exceeds her biomass. When I walk into the lodge at the ranch, Eisenberg is herding scientists and journalists, and she herds me, too. Men twice her weight bend their heads and heed her. "You," she says to me, "are not hunting. You will visit with Scott [ranch manager] at breakfast and between 10 and 11 with Paul [Vahldiek, ranch owner]." The science hunt has been conceived as a communications effort, to help change a widespread assumption in the hunting community that scientists are anathema to their sport. For this purpose Eisenberg has invited four scientists, including Michael Soulé, who are avowed hunters to come do their thing on the ranch, and she has invited three journalists, including me, to observe and report on this. The message is that scientists actually like hunting and believe in it; some of them would even like to see hunting of elk in particular, stepped up quite a bit in some areas, to cull the herds.

"I'm not hunting?" I squeak. I didn't actually expect to shoot at anything, not just because I don't know how to do it, and have negative interest in killing an animal. But at home I had been dining out for weeks on the prospect that I would be tagging along on a guts-and-glory expedition and would report back to my similarly citified and sissy friends about what it's like out there in the snow, with guns. "You'd scare the elk," Eisenberg says. Since she de facto associated me with her favorite predator, the wolf, I decide to accept her judgment in this matter as a supreme compliment.

Another revelation presents itself in front of the fireplace at the lodge: Michael Soulé knit tightly together with his newlywed (and third) wife, Joli Sharp, whom I had not previously met. Joli is, as her name connotes, very pretty and approximately forty years old. I have also come in on the tail end of a discussion in which a young forestry academic from Oregon State, John Lennon Campbell, had boldly taken on none other than Jim Estes in the matter of trophic cascades, terminology describing the way the balances of ecosystems are managed by top-down predation (more to come). Arguing otherwise, that ecosystems establishment occurs bottom-up, starting with the photosynthesizing plants (*pace*, bacteria and fungi), Campbell's challenge was tantamount to proposing to Paul Ehrlich that human population keeps increasing because there are so many resources to go around. Estes is another of the famous elders in the conservation biology tribe (younger than Soulé, he still teaches at UC Santa Cruz), and he got that way based on his trophic cascade research. I am thinking, wow, this is going to be an interesting trip. I am right.

In addition to her other attainments, Eisenberg is what Malcolm Gladwell calls a "connector," and she is responsible for bringing the blue-ribbon scientific imprimatur of Michael Soulé to the High Lonesome Ranch. She is also helping Vahldiek build the High Lonesome Ranch Science and Conservation Institute, one goal of which is to measure the restoration efforts underway there. By quantifying results according to the highest academic standards, the institute will create data and guidelines that will be highly useful to helping heal other degraded western landscapes. Eisenberg met Vahldiek while she was giving a talk on trophic cascades to the Boone & Crockett Club at the Theodore Roosevelt Memorial Ranch in Montana. "At the end of my talk this big man stands up and says, 'Now I know what's wrong with my ranch! Come heal my aspen!'" Vahldiek had been trying everything for eight years, spending millions of dollars on experts, on riparian restoration, on moving earth around, and his aspen were still sickly, his stream channels barren and steeply incised.

THIS LAND IS MY LAND

It is not a slam-dunk to do the right thing, even when you possess the dispatch of Paul Vahldiek. He directs what happens on his land, but because everything is yes, connected, the land around his greatly impacts the health of his ranch. Over the years Vahldiek has developed relationships and working agreements not just with the BLM, but also with the oil and gas companies that have BLM mineral and gas leases adjacent to his property. Like other big ranchers Vahldiek is engaged in a web of issues that are of vital interest to conservation, the intricacies of which NGOs don't usually have access to.

It is axiomatic that wealth minted elsewhere is a blight on the West when it comes to buying up land, but an infusion of political and cultural diversity could potentially loosen the vise of traditional "values" in the region, including the seemingly reflexive attitude that people should be able to do whatever they want on the land. Vahldiek may call himself a rancher and a conservationist hunter, but he is also a trial lawyer. In the matter of batting back oil and gas pressures, he says he couldn't have done it without his knowledge of the law. Your stereotypical rancher in the West is usually concerned with circling the wagons around long-held provenance, other considerations be damned. Vahldiek is cut from different cloth. While most certainly personally enriched by his law practice, he speaks about it in rather bleeding-heart terms; from big, bad corporate interests, he has won much recompense for his fair share of widows and orphans. Virtually everyone who talked to me about Vahldiek before I met him described him as a good-old-boy Republican, marveling all the more that such a creature would be interested in doing right by the land. He tells me he is more of an Independent than a Republican. "I'm like most Americans," he says. "I'd like both parties to behave."

The High Lonesome Ranch is emphatically multiuse. It is a destination for adventure travelers, offering high-end fly fishing, shooting sports, biking, birding, and hiking. The food and wine are such that even a snobby San Franciscan can rave about it. The accommodations strike a perfect balance between rustic and luxurious. In the summer months, these include *Out of Africa*–style tents replete with hardwood floors, granite baths, and interesting artwork. The ranch is also perfectly situated between Aspen on one side and Telluride on the other, for those who would like add forays into these glittering western precincts to their luxury vacations.

From the beginning of his High Lonesome adventure, Vahldiek has had stewardship intentions for it. He credits David Ford, a former managing partner of Goldman Sachs, with mentoring him in science and conservation matters. (Ford owns a small share of the High Lonesome Ranch.) Before Eisenberg came along, Vahldiek had instigated a large stream restoration project and brought in scientists from Philadelphia's Academy of Natural Sciences to inventory biodiversity on the ranch. In the nearly two decades that he's owned the place, Vahldiek has tried various ways to restore native grasses, some more successful than others, and done Herculean, but largely inadequate, stream restoration—including reintroducing beaver onto the waterways. There is talk of reintroducing bison, since it is likely that bringing them back would bring back the plants and animals that historically make a healthy flow here. On the other hand, the High Lonesome is a guest ranch, and bison can be dangerous to people.

Talk of prescribed burns on the land is similarly restrained by the fact that even the most carefully attended fire can easily leap out of control. Before it was suppressed, fire cycled through the landscape and rebooted the ecosystem. Fire plays an integral role in the long-term health of aspen in particular, and Eisenberg's research in Canada reveals that fire plays a key role in trophic cascades. As essential as fire is to forest ecosystem health, however, there is so much understory and debris in western forests now that fires burn too hot, destroying even the biggest trees that would have withstood lesser fires if they had been allowed to occur naturally. Fire is one of the biggest Catch-22s on the western landscape today.

Conserving with the Enemy

In researching *The Wolf's Tooth,* her book on trophic cascades, Eisenberg made a trip to interview Michael Soulé, one of the concept's leading proponents. The title of her book references a Robinson Jeffers verse: "What but the wolf's tooth whittled so fine the fleet limbs of the antelope?" Which tells you quite a lot right there about natural selection. It means that the antelope evolved its ability to run fast in response to the jaws snapping at its heels.

Soulé had been talking with his strategy director, Kenyon Fields, about making a paradigm shift for the Wildlands Network to bolster work on the Spine of the Continent. "The scales fell from my eyes," Soulé says. "This cannot be just about protecting public reserves. We are fiddling while Rome is burning, and Rome is burning up." Soulé's revelation was that as good conservationists do, Wildlands Network had focused its efforts on educating and cajoling and standing on its head to get the Forest Service, the Bureau of Land Management, the state wildlife agencies, and local communities to protect important landscapes and to adopt healthy management practices, to build sufficient cores and corridors so that nature, particularly large predators, could flow up and down the Rockies and thus constitute resilience. The assumption was that the right thing would be done on public land. "But we have learned public land is in many ways impossible," Soulé notes, referring to the often truly endless bureaucratic end zones found in state and federal agencies. Meanwhile, nature has not been protected fast enough; the work of the Wildlands Network and its brethren NGOs has not kept pace with development. Add climate disruption into the picture, as we must, and the clock is striking twelve.

While not at all abandoning the public approach, Soulé and Fields realized they were ignoring a hugely significant part of the landscape: working lands that are privately owned. Wealthy people like Paul Vahldiek who buy up huge acreages are quite often sincerely committed to the health of their investment. "I didn't buy this ranch for it to be covered in sagebrush," Vahldiek mutters to me while I tag along with him one day. Sagebrush tends to take over the landscape in these parts when species with differently attuned adaptation systems start to disappear, due to climate change or some other exacerbation.[48] "I want to look out at aspen," he grouses. To actually address what is happening on his land, Vahldiek has three things that public land stewards typically lack: money, will, and relative freedom from organizational runarounds.

With examples such as Ted Turner in mind, Soulé and Fields had been developing the idea of a private lands conservation network. The model is profitable business coexisting with progressive environmentalism. They noticed big-time that one superempowered individual could do more for conservation with a single pen stroke than hundreds of sweating NGOs over decades. So, what about encouraging many more ranches to become similarly aware of the importance of conservation-minded strategies on their land? What about connecting them with each other so that the greater resources of one could be leveraged by the good intentions of another? Private lands can become isolated islands as easily as national parks can, in which case individual owners are threatened with great loss. In other words, owners need connectivity, too.

Soulé and Fields envisioned an umbrella structure in which participating ranches, or other kinds of large property owners like private timberlands, would agree to steward their lands according to science-based management principles. Member ranches would adjust their grazing practices and work to restore their riparian areas. They would manage the roads on their properties with a mind toward reducing traffic near or across core roadless areas, and make sure their fencing is the kind pronghorn antelope can slip under (pronghorn don't like to jump over things). They would implement controlled burns to bring fire back to the ecosystem in a manageable way. And parts of the property that abut other natural areas or are otherwise good corridor candidates would be so managed. Since these are the fundamentals of taking good care of land, something lots of private property owners are highly interested in, the deal would be a good one for them. "We all care about the health of the land," says Fields. "That includes wildlife populations and the human communities that depend on these resources." Oh, and another thing private property owners who become part of this network would be wise to consider: allowing top predators (i.e., wolves) to not only move through their property, but also hang out on it.

Eisenberg introduced Vahldiek and Soulé, and in 2009, Vahldiek attended Wildlands Network's Western Conservation Summit, along with NGOs and agency personnel, and scientists such as Healy Hamilton and Paul Ehrlich. Fields tells me, "Michael gathered all these people together to remind them that their best intentions to save nature are not working. All ecosystems are still in bad shape and land is being lost every day." Vahldiek says, "I had to keep quiet, you know, around all those enviros." He raises his brows and flashes a mischievous, gap-toothed grin. When Kurt Menke's 6-foot map of the Spine of the Continent was unfurled, Vahldiek says, he laughed to himself. "These people been smoking something funny," he thought. But he is not a man to shirk the big picture. Vahldiek is a self-made man, the son of a butcher; Neil Armstrong was his neighbor growing up, and the young Paul would sit on his roof, looking up at the moon, and dream: The big picture was made for him. "I saw that my ranch takes up about the size of a half dollar on that map. That's a lot of land—it's a big piece of the Spine. I have friends who have other big pieces. I realized it could be done." Vahldiek has since hosted Wildlands Network's inaugural Western Landowner Network (in July 2011), proffering the High Lonesome Ranch as a prototype where commercial endeavor mixes productively with conservation-minded stewardship. Thus far the effort has attracted participants from nine states and Alberta, Canada—together, these people steward more than 8 million acres of land. A significant enthusiast in this effort is Idaho's Lava Lake Ranch, (owned by Kathleen and Brian Bean), where a grass-fed sheep operation coexists with a multitude of other healthy land practices.

HOWL

In April 2009 Eisenberg was well under way with developing her elk-predator-aspen study of the ranch. One day one of her biologists noticed a piece of scat unlike those they were accustomed to finding on the ranch; it was as long and thick as a banana. An hour and a half later, they found similar scat about 500 yards away. Over the ensuing months, Eisenberg and her crew found several more examples of scat that, based on her long observations at home in Montana, clearly told of the presence of "the visitor from the north." In the same way that actors cast in *Macbeth* avoid actually naming "the Scottish play," so do those who study the lupine species avoid its moniker, lest those pitched to destroy it whiff the scent—in Colorado, that is, where the mighty fanged beast of nightmare and fairy tale has been resolutely extinguished for more than seventy years.

If I'm walking in the woods, I'm not so happy to come upon evidence of the Big Bad Wolf, but others could not be more excited. The press jumped all over the possibility, and Eisenberg found herself besieged by reporters from papers such as the *Denver Post*. CBS News interviewed her and Soulé. Environmental NGOs also knocked on Eisenberg's door at the High Lonesome Ranch, eager to leverage a new wolf presence in the state to help raise their own public profiles, but they were rebuffed. For the High Lonesome Ranch, a colonizing wolf could signal that a beleaguered species is making a comeback. The good news for reporters is that emotions around wolves instigate conflicts that often result in a story. The story of wolves in the United States has been a cultural one, a political paradigm; it is now, also, a story about environmental degradation and its potential restoration. As it so happened, DNA analysis suggested that the scat belonged to a coyote.

TROPHIC THUNDER

"I thought I'd take my usual contrarian stance and challenge these guys from the perspective of the plant ecologist," explains John Lennon Campbell about the saucy argument he leveled at his elders in the matter of wolves. "Jim Estes was amused by my deliberate belligerence—he makes a very good case that not only does it make sense that higher organisms shape the ecosystem from the top down, but you always find it going on." Michael Soulé, whose stalwart championing of the wolf comes with a resolutely emotional charge, was not as tolerant of Campbell's parrying. But this is just the attitude that provokes Campbell to take exception. "I get worried that such an important thing as trophic cascades are being used by conservation biologists to save wolves. I might say there's a brain worm that controls elk that's more influential on a particular population than wolves are—why wouldn't we get excited by that? We're scientifically enshrining top predators, almost exclusively charismatic ones." Campbell says, "I was brought up by socialists who said labor is the source of everything; the primary producers. I say labor is the source of all wealth to invite the obvious; there is no economy without capital, just like there's no ecosystem without bottom-up effects. Plant production may start it all."

"Trophic" is from the Greek *trophikas,* meaning "nourishment"; "cascade" is from the Latin *cascare,* "to fall"; and the term "trophic cascade" was coined by Robert Paine to describe how carnivores, at the top of the food chain, impact the herbivores, at the next level down, which impacts the plants and phytoplankton at the bottom of the food chain. That the critters with big, sharp teeth eat those with leaves in their mouths is an observation not in need of a scientific imprimatur, but in the 1960s a trio with the names of Hairston, Smith, and Slobodkin (sounds like a Beckett scenario) proposed in a short paper that the reason terrestrial earth is covered in plants is that predators keep the herbivores from eating it all.[49] The paper stirred up enough debate that the authors became collectively known as HSS, and their idea "the green-world hypothesis." What people found so much to argue about was its directional change in thinking, since it was customary to view the dynamics of the food chain from the bottom up, probably since photosynthesis happens first in earth history, making phytoplankton and plants possible to begin with; and the existence of these also predates the herbivores and predators that have taken such advantage of their bounty.

What Robert Paine did was test the hypothesis by removing sea stars from a defined area off the coast of Makah Bay on Washington's Olympic Peninsula. (Formerly known colloquially as "starfish," these multiarmed beings are not fish at all but animals: echinoderms. Despite their decorative demeanor, these are formidable predators and when it comes time to eat, the sea star throws its stomach over its prey and begins digesting.) Paine then watched what happened there and in a control plot where he did not remove them. Left to their own devices, sea stars dined on mussels; in the area where they were removed, the mussels flourished. And then the mussels kept on flourishing, until they had decimated all the vegetation and crowded out all the other species on the water-washed rocks. Paine showed a deeper level of functioning going on in the linear sequence of predator-herbivore-plant, in which the predator's role is intimately implicated in the persistence of the plants. This regulating and dynamic relationship among members of a food group brought the green-world hypothesis to dynamic life, with those at the top exerting demonstrable effects on those at the bottom.

THE DALLAS HUNTERS

While the others are off hunting, I happily divide my time at the High Lonesome Ranch among very comfortable locations, including the lodge, where I sit with my laptop in front of a fire. Other visitors include two groups of hunters from Texas—all male, employees in one case from a construction company in Dallas, who are at the ranch to shoot birds. Driving up to the Homestead House where I am lodged, or while taking a walk, I periodically see the Dallas hunters in a field (at a safe distance), hear the sudden flapping of dog-rousted birds, and then watch as shotguns tilt up in concert to the sky like magnetic filings. The quick motion of an emphatic aim and then the bang of the shot remind me both of a pitcher's throw and the crack at the center of a bat.

One day after lunch Eisenberg and Estes give the Dallas hunters a brief presentation on trophic cascades. The Dallas hunters don't quite realize they are getting a tutorial from a famous scientist, but they are certainly all eager to hear what Estes and Eisenberg have to say. Estes is tall, fair-haired, laconic; as someone said of Humphrey Bogart, his fires are banked. He shows a slide of a man submerged in open water and says, "It was cold. This is the Aleutian Islands, in the '70s, before they made dry suits." He takes another look at the slide, at the slim figure therein, and smiles. "I was a lot younger then."

He's still in fine form, the first of the scientists to shoot an elk; he'll be driving back to Northern California and has come to the ranch prepared, with a trailer to transport his quarry home. Estes grew up hunting and to him there is no argument or apology to be made about that; he would certainly never pass up the opportunity that has been proffered to come hunt here. In a previous dinner conversation about the relative humanity of the practice, Estes argued that shooting an elk was a lot more compassionate than letting it die of starvation or disease resulting from overpopulation; then he says he knows his argument is self-serving. "I more than concede that," he says. Where many another of his conservation biology generation of senior males make a big puffing-of-the-chest testament to their Y chromosomes, Estes simply embodies something of the ideal of the form, carrying it lightly. The Dallas hunters are riveted.

BOTTOMS UP

He tells them about his work in the Aleutian Islands with sea otters. Otters are another of those animals whom in cartoon outline have come to represent something juvenile and benign, when in fact they are unreconstructed predators. Embarking on a study of how kelp forests support sea otters, the story goes that Estes ran into none other than Robert Paine in a bar, who told him, "Jim, that's stupid." He directed him instead to work on otters eating sea urchins, and sea urchins eating kelp. This would amplify Paine's own sea star work on an oceanic scale. As you have by now likely anticipated, Estes found that in the absence of sea otters—he found locations in the Aleutians that had them and locations where fur hunters had extirpated them—sea urchins, which sea otters eat, had decimated kelp beds. And with the kelp gone, so too all the myriad life-forms it harbors: not just big crowds of fish, but seabirds who feed on them from above. So far so good. Trophic cascade, check. Estes leaves it right there with the Dallas hunters. Paul Vahldiek is listening in and he interjects, "Now back to Cristina and the whole Aldo Leopold healthy-mountain thing."

LITTLE SHOP OF HORRORS

Over the years since then, the phenomenon of trophic cascades, or top-down control, has been evidenced in every major ecosystem, both marine and terrestrial. Of course it is even easier to draw the diagram moving in the opposite direction. John Terborgh conducted a famous study Kafka might have liked on islands created by the establishment of what is now called the Gurii Dam in Venezuela; the resulting lake created islands out of the highest peaks of the countryside, and they came in all different sizes, many too small to support the top predators in the area. Jaguar, cougar, and harpy eagle: all absent. I myself can imagine that the famous howler monkeys of Venezuela might be kind of freaked out by finding themselves abruptly marooned on islands, the landscape they were adapted and accustomed to summarily shape-shifted, but whatever instigated their resulting degeneration, the results fall into the trophic cascade outline. They stopped howling. Instead of hanging out together in groups and grooming each other, they split off into separate trees. They browsed the vegetation mercilessly, not one of their number ever checked by the threat or deliverance of hungry jaws, and the vegetation bit back. The trees adapted where the monkeys could not, and started spiking their leaves with poison; the hungry monkeys ate them anyway and then threw up. The scene is unnervingly similar to that imagined by Yann Martel in his wonderful novel *Life of Pi*. Remember the island poor Pi Patel comes to and it seems to offer succor, a place to recover from his travails, but then he registers that the grassy sward is actually burning hot and that at the center of every tantalizingly abundant fruit there is a human tooth? The island's carnivorous plant profile is not metaphorically distant from what actually happens when you remove a top predator from an ecosystem.

MIDDLE MAN

Given his frequent role as moderator and synthesizer of polar positions, it seems fitting that Michael Soulé's scientific contribution to the trophic cascade line of inquiry involves what are called mesopredators, from the Greek *mesos* meaning "middle." Mesopredators are the putative second-string carnivores, smaller than the heavy-hitting wolves, grizzlies, panthers, and so on, and include raccoons, cats of the in-your-lap size (both domestic and feral), skunks, foxes, crows, and so on. In many ways the mesopredator dimension of trophic cascades brings the consequence of the dynamic up close and personal. Soulé figured it out equally through a field experiment and by the behavior of his own house cats. (Despite his professional identification with the iconic wolf, he's more of a cat than a dog person.)

In the mid-1980s, Soulé was living north of San Diego and approached developers to suggest they do the right thing by wildlife and put some corridors in their blueprints. He explained the ecological peril of isolation and said that if they incorporated connectivity on the landscape they were about to transform, the critters who lived there would have a chance at survival. Since those critters were not about to invest in the development and could not themselves go to a planning board meeting to protest, their interests were summarily dismissed by the developers. "I got mad," says Soulé. "I decided to do a research project." Over a period of two years Soulé conducted surveys of birds in the chaparral, quantifying their expected decline, which corresponded like clockwork to the predictions of island biogeography: the smallest fragments lost the most birds the fastest. While analyzing the data, one point leaped out at him: There were more species of chaparral birds singing away in patches where coyotes still did their thing. Remembering how his pets came flying through their cat door, chased by coyotes, he immediately understood why. "Ecologically speaking, when the top dog was away, the undercats would play," he says, and without coyotes to keep them in check and on the move, house cats and their feral brethren were advancing the demise of the songbirds, big-time. Coyotes don't generally prey on birds, and their presence actually supported the populations. He dubbed the phenomenon "mesopredator release," and it's kind of like what would happen if the locks fell off prison doors and the guards disappeared. Let the predation begin.

CHAPTER 11

Take It from the Top

ONE DAY AT BREAKFAST AT THE RANCH EISENBERG SAYS THE CARCASS
of a recently killed elk has been spotted not far away, and a bunch of us
climb in a truck with her to go see it. Each day the hunting scientists and
journalists (except for me), had gone out in pursuit of their quarry at 4:30
a.m., and then again at around 4 p.m. After Estes got his elk, there was
something of a lull in the takedowns, and there were some bleary and yet-
to-be-satisfied eyes in that truck. Hal Herring, a columnist for *Field &
Stream* and author of *Famous Firearms of the Old West,* explains to me that
what these guys and gal (Eisenberg is hunting) are doing every morning
and evening is not hunting. Herring is rather a sweetheart. With a big
swatch of black hair and a friendly squint, he's like an adult-size Alfalfa
from the Little Rascals. His flushed, outdoor-grizzled complexion attests
to the hunting-fishing-writing life he lives in Montana with his wife and
two kids, but he also has a very thick Alabama accent.

"Not hunting?" I ask. "No, Mary Ellen, no, it's not hunting," he says.
"It's some kind of sport. It's culling the herd. It's taking out meat. It's
fun. But it's not hunting." Herring explains that hunting is not driving
around in a pickup truck, looking for a herd of elk. The science hunters
were splitting into two groups, each accompanied by one of the ranch's
hunting guides; another guide was similarly leading the Dallas bird hunters. By every account the guides were superb and rather preternatural
in their abilities. One of the hunting scientists described to me how his
guide had stopped their truck across from a hillside upon which a herd
was gathered. "He said, 'I'm going to make a call, and that elk will stop,'
and he pointed to one. 'Then I'll make another call and its head will turn.

Then you shoot.'" And then that's just what he did, one call, two calls, the elk stopped, turned, and he fired.

Herring explains that real hunting is when you go out with a buddy or two and you track elk on foot. "The whole point is to track the animals," he says, his southern cowboy voice something like a shout through a mouthful of cotton. "Attuning yourself to what they're doing, how they're moving, looking for signs of them, and anticipating their next move." This is how you reconnect with your primitive, more alive self; this is how you become one again with nature. The pursuit can take days, involving camping out in the cold and the snow, in some cases—clearly the most satisfying ones to a hunter like Herring. "Then when you shoot your animal, you have to carry it on your back." This can mean several trips of several miles each. It can mean camping out with big hunks of raw meat by your side, and you'd better know how to deal with that if you don't want a crowd of coyotes, bears, wolves, and whatnot trampling your campsite. In the unlikely event I ever decide to hunt, I'm going to do it the High Lonesome Ranch way, with a hot meal and a bed at the end of the day.

We pull up in the truck on the top of an embankment, below which a moderate trickle of water flows. A big flapping of wings takes off from the body of a large elk lying by the side of the stream. There is expectation in the truck that the elk will show signs of having been felled by a wolf, but the indications prove otherwise. In the snow above the elk there is an unnerving indentation where the cat—for this was in all likelihood a cougar kill—had evidently belly-flopped midpounce and slid downhill before nailing its quarry. Cougars lie in wait for their prey near steep banks like this one. They surprise their victims and often kill with a lethal wound to the throat. By contrast, wolves typically hunt in small groups of two or three and work together to run down and eventually immobilize their dinner.

Another telltale sign of cat is an almost dainty array of tawny hairs in a curtain formation on the snowy embankment. Like house cats, the big ones don't like to eat hair, about which wolves and coyotes don't quibble. It is something to imagine, this big fastidious cat removing hairs from its dinner. Soulful hunters all, the group observes the sight with some awe. One big animal killed by another big animal: redness, tooth, and claw.

Reprising the theme of the science hunt that predation is fundamental to healthy nature, Herring quotes Tennyson: "So careful of the type she seems, So careless of the single life."[50]

The group's eagerness for wolf is partly an accrued emotional reaction to the venomous persecution perpetrated on them in the West for more than a century. It is also (in the opinion of scientific consensus) an eagerness for their presence to start healing the ecosystem on the ranch, its woes so typical of the entire region's. John Terborgh calls the three C's—carnivores, cores, and connectivity—"the proudest achievements of conservation science . . . practical applications that follow directly from established theory," and further asserts that of the three, "carnivores top the list, for without them all else will fail."[51]

THE TAXONOMY OF DESIRE

Soulé joins the science hunters each morning and late afternoon but leaves to take home his wife, Joli, before shooting an elk (they live fairly close by). I am reading one afternoon in the idyllic Homestead House, one of the guest lodgings at the ranch, an occasional couple of deer pronking by the living room's big picture window, when the phone rings. I uncurl myself from the couch in front of the fireplace to answer it and stop as sock-muffled footsteps come closer. I'm surprised to find Michael Soulé gliding down the stairs. "It's for me," he says. "I've come back to get an elk."

Soulé's appearances are indeed like Gandalf's, intermittent and opportune; they put me in mind of "stochastic" natural processes and "presence absence data." We sit and chat for a while in the Homestead House, and Soulé asserts that "there's something deep about hunting like there is with bodily functions. For millions of years, that's what men did. You had to have meat, so you could provide the lactating mother with milk. I believe it's in our genes, to go out and kill something big." Soulé connects pride with the hunt, and pride along with its cohorts envy and greed, are those über-deadly sins standing in the way of our saving nature. At the same time he makes a point of showing himself to be an eager hunter. A 2003 profile of him in the Buddhist publication *Tricycle* is titled "Buckshot Bodhisattva"; in it he recognizes the role of killing in enhancing diversity.

In the Homestead House living room he tells me more about his investigations into the seven deadly sins. He talks about the problems that conservation addresses: overexploitation, deforestation, exotic species, invasive species, habitat fragmentation, and so on. "These are what ecologists call proximal problems," he says. "I realized over the last decade or so that we're trying to deal with therapies, but not with the underlying problem, which has to do with human nature. The population explosion is about human nature—our desire to reproduce, and our greed." As much as we need to address the land, "we need to deal with people because people are the problem."

One of Soulé's favorite sources of thought is Jonathan Haidt's book *The Happiness Hypothesis,* particularly its cover, which shows a tiny human body perched atop an elephant submerged in a body of water. According to Haidt, a social psychologist concerned with morality and positive psychology, "Like a rider on the back of an elephant, the conscious reasoning part of the mind has only limited control of what the elephant does." Soulé says, "The elephant is the emotions. We think our decisions and our actions are rational, but they aren't." There is often a major disconnect between what we think we are doing and what we are actually doing.

Soulé observes with a scientist's eye that the first five sins—greed, anger, gluttony, sloth, and lust—evolved hundreds of millions of years ago, and these impulses—survival instincts gone haywire—"are found in all other vertebrates and some invertebrates." He dates the roots of sin prior to the invention of the word, which is relatively young. "Sin is biological, as old as desire; it extends back billions of years because the need for energy is essential for life. Desire is the core element of fitness—bringing us reproduction and survival. Life is grasping. The life force—*élan vital*—is really desire."

But it is the remaining two sins that really do us in, "the two that require theory of mind: pride and envy." Theory of mind marks the development in human history of our ability to observe the feelings and desires of others, which in turn led us to modify our behavior to better achieve the aims of the primary sins. In Soulé's view, pride and envy are the worst, since they feed our desire for more and more stuff with which to display higher status. Pride and envy fuel the arms race of human regard.

READY, AIM

With the exception of Jim Estes, by the looks of them I wouldn't have pegged any of the scientists at the High Lonesome Ranch as hunters. To a one, they are very deliberate, and even agonize over the ethics of hunting and the proper place of killing. Trent Seager, who came to study forest ecosystems after a career as an AIDS activist, wears a skullcap and a decidedly soft and friendly expression. He tells me that he came to hunt as a result of struggling with the idea that for him to eat meat, someone had to kill it. "If I'm going to eat it, I want to kill it myself." Seager performs a short ceremony over an animal he's just killed, to honor the animal.

John Lennon Campbell offers the downed animal a drink from his water bottle. "It's my way of signifying the transfer," he says, "acknowledging that it's moving on to its next life." He also discusses an undoubtedly resonant part of the hunt, which is that when you kill an animal, it becomes yours. "You know, there's an ambiguity as to when laundry becomes clothes in your drawer: When does an elk become meat? Is it the moment when the bullet hits? Is it when you take it apart and it no longer has its form? You kill it, and as the lawyers say, it becomes 'reduced to my possession.' You kill it, and it is your property."

Perhaps most hunters are not thinking about all this to the degree Campbell is, but his remarks get at something of what makes hunting so compelling a sport. Understanding the perspective of hunters is extremely important in the quest to conserve habitat and species in the West. The hunting community often opposes pro-conservation initiatives, taking the position that conservation is in competition with them. The truth is somewhere else. In fact, it can be argued that conservation aims to support ecosystems in which hunting can play a vital role. But there is little doubt that as with cattle ranching, the rules and expectations around how hunting is done, which species are appropriate quarry (elk) and which are not (wolves), has to change if our ecosystems are going to continue to support anything worth shooting at all.

Look at That Body

I am sitting in the lodge when Campbell comes in, right after he has shot his elk. He is slim, with long, brown, curly hair and bright eyes that are even shinier than usual. "So what happens after you shoot the elk?" I ask. "The first thing you do is remove the guts. You leave that behind; you have to. And then you take the animal apart." Hal Herring sits down with us around the fire. Campbell's eyes are dilating and I wonder whether he remembered to hydrate on the hunt. He explains that by the time you draw and quarter the animal, it is bled out, which is the actual cause of death, whether the fatal blow has been administered by bow or rifle. "You can reduce a recently killed animal into several packs in an hour and a half, but it can be done in forty minutes." The work this morning had been leisurely, since the elk had only to be field dressed. "Afterward, we took the organs out and put the whole animal onto the truck—I have to laugh at this convenience because usually I have to take animals out on my back. How much you can take at a time depends on how big and tough you are. The most I can carry out on my back is a fifth of an elk, one of the legs, or the spine." Lest Campbell's download seem cold, a lengthy appreciation of the animal's body as revealed through the literally visceral experience of taking it apart follows.

"The form of the animal is just so beautiful, and we are built the same way. We are this giant invaginated organism, and you really see the organization when you gut an animal, you really appreciate it." "Invagination" describes the way elements of the body form spaces in which the next part of the body is enfolded; Campbell is figuratively peeling back layers of an elk with a knife, but if he could keep going, this basic pattern of folding and containing would continue down to the cellular level of the animal. Its ultimate point is at the beginning of the animal's conception, in the embryonic cells that first gave rise to it. "There are two systems," Campbell says. "There's an inside of an animal and an outside, and that's established soon after the zygote starts separating at germination. Some cells envelop themselves or invaginate, and the genes expressed inside the cells tell them to develop insides, and those expressed on the outside tell the cells to form the outsides."

Campbell is talking about the basic blueprint and building plan for most body forms, otherwise known as "evolutionary development," or evo-devo for short. Recent advances in evo-devo research build on observations made back in the day by Darwin and crew. Most notably Sir Richard Owens, famous for naming the species of a bizarre set of fossils "dinosaur" (in 1841 or 1842), had noticed profound similarities between the structures of bodies among species as otherwise wide apart as birds, amphibians, and *Homo sapiens*. In "On the Nature of Limbs," Owens pointed out a fundamental design in the skeletons of all animals, with flippers and wings corresponding to arms and legs. This uniformity in architecture, to him, evidenced the plan of a Creator. Darwin responded by proposing that this homology, which was Owens's term for "the same organ in different animals under every variety of form and function," was explained by way of a common ancestor. Thomas Huxley, aka Darwin's bulldog, proposed that the "perennial miracles" of nature were born in the embryo, but neither Huxley nor Darwin nor many subsequent generations of scientists had any way of getting at how exactly this happened.

To Owens's observations about similarity among body forms, William Bateson added the observation that many large animals are composed of repeating body parts—like vertebrae. He also noticed this pattern in insects, which are formed of repeating segments. Bateson was a main rescuer of Mendel from obscurity, though he had his own battles to wage. He is credited with the very term "genetics," from the Greek *genno*, which means to give birth, but it took some time to establish genetics as a viable field of inquiry. While embryology and heredity were clearly all part of this early evolutionary thinking, after Darwin they went down their separate roads.

When genetics did get under way again, it concerned itself with variation in traits, but in just a few species. At the other end of the spectrum of scale, paleontology was concerning itself with the longest time frames and the evolution of higher taxa. The disconnect between these two was resolved in the early 1940s, by way of the modern synthesis, which posits that small genetic changes produce the variation natural selection acts upon, and that evolution of greater magnitude in higher taxonomic levels occurs by the same processes over longer periods of time. So now it could be said that forms do change over time and that natural selection is a force in this, but again, it could not be said exactly how. Darwin and Huxley (and others) put down embryology as the place where forms actually change, but that marker didn't move until just a few decades ago.

Population genetics, to tack back to Michael Soulé's original field, had shown that evolution is caused by changes in genes, but in the words of one of evo-devo's main practitioners, Sean Carroll, "this was a principle without an example."[52] Using the amazing tool offered by molecular genetics training its sights on the doings of DNA, scientists have since cracked the "black box," and yes, shown without question that here in the embryo is where form is born. In very short surmise, gene expressions in the embryo give cells instructions about when to divide, and what they should eventually become: You are a foot; you are a leg; you are an antenna. Given their marching orders, the originating cells start making up the body. Fins and arms are homologous because the genes that tell a fish to develop a fin *right here* evolved from the same genes that tell a human body to develop an arm *right here*. The same gene mutates slightly differently in different animals over evolutionary time.

FATE MAPS

"Fate maps" is the actual scientific term for the temporal geography of the embryo, the map upon which developmental cells are arrayed in specific positions that are as defined by latitude and longitude as your location in traffic by GPS over time. Populations of cells that will become organs or other specialized structures first deploy themselves into groups by geometric designs: bands, stripes, lines, spots, and curves. Then they continue organizing, subdividing, and specifying. The serially repeated body parts are largely controlled by a set of similar genes called the homeobox, or Hox genes for short, and the Hox genes preside over the sequence of steps that proceed to the full deployment of the form. When a step is missed, all the subsequent steps are abnormal. Form is first encoded, then built, as Carroll says, "stripe by stripe that becomes bone by bone."

And the actual craft of this form-making is achieved through the formation of cells into layers. The process by which a tooth becomes a tooth is similar to that which makes a feather a feather. Cells tell other cells what to become, forming layers that layer again and again, until you have, in the case of an elk, fur, bone, and muscle; an outer body; and innards that are its engine. The marvel of body parts is in evidence at the High Lonesome Ranch, where decapitated elk carcasses hang on hooks, the quarry having been tested for brucellosis. (The term "quarry" is influenced by both the old French *cuir* for skin and *corée* for entrails—capturing the outside/inside theme of evo-devo.) Admiring especially their ample haunches, a veritable herd reduced to its galloping mechanism, I'm reminded of Sarah Stein's note of instruction from a class with Matisse, who directed that his pupils attend to "the plenitude of essential parts."

The Ultimate Microcosm and the Ultimate Macrocosm

Different body parts make the world go around. Both invertebrate (insects) and vertebrates use specialized body parts to take advantage of every worldly realm: air, earth, and water. To see, to sense, to eat, to move: These are capacities that run life as we know it, and they are made possible by homologous genes, operating by different instructions, whether in fish or fowl or insect or ape. All bodies are built from a single cell, and all are built with the same tools. As taxonomy studies the body shape and genetic profile of an organism, relating it to the species it descended from by comparing which parts are the same and which are different, so evo-devo research examines life-forms going all the way down to their Hox genes. The existence of Hox genes can be traced back in time through the fossil record. They are locatable in organisms that predate the Cambrian explosion, which brought about such a proliferation of form to begin with. They date back to before there *were* vertebrates or insects.

"And in this development," John Lennon Campbell continues, "ontogeny recapitulates phylogeny." Easy for him to say. What this axiom means is that the development of embryo to adult in a single animal follows the same game plan as its entire genera, or taxonomic group, in developing from its ancestors. That fundamental body design noted by Sir

Richard Owen has a history—and as the spinal column is one of the first structures to get laid down in that embryonic fate map, so is it one of the earliest structures that laid down the blueprint for all vertebrates to begin with. Neil Shubin, one of the paleontologists responsible for finding the fossil definitively connecting human ancestry back to a fish with rudimentary legs, says all "living things can be organized and arranged like a set of Russian nesting dolls, with the smaller groups of animals comprised in bigger groups of animals." He can prove this to you via the fossil record, and he can also prove this to you on the genetic level, by tracing the trajectory of historic DNA—Hox genes—in successive groups of organisms through time. In his fun book *Your Inner Fish*, Shubin traces the body parts we humans have that directly evolved from fish body parts. The proof is definitely in the skeletal pudding.

"So the way the elk is put together reflects her own development, but it also represents the way vertebrates developed—the result of eons of evolution," Campbell says. "And shaped by predation," adds Hal Herring. "When you see an elk you think, 'That's beautiful, I want it on my wall'"—well, I guess *he* does—"but you don't feel that way about a cow. There's something lost when the predation is lost." Back to you, Robinson Jeffers.

Campbell makes the connection that the way a hunter takes apart an elk mirrors the way the animal both evolved as a species and developed as an individual. "Taking things apart reveals 'creation,'" he says. He opines that processing the kill is even holier than making the kill. "I think we also get a resolution of the top-down, bottom-up controversy right here in the body of the elk," Campell concludes. "The gut is the animal's bottom-up function, digesting the grass and leaves and purposing the photosynthesizers into a beautiful body that goes running around, chased by wolves," ultimately transferring the food created by sun and plant to another trophic level. "Without wolves around, elk would be running balls of guts consuming forage."

Vahldiek has been listening in and he shakes his head indulgently. "I think elk is my dinner," he says. "You're the one who wanted a science ranch," mutters Hal Herring.

JIMINY!

When I visited the High Lonesome Ranch in December 2010, finishing touches were being put on Vahldiek's new house on the property. "I'm a little embarrassed," he says, showing me around the place, "about the footprint and all." I doubt that Vahldiek has an embarrassable bone in his body. His kitchen counters come up to my armpits. "I don't like to bend over when I'm cooking," he adds, "and I love to entertain." He is certainly a gifted and generous host. "What do you like to cook?" I ask him. "Oh, hamburgers, hot dogs," he says.

One afternoon while the gang is out hunting, Vahldiek parks me in his living room with my laptop, and I enjoy a long afternoon of work in a wingback chair, looking up like a vigilant elk with some frequency as the light changes outside the enormous floor-to-ceiling windows. The main purview of the house faces east, because Vahldiek prefers watching the sunrise to watching the sunset. Even without the distinct orange ball slipping behind the low-slung mountains, the darkening landscape presents portrait after portrait of color studies, amber and orange eventually becoming indigo and then finally black.

At about five o'clock a visitor comes to the door. Vahldiek greets him and exits. A man of about Vahldiek's age and half his girth, with a cropped, disciplined demeanor, advances and sits down next to me. He introduces himself but as names often do, his bounces off my eardrum into the void. "A writer?" he inquires, and begins to ask some very specific questions about how the publishing process works. I imagine he will ask me any moment now about how to get something he's written into print.

It turns out I am chatting with Scott McInnis, a former member of the US House of Representatives, a Republican from Colorado's Third District, who served six terms from 1993 to 2005. He is an old friend of Vahldiek's; they went to law school together. "I have never done anything, anything, that wasn't in the service of my country," he pledges to me. He tells me he was in the process of running for office in the election just past when the *Denver Post* alleged he was guilty of plagiarism. After leaving office in 2005, he received a $300,000 fellowship from the Hasan Family Foundation, for the purpose of writing about water issues in the West.

He shakes his head with rue. "My whole career, a lifetime of serving my country, and I have been completely smeared." He goes on to tell me that it was Rolly Fischer, an octogenarian retired engineer who once worked at the Colorado River Water Conservation District, and whom he had hired as a research assistant, who apparently plagiarized a twenty-year-old essay by Colorado Supreme Court Justice Gregory J. Hobbs. McInnis has been cleared of ethics violations by the Office of Attorney Regulation Counsel, which cites insufficient evidence in the matter.

To his credit, McInnis is eventually able to get off the subject, and he asks me pointed questions with apparent sincerity about my children, and tells me about his, especially praising Outward Bound for instilling his daughters with ballast to withstand the prickly eruptions of young adulthood. Vahldiek comes in and we drive down to the lodge together in his big truck, followed by McInnis. We are joined for cocktails and hors d'oeuvres by the scientist-hunters and journalists in front of a roaring fire pit. With the Rocky Mountain backdrop, it is a pretty spectacular setting.

Now, before I go on I want to point out that McInnis does not drink, because if he did, it would explain things in one way. Most of the men have some distilled spirit or other in their hands out by the fire pit, and when we convene for dinner wine is served. Can you tell that I'm about to declare that all hell breaks loose? I am seated next to McInnis and we are talking together amiably, when I am emboldened to hazard an opinion. "I'm a coastal person," I admit. "I grew up on the East Coast and I've lived in San Francisco for twenty years. So I don't pretend to have any kind of intuitive or instinctive feeling about the West. But I feel that westerners are kind of spoiled."

The chatter at the table ceases. No hurricane has had a shorter lull. Next to me McInnis ejects himself straight out of his chair. And then every single person of the ten or twelve at the table start to shout, to point, to harangue . . . but even this din fails McInnis's nearly broken-blood-vessel rage. "*You* get subsidies!" he rails. "Why can't we?"

Subsidies? Does he mean the way I deduct the cost of my *New York Times* subscription from my income taxes? Is that actually the equivalent of the Farm Bill? But McInnis moves on, and the rest of the table joins in, everyone going nuts over immigration, the Second Amendment, and socialism. Hal Herring is halfway out of his chair. Vahldiek pushes his chair back and makes some big dares to the powers that be. Eisenberg and Soulé are yammering on about all this as well, and as I can't hear them, I am thoroughly confounded about what positions they might be taking. It is as if the cultural conflicts of the West have been thrown up like confetti at this one dinner table, for all to grab at.

At some point I get a chance to explain. "All I mean is that on the coasts, we are used to sharing our land and our public spaces with new-comers. The argument in the West is always that things are the way they are, because that's the way they've always been. We don't think like that on the coasts. It would be like saying, 'The Mafia has always enforced its own rule of law and so it should always be able to.'" The shouting has subsided to a similarly deafening silence. These people don't know what the heck I am talking about. So I put it this way: "Cattle grazing is ruin-ing the West."

"Well, that's true," assents Soulé.

Order restored, dinner proceeds. When it comes time to bid adieu, Vahldiek gives me a hug. Not just any hug. He lifts me several feet off the ground and holds me there for several long minutes. "Wow!" I say, enjoy-ing this immensely, while the others look on, impressed. Vahldiek says (huffing a little) that in his day, he used to be able to hold a gal under each arm. I'm thinking, no wonder Paul Vahldiek is not afraid to have wolves on his property. The guy is alpha through and through: He's an alpha *hugger*. Scott McInnis gives me a hug, too. And a mournful look. "Mary Ellen," he says, "my parents are *permittees*."[53]

CHAPTER 12

Wolf Sign

I KNOW IT ISN'T FAIR, BECAUSE BOB BESCHTA IS NOT VERY OLD. I'VE never met his longtime colleague Bill Ripple, but he isn't old either. Still, when I picture these two men tirelessly tromping around four national parks—Yellowstone, Zion, Apache, and Olympic—coring trees and circling trunks and methodically taking the measure of age structures and recruitment levels, I persistently envision them as Statler and Waldorf, the grumpy Muppets who stomp around and crack up at their own jokes. It's because Bob Beschta's eyes are always wide open, as if he can't believe what he sees, and he just keeps on seeing it. Now an emeritus, he was for many years a professor in the forestry department at Oregon State University, and a hydrology expert. He studied watershed processes in forests. "I'm a water guy!" he says. The story of Bob Beschta's enlightenment goes something like this.

As we know, the cycles of nature are constantly subject to disturbance events that seem to throw its works all out of whack, but that are actually reordering the flow of things to the overall benefit of the system. In the ubiquitous water cycle, precipitation creates rain and snow, which run into rivers and creeks and streams. By eroding the ground beneath it, water makes soil. Plants need sunlight and water, and most of them take root in the soil.

Taking a field trip to Yellowstone in 1996, Beschta visited the Lamar River and saw its banks were barren and incised, as if someone had thrust a fork all along the middle of a cheesecake and scooped most of its contents into the trash. Few trees remained alongside it, so there were no roosting places for birds, no shade to keep the water cool, no insects to drop into the water for fish. The cacophony of critter life was stilled. "It broke my heart to see it," Beschta recalls. "I watched dark, rich soils that had taken tens of thousands of years to create just get washed away. This is Yellowstone. The grandmother of all national parks, and I'm seeing a river of degradation."

There had been concern in the scientific community about how badly aspen were doing in Yellowstone, and it seemed clear that the culprit was elk. Beschta has a series of photographs recording aspen decline in the park. A 1954 photo shows an evidently healthy stand; by 1992 this same stand has fallen apart. A few old trees remain, but there are no young-sters, nobody growing up to inherit the store. A photograph from the '70s shows elk hanging out like fat gangsters in a safe zone. The same thing was happening to cottonwood. As we know from our beaver foray, willow, aspen, and cottonwood are the woody foundation of most of the biodiver-sity in the West. On Beschta's 1996 visit to the Lamar Valley, willow were browsed so low they appeared not to be there at all.

Beschta's colleague from Oregon State, Bill Ripple, was meanwhile studying Yellowstone's aspens with his then graduate student Eric Larsen. Coring hundreds of trees (by which you assess their age) and consulting historic data, Ripple and Larsen established aspen regeneration proceed-ing along a healthy course until the 1920s, when, says Larsen, "it just fell off a cliff." Biologists had been studying predator-prey dynamics in other places, most prominently Rolf Peterson's documentation of a pro-longed and intricate moose-wolf dance on Isle Royale in Wisconsin, and Joel Berger's observations correlating grizzly populations with songbird diversity in Grand Teton National Park. Larsen and Ripple wondered if the aspen interruptus could have something to do with the extirpation of wolves from Yellowstone in 1926.

REMEMBRANCE OF THINGS PAST
"But I did not go back to Yellowstone to look at wolves," says Beschta, of his return there. Looking for an answer to what was destroying the plant community, he thought about elk herbivory, fire, and climate change. He set to measuring cottonwood stands, assessing the age and health of stands by coring some trees and measuring a whole lot more. The question

of wolves came up because his work coincided with a watershed moment in Yellowstone: the reintroduction of the gray wolf in 1995.

The release of an initial fourteen wolves in Yellowstone was the culmination of efforts undertaken since the gray wolf was put on the landmark 1974 Endangered Species Act's very first list. In 1991 congressional funds supported some preliminary studies, and hosts of committed individuals pushed the boulder of reintroduction up the hill of resistance. "The stars and planets lined up when Bruce Babbitt became Secretary of the Interior," writes Bob Barbee, the superintendent of Yellowstone from 1983 to 1994. He "personally stepped up to the plate, leading Clinton administration support, and the rest is history.[54]" The slam-dunk, however, came only after a last-minute foul: The American Farm Bureau Federation filed suit, imposing a restraining order on the wolves in their prerelease cages. Babbitt warned these cages might soon be coffins. After a fight to the finish, the restraining order was lifted. Babbitt helped carry the first wolf to its acclimation pen. The next year, seventeen more wolves were brought in, without the drama. The recovery plan stipulated that fresh recruits would be added to Yellowstone for five years, but this turned out to be unnecessary. The first transplants established a successful population, a testament to the resilience of wolves.

THE ECOLOGY OF FEAR

But how many elk can a relative handful of wolves actually kill? Enough that the corresponding diminishment in herbivory actually makes or breaks an ecosystem? For one thing, contrary to superstition, wolves are not killing machines. It's not that easy for a wolf to down an elk, and most of their encounters end up with no loss of ungulate life. Often the elk does damage to the wolf. The fact does remain, however, that wolves eat elk, and the elk understand this, which is why they behave quite differently when they know their hunter is in the 'hood. And their changed behavior is what affects the landscape. (By now you have realized we are talking about a critical juncture in a trophic cascade.)

Joel Brown and colleagues dubbed the behavior of prey in the perceived presence of its predator as "the ecology of fear." The formulation is a reminder that nothing in nature is truly inert. Everything has its cause and effect. We are accustomed to thinking of prey like chickens we pull out of the refrigerator—with zero agency. And it's true that prey quite often run away, and that behavior doesn't seem like a driver of consequence. Brown and company pointed out that in an overall analysis of the predator-prey transaction, the prey behavior is intertwined with the number of predators, and that the number of prey actually influences the effectiveness of predators. Usually, things are working optimally when a small number of big predators are on the landscape with a big number of prey. The fact that predators control prey not just by eating them, but by threatening them, has at least as much impact on the overall balance of the players than as the number of carcasses at the end of the day.[55]

Wolves are the protectors of aspen, cottonwood, willow, and all the ecosystem players who depend on them, because in their perceived or expected presence the elk don't hang around eating. They take a bite, they look up. They take another bite, they look up and over their shoulders: Any wolf coming around? Not going to find out. Elk that know wolves are around and are constantly on the move. This is ultimately what Robinson Jeffers's line of poetry about the wolf whittling so fine the antelope's fleet limbs and so on refers to. Wolves don't often do the high-speed chase that such an image might invoke. Instead they stalk, they harass; they can come from anywhere. In response the elk keep moving, which keeps them in great shape.

In the end, the extirpation and reintroduction of the wolf to Yellowstone has done some tremendous things for science and our knowledge of ecology. The 1994 Environmental Impact Statement advocating for the return of the wolf posited that the species "is the only member of the mammalian biotic community of Yellowstone National Park that was present in historic times that is missing." It argued that wolf recovery would restore the food chain. "Prey populations will likely fluctuate slightly less, because of reduced winterkill, and fewer injured or unhealthy individuals will be present in the general prey population." The understanding even such a short time ago was that yes, predators have an important function in that they cull prey species of weaker individuals, not only enhancing the fitness in this case of an entire herd, but also in

honing the gene pool. But the extent and reach of the effect of one species on an entire system was not anticipated; nobody would have guessed
that, as Bob Beschta, who has long studied the effect of wolves on keeping
riparian areas healthy, says, "Holy smokes, wolves control the river."

SHADOW DANCE

"'It's wolves, Jimmy,' Antonia whispered. 'It's awful, what he says!'" The
scene is a deathbed confession by a character named Pavel in Willa Cath-
er's novel *My Antonia*. While the young girl listens in, Pavel recounts a
wedding party in the midst of a Russian winter. When it comes time to
go home, in the middle of the night, the sledges carrying the participants
are beset by hundreds of wolves:

> *Another driver lost control. The screams of the horses were more ter-
> rible to hear than the cries of the men and women. Nothing seemed to
> check the wolves. It was hard to tell what was happening in the rear;
> the people who were falling behind shrieked as piteously as those who
> were already lost. The little bride hid her face on the groom's shoulder
> and sobbed.*

Eventually Pavel, driving the sledge carrying the bride and groom,
indicates to the groom that their load must be lightened, and points "to
the bride." The groom refuses this directive, and Pavel throws them both
off the sledge. Peter and Pavel arrive in their village alone and are summarily disowned and ejected. They wind up in America. And thus is dra-
matized the wolf nightmares of European peasants settling in the West.
Such a tale goes a long way toward explaining the stark and exaggerated
fear of wolves still prevalent here.

In fact, wolves seldom kill humans. Sometimes they kill each other,
but not often. They are as socially organized as people. Pack sizes are
two to twenty, in general, and the order beginning with alpha and beta
proceeds down to omega—every wolf has a rank. Barry Lopez, in his
book *Of Wolves and Men*, muses that as Joseph Campbell said that "men
do not discover their gods, they create them," so do men "create their
animals." Wolves have much in common with *Homo sapiens*, perhaps

nothing more important than our top-predator status in the ecosystem, achieved through means of the hunt.

Here Lopez meets Michael Soulé, who posits that human hatred of wolves is based on competition—they do what we do, and go after the same animals. Lopez notes, "In evolutionary terms, of course, wolves and men developed along similar lines as social hunters and were in competition for the same game. Undoubtedly there were encounters in prehistoric times that resulted in death." And also consonant with Soulé's surmise of the deep resonance of hunting in the human soul, Lopez writes, "Hunting is holy." Looking up at the Lascaux cave paintings of hooved animals on the run, he finds in the transaction between hunter and hunted an ancient covenant, a sacred center where life and death meet.

LEADER OF THE PACK

The alpha male and the alpha female frequently mate for life, their first conjugal joining lasting about thirty minutes and sealing the deal. The main privilege and rule enjoyed and enforced by the alpha pair (though there are exceptions, as always) is that they are the only members of the pack who get to breed. "In general, the female is more in charge than the male," says Doug Smith, whose official title is actually "leader" of the Yellowstone Wolf Project, and who has monitored Yellowstone's wolves since their reintroduction. "It's not a matter of dominance between the alpha male and the alpha female. His behavior hinges on hers. She tends to take the initiative, and he lets her. We thought that it varied pack to pack, but I can't think of a single example where the male has been in charge." Smith says the assertion that the alpha male is top dog can be traced to the fact that early observers of wolf behavior were all men.

The way the alpha female rules varies widely from animal to animal. Smith refers to wolf "40," head of the Druid Pack, who "bared her teeth and showed her dominance all the time, at the least provocation"; he contrasts 40's leadership style with that of "7." "She [7] was as firmly in control of her pack as 40 was; her position was never in debate. Yet we never saw her behave like 40 did." As to the preferential place of the alpha female, Smith attributes this to the "huge reproductive value of the female; when momma's happy, everybody's happy." Years ago on the eve of becoming a parent for the first time, Smith told a journalist he hoped to emulate wolves in the matter of bringing up progeny. Wolves, he said, "are able to give discipline and structure to the pups without punishment."

Now that his kids are six and eight, I ask Smith for an update, and he tells me that yes, he still parents based on the wolf model. "There's always conflict," he tells me. "Children have all the time in the world; you don't. But what matters is how you handle the conflict. When wolves are annoyed by their pups, they just get up and walk away. They go sleep somewhere they aren't going to be bothered." Smith admires the way wolves set good examples but don't do everything for their pups. "They're not dragging them around by the paws telling them to do this and do that, because they have to learn. For a wolf, if you don't do it right, you're going to die. By contrast, we're safety net all the way." Not only do wolves make good moms and dads, they also make good "alloparents," as anthropologists call relatives who assist in raising the kids, and they help out when an alpha has lost a mate, male or female. "Watching wolves, they have great messages," says Smith, "if you're not always looking at them through the scope of a rifle."

I also ask Smith about a claim I've heard several times, that wolves are surplus killers; that is, they kill to kill, and kill more than they can eat. "No," says Smith. "In thirty-two years of handling wolves, I've never felt a fat one. Your average wolf weighs 100 pounds. Your average cow elk weighs 500; the bull is 700 pounds. A bull bison is 2,000 pounds." Again, it is not easy to kill an elk, even if you are a wolf, and Smith tells me he has seen the effort to kill a bison go on for eight hours. "Wolves are programmed to kill. Even killing all they can, they just get by." Smith says there are occasions when a wolf will come upon a herd of elk belly-deep in snow and will kill a couple of them. Usually the wolf will be set upon by grizzlies and other opportunists, such as wolverine, who take over the carcasses. "But they will circle back to those kills," Smith says, until "there's just a hoof left." Smith says people send him photographs of eviscerated ungulates that have not been fully eaten, and he observes, "There's always tire tracks or human footprints around it. Somebody shooed the wolf off the carcass."

Wolf antagonism, in Smith's view, is not so much located in the ranching community as it is with the hunting. "When a wolf kills livestock, it gets shot," he says. "It's the elk hunters. They resent the competition. They say wolves are ruining their enjoyment, their recreation." When an ecosystem is at its true carrying capacity for carnivores as well as ungulates, there are fewer elk around, because the population is culled, which is better for the aspen and so on. "Things are more 'in balance' at a lower number" than hunters have come to expect, says Smith. "Humans have a hard time with the concept of 'less is more.'" I ask him whether human hunters could potentially shoot enough elk to keep their populations at a healthier level and so have a healthier ecosystem.

Smith tells me human hunting practices are not integrated into the overall cycles and balances of wilderness. "Humans hunt seasonally, and during the day. They hunt from road heads. They take the meat home." Wolves, on the other hand, are on the landscape everywhere, 24/7, and so the pressure on ungulate behavior is constant—thus, they change their behavior. A multitude of animals depend on the carnivore kills, not just grizzlies, but smaller mammals, birds, and certainly abundant insect and microbe life. Additionally, wolves tend to kill calves, or cow elks that are past their breeding time. "They're slower and easier to get. But the bullet gets the seven- to eight-year-old." Human hunters shoot the animals that are in the most prime condition, and the males with the big racks. They take out the cream of the genetic crop at its peak breeding age.

When you get yet another "stop the wolf killing now!" e-mail from one of your favorite NGOs, you may send in $25 or sign onto a petition, or you may hit "delete," because you choose to support saving the redwoods, and you personally can't finance the saving of every species. Here's the problem. Saving the wolf is connected with saving the redwood. There is a longer chain of causality perhaps than can be traced between wolf and aspen health, but by now you get the drill. One serious problem with conservation today is that the message about how the pieces of nature work together is virtually never communicated to the public. Some citizens may be inclined to give antiwolf sentiment a pass because there seem to be more important issues in the grand scheme of things. The grand scheme of things needs a better general definition. Let's start with geological epochs.

THE AGE OF MAN

There is current discussion afoot to amend our place in the historical epochs of Earth history; instead of our being part of the Holocene, which began 10,000 years ago, some scientists are calling for us to locate the present time in the Anthropocene, or the age of man. Charles Lyell himself came up with the term "Holocene," which means "recent whole," and it was adopted by the International Geological Congress in 1885 to describe the first postglacial geological time period. As far back as 1873, Italian geologist and paleontologist Antonio Stoppani called human activity a "new telluric force which in power and universality may be compared to the greater forces of earth" (*tellus* means "earth" in Latin), and he referenced the "anthropozoic era." The idea of formally declaring the age of man has been in the air for several decades, and when in 2000 Nobel Prize–winning Dutch atmospheric chemist Paul Crutzen suggested with Eugene Stoermer that that time truly is now, the conversation heated up.

Geological eras are not named lightly. In "The Anthropocene: Conceptual and Historical Perspectives," Crutzen and colleagues argue that "the human imprint on the global environment has now become so large and active that it rivals some of the great forces of Nature in its impact on the functioning of the earth system."[56] Some of the results of this activity include the population explosion of humans and cattle—the biomass of the two now outweighs that of all other large animals taken together, by far. Part of the "success" of this population increase is due to our fixing of nitrogen in synthetic fertilizers, causing disruption in a natural cycle on a par with the damage done by greenhouse gases. We are all fairly aware that in the past several hundred years we have shifted huge quantities of fossil carbon from their place underground into the atmosphere. Crutzen points out that more than half of all accessible freshwater is used by us.

Lights Out

One of the darkest shadows on the Anthropocene is the *Homo sapiens*–induced extinction rate taking out so many branches on the tree of life. We look at the destruction of indigenous culture that helped speed Manifest Destiny on these shores, and we look at historic and current genocides around the world; we say wouldn't let that happen again, or here. But of course we are all letting something equivalent if not more devastating occur, and that is the sixth mass-extinction event. The major epochs in Earth history are defined by extinction: The big five are the Ordovician, 443 million years ago (mya); the Devonian, 359 mya; the Permian, 251 mya; the Triassic, 200 mya; and the Cretaceous, 65 mya. To help answer the question, "Has the earth's sixth mass extinction already arrived?", Anthony Barnosky, a paleontologist at the University of California–Berkeley and colleagues examined the differences between modern and fossil data to better quantify the relationship between what is happening now and what happened then.[57]

As with so many questions in conservation biology, this one begins with species distribution. Barnosky points out the "severe problems" in making data comparisons between prior extinction events and what is happening today: While modern global distributions are well known for many species, the fossil record is sparse in many places and usually includes only species that left behind hard parts that fossilize well. Fossil analysis has often been done at the genus, not the species level, and when species are identified it is usually based on morphology, or what the body looks like, which is vulnerable to identifying either too many species or too few (by lumping species together or by over-splitting). Since many taxa have left no fossil record, the actual number of historic extinctions is underestimated.

By the same token, we have by no means identified all the species currently on earth now, many of which are likely to be extinct before we name them. And then there's the problem of time; the fossil record hasn't been left according to a statistical model evenly distributing its data across the eons. We have more fossils for some times than for others. Our modern records are relatively dense samples from over very short time frames.

Extinction is measured by rate and magnitude; essentially the number of extinctions is divided by the time over which they occurred to reach a proportional rate. Mass extinction is when rates accelerate such that over 75 percent of species disappear within less than 2 million years. To the number, speed, and size questions is added the context for extinction events, the climate dynamics, and other ecological stressors that push species loss into overdrive (there's also the random accident scenario, as with the asteroid that brought us the Cretaceous, but we can't exactly measure for that). As Barnosky says, "Once again the global stage is set for unusual interactions."

Barnosky concludes that even given all of the above-referenced bad news, "the recent loss of species is dramatic and serious but does not yet qualify as a mass extinction in the paleontological sense of the Big Five." He reiterates that saving the world's remaining biodiversity "will require the reversal of many dire and escalating threats," and he warns that losing species now from the "critically endangered," "endangered," and "vulnerable" categories "could accomplish the sixth mass extinction in just a few centuries."

Call it Anthropocene or whatever you want—we have reached a new threshold in the ancient balance between life and death.

Nature, Red in Tooth and Claw

And it would seem we need to tolerate and even safeguard nature's savage ones if we are to stem the losses. In the July 2011 issue of *Science*, Jim Estes is the first author of a short, extremely pointed article, "Trophic Downgrading of Planet Earth."[58] There are twenty-two more authors on the paper, including Soulé, Joel Berger, John Terborgh, and Robert Paine—the paper summarizes the work of all these people, trophic cascade findings in "all the world's major biomes, from the poles to the tropics and in terrestrial, freshwater, and marine systems." The article takes the position that we are currently in the early to middle stages of the sixth mass extinction, and points out that this one is different than those that have come before. In the first place, it is being caused by a single species, *Homo sapiens,* and in the second place, it is characterized by the loss of larger-bodied animals, the apex consumers in particular—like the wolf. And the article goes on to give a brief outline of the "downgrading" effect this loss is having on the structure and dynamics of ecosystems everywhere. Another reason there are so many authors on this article is that they are making a big, concise statement together about what is going on. It is a strategy to get this message heard.

PROVE IT

Jim Estes is a very patient man and takes it in stride when I ask him yet again to tell me what on earth "basins of attraction" are; the phrase makes me see a crowd waiting to get into a nightclub. "Basins of attraction" is a term from physics, and Estes uses it to describe the coherence of pieces of an ecosystem that shift into a new way of operating together, pushed by "perturbations of sufficient magnitude and direction." That is, you can mess with an ecosystem for only so long, and it will start to function differently, and you probably won't recognize it or like it. So to use the example of the wolf's salubrious effect on the rivers of Yellowstone, in the absence of that big predation, the system still worked, but badly. A healthier Yellowstone was restored by reintroducing wolves, but this sort of recuperation will not necessarily happen so easily in other degraded ecosystems, where new "basins of attraction" will stubbornly persist, like toxic waste sites where only thorny vines will grow, not letting native plants recolonize.

Breaking down the resilience of an ecosystem by removing or crippling its parts in many cases also invites a proliferation of infectious disease. One example of this is a "mesopredator release" of olive baboons in sub-Saharan Africa following reduction in the lions and leopards that kept them in check. The baboon population blossomed, and this swaggering and imperious creature began to raid crops and terrorize people; both baboons and *Homo sapiens* in the area developed a higher rate of intestinal parasites linked to their increased proximity.[59]

Estes and coauthors warn that ecosystem "decapitation" by removal of top predators has effects that penetrate both the atmospheric and geological carbon cycles that make our world go around—that's atmosphere, soils, and waters. Impacts on soil are like those of bad grazing, which reduce the ability of the ground to sequester CO_2 or grow anything in it, and the effect on water is like what happens when man-made dams replace beaver dams. Effects on the atmosphere are exemplified by places where the top predator fish has been extirpated from a lake. It impacts phytoplankton density, affecting primary production, or the purposing of inorganic sunshine into fat, carbohydrates, and protein by plants, which impacts "the uptake rate of CO_2, and the direction of carbon flux between lakes and the atmosphere."

The paper makes a reasoned argument that top predators have been seen for a long time as "passengers riding atop the trophic pyramid but having little impact on the structure below"; not only is this wrong, but the authors "propose that many of the ecological surprises that have confronted society over past centuries—pandemics, population collapses of species we value and eruptions of those we do not, major shifts in ecosystem states, and losses of diverse ecosystem services—were caused or facilitated by altered top-down forcing regimes."

The paper calls for a readjustment in the way ecology is understood. It might also call for a change in the way endangered species are understood. When you are trying to save an endangered jaguar, for example, not only are you doing this for general moral purposes; you are helping to save the ecosystem.

CHAPTER 13

Borderline

THE CABDRIVER TAKING ME FROM THE AIRPORT TO THE BED-AND-breakfast where I'm staying in Tucson turns around and looks at me when I tell him I'm going with a conservation group to learn animal tracking on a ranch in Sonora, Mexico. "You're worth about $30,000," he says. "Better let your family know to have the cash ready." Frankly, I'm kind of insulted at this evaluation. "I'm worth more than that!" I say, adding, "Nobody is going to kidnap a bunch of wilderness geeks hunting for jaguar tracks." "What about those hikers in Iraq?" he retorts, and asks me to phone him upon my safe return to Tucson, just to ease his mind. (In fact, I do that and he drives me back to the airport five days later.)

Since the woman who runs the B&B where I stay opines that maybe I ought to cross the tracking workshop off my calendar and go do some bird watching on nearby Mount Lemmon instead, I am feeling rather queasy about where I'm headed the next day in a van driven by Sergio Avila, who is the northern Mexico conservation manager for the Sky Islands Alliance. By Avila's side in the passenger seat is Jessica Lamberton, wildlife linkages program coordinator for the organization, and three other would-be trackers are in the back with me. We'll be joining several more at Rancho El Aribabi. El Aribabi is privately owned by the Robles family, divided between three brothers: Carlos Robles has been gradually rehabilitating a third of the estate from its original incarnation as a cattle operation into a biodiversity destination, with some seasonal trophy hunting activity in there, too. El Aribabi is not anywhere as developed on the "science hunt" trajectory as the High Lonesome Ranch in Colorado, but the place is thronging with wildlife and was recently designated a Natural Protected Area by the Mexican National Commission of Natural Protected Areas. Setting aside private property for wildlife conservation is not as widespread a practice in Mexico as it is in the United States, as there is no explicit financial incentive for doing it. While the property is not Robles's sole source of income, giving up the cattle business has an impact he feels. He's not necessarily crazy about running a hunting operation on the land, but since it could be done seasonally, provides cash flow, and potentially helps sustain the health of the deer herd through culling, hunting remains in play as an adjunct to ecotourism there. While all conservation-minded landowners deserve tremendous credit for doing the right thing, in the context of Mexico, Robles is a real trailblazer.

"Nothing to worry about," Avila assures us in the back, because I'm not the only one talking about the likelihood we will get caught in the crosshairs of the drug war raging in Mexico. "We will be far from the areas where this is happening," he says. "Worry about getting pounced on by a jaguar instead!" The van is a long one, but Avila's exuberance bounces all the way to the back of it regularly on the journey, which takes a few hours. We are going 30 miles south of the border and our crossing is uneventful.

CITIZEN TRACKERS

As with my trip with the Grand Canyon Trust, I'm amazed at the diversity of people who are ready to get their hands dirty for conservation. My fellow trackers include an elementary schoolteacher, an architect, a former prison guard, and a software engineer. They are male and female aged mid-thirties to late sixties, single and married. In addition to Avila and Lamberton, we will be trained by three more professional trackers. The workshop is part of a Citizen Science program; after these Tucson residents learn what to look for, they will be assigned transects in the Sky Island region and will be charged with inventorying the wildlife on them. Citizen Science is a broad designation in which volunteers collect data for use in the aggregate for science or conservation projects. An example is Cornell University's Great Backyard Bird Count, the yields of which have contributed to lots of scientific inquiries, including how avian flu spreads. In Tucson, data on what wildlife are actually out there will help inform decisions about where to develop land and where not to, and will help in deciding where to designate wildlife corridors. It also may influence an Endangered Species Listing or two, because jaguar and ocelot miraculously are making their way up over the border.

SKY PILOT

The Sky Islands were the first geographical area for which a Wildlands Network design was initiated; the process, however, took more than ten years. Dave Foreman knew the area intimately from having evaluated chunks of it for RARE II, the Forest Service's Roadless Area Review and Evaluation. Wildlands started to map its intentions before GPS and GIS became readily available to civilians (the military had them first), the work identifying the terrain and the species inhabiting it basically had to be done all over again to verify it. Apparently Foreman's ground-truth knowledge was pretty much 100 percent borne out by the latitude and longitude coordinates provided by satellites.

"Sky Islands" is a romantic name, and these mountains deserve it. The term was coined by Weldon Heald in 1967 to specify mountain ranges that are isolated from each other by intervening valleys and grasslands. The mountains stand singular and tall, yet keep each other's distant company, and have a remote feeling even when you are fairly close; it's that hazy southwestern light, full of dust, its pastel glow a penumbra around the green heights. From a lookout one day on Mount Lemmon,[60] which is right outside Tucson, and arrayed around which are others of the Santa Catalina range, I remark to my scientist companion that the view looks aquatic. The land dips down, flat and scrubby, dotted with tangled, low cacti that in the light could almost be hunks of kelp. A former marine biologist (now working on insects in the desert), he tells me the sight often reminds him of big, empty coral reefs off the coast of Hawaii.

The fifty-two Sky Islands are where nature gathered her treasures and piled them up in one place. They join tropical, subtropical, and temperate montane systems, overlapping and blending these at their edges at the conjunction of the Chihuahuan Desert, the Sonoran Desert, the Rockies, and the Sierra Madre Occidental. They embrace this great diversity not only across the breadth of the range, but elevationally. Going from the bottom to the top of one of them, you find "life zones" or biotic communities starting with desert scrub at 2,000 feet; moving up to oak woodland and chaparral at 4,000 feet; pine-oak woodland at 6,000 feet; ponderosa pine at 8,000 feet; and spruce fir at 10,000 feet. On a single mountain is thus stacked a gradation that latitudinally represents the way these life zones progress from Mexico to Canada.

Species that ordinarily would be separated by great distances are in close quarters on these mountains, so you will see, for example, huge saguaro cactus at one elevation and, as you hike farther up, find yourself in conifers. There are more species of hummingbirds here than anywhere else in the world. Heck, half the bird species in North America reside in the Chiricahua Mountains alone. There are approximately 130 vertebrate species found here; 117 reptiles; I could go on. The Sky Islands have been designated by Conservation International as one of the world's "biodiversity hot spots."

INHERIT THE EARTH

The ranch house at El Aribabi is largely made of stone and is very cool in the hot Mexican sun; an enormous veranda surrounds its perimeter, and some of my fellow trackers set up their sleeping arrangements here, under its overhang. I have brought a sleeping bag and claim one of the rooms inside. There are more to go around, but most of the gang choose to sleep outside, and many have brought along cots for the purpose. Avila hustles around helping everyone get set up, greeting those who drove down under their own steam. While he's got that masculine Latin thing going on, it is more than balanced by the general mother-hen approach he takes, making sure things are smooth for everyone. He's a supervoluble talker who launches into passionate disquisitions on subjects like Rancho el Aribabi, "where by protecting 10,000 acres along the Spine of the Continent, Carlos has made it possible for jaguars to be here!"

THE JOURNEY, NOT THE ARRIVAL

The greening of El Aribabi began in 2004, when the Sonoran Joint Venture approached Robles about studying winter bird populations in relation to riparian habitat on the ranch. The Sonoran Joint Venture is a binational group devoted to preserving bird diversity and habitat along this incredibly rich migration pathway. In 2005 funding from the International Migratory Bird Treaty allowed Robles to put up fencing on the ranch to keep his brothers' cattle out. Robles avers that he had a general interest in protecting his land and never liked cattle anyway; he was more or less an intrigued observer of the data the scientists, including botanists as well as bird people, began to accrue based on the Sonoran Joint Venture work. Avila was in the process of cultivating conservation-minded property owners south of the border for potential cooperative work with Sky Island Alliance when he heard about Robles and El Aribabi. The two men, who communicate in a warm yet formal father-son style, hit it off immediately (although it must be said that most people hit it off immediately with Avila).

"We had photographs of jaguar in Arizona," says Avila, "and evidence of them 150 miles south. So we thought, let's look in between." Since jaguar are top predators occupying territories up to 525 square miles, a landscape that supports them is likely a healthy one, and it is a priority of many an environmental NGO to help facilitate their movement north from established southern populations. With jaguar, it is not just a matter of shifting distributions due to climate change, though that is happening, too; they lived here for a long time a long time ago. With Robles's permission, Avila began to set camera traps on the ranch and in the past year alone has photographed a jaguar on the property, as well as puma, ocelot, bobcat, black bear, and badger. "Carlos had no idea he had all these creatures living here," Avila says. "It has greatly spurred on his conservation."

ON THE TRAIL

The act of tracking animal movement is perhaps the very first human activity in which an overall attention to space, including the features of the terrain, was combined with data point observations and used together to form a template from which an important question could be answered: What are we going to eat tonight? And this created something of a map. Tracking is satisfying business, even when you don't quite know what you're looking at. Following suggestive narrative threads, as in three paw marks seemingly headed in the same direction (are they all from the same animal?); figuring out roughly whether you're looking at a dog, a cat, an ungulate, or what; then putting your head up and thinking—where is this animal now, what was it doing and how long ago did it step here?—an altogether deeper dimension of life becomes apparent in the landscape. Tracking is familiar to us and animals do it, too. One researcher tells me coyote will approach tall grass where calves are hidden by their mothers with the deliberation of scientists measuring transects. Virtually every field biologist who has stalked a big cat, a wolf, or even a grizzly bear will tell you that at some point, they realized the object of their quest was simultaneously tracking *them*.

We learn to walk on the sides of the trails to avoid destroying tracks as we go, and to use a mirror attached to a compass to create horizontal light, which has less contrast than light coming straight down from the sun. We spend a great deal of time poised over marks in the dirt and also evaluating scat. Since there are no wolves here, we do not engage in the fascinating discussions that sometimes ensue around canine scat: Is it coyote, or the visitor from the north? There is deer scat, there is coyote scat, there is fox scat, there are a variety of cat scats. Field biologists have an unnerving habit of picking up scat in their bare hands and rubbing it between their fingers.

As to the truth about cats and dogs: Their tracks are similar. Cat claws are retractable and so rarely show up in the tracks. Cats have a more obvious lead toe. The professional trackers get out their rulers when trying to distinguish cat from dog: You can draw an "X" through a dog track that will cross above the top of the palm, or metacarpal pad, which is usually much bigger and rounder in shape on a cat track. It's similarly hard to distinguish coyote from domestic dog tracks, but one hint is to notice whether they move in a linear direction. Wild animals don't mess around as domestic dogs are wont to do. They conserve their energy, and they know where they're headed.

Looking for animals has contributed to the fine-tuning of our sense perceptions, most obviously, of course, our eyesight. Moreover, discernment of all kinds may trace its roots to the finding of prey or the avoiding of predators. Consider the snake. In *The Fruit, the Tree, and the Serpent: Why We See So Well,* University of California–Davis anthropologist Lynne A. Isbell traces the advanced development of human eyesight to spotting deadly snakes in the grass. Further, she marshals brain mapping and social development research to make her case that "declarative pointing," a gesture that underlies language acquisition, similarly evolved from the impetus to warn each other about snakes. While vocalizing and gazing would have been sufficient to draw attention to other types of threat, it really helps to point at a snake.

KILLING FIELDS

We head into precincts of El Aribabi where camera traps are set. These areas have documented high levels of animal activity, and a great deal of it is apparent, in scattered bones and tufts of wayward fur. Cats, in particular, like narrow canyons with lots of cover, and in one we come upon the partial remains of a gray fox. The fox's furry tail is seemingly tossed aside; Avila picks up pieces of the skeleton, still evidencing bits of tendon or something, and explains that the wideness of the pelvic bone corresponds to the width of the animal's gait. "Foxes didn't read the rule book about canids and cats," he says. "They have semiretractable claws and can climb up trees." Another professional tracker muses on "how little this fox is and how little of it was eaten," and then identifies a healthy deposit of bird guano nearby, thus conjuring the picture of a big raptor having a bite of foxy lunch.

Avila elucidates the features of the remote camera, which is set up on a tree and pointed at the trail. You can set it to be motion-activated or to take photos at timed intervals. Remote cameras are developed to the degree they are, he says, because hunters use them, and "not enough biologists can afford them." The camera assigns each photo with its GPS point and the time it was taken; whole maps are constructed from camera trap data. One evening Avila treats us to a slide show of selected camera trap photos from the ranch that include jaguar, coyote, herds of javelina (which look like cartoon versions of pigs), groups of coati with their tall tails held high. It is like observing the life of a whole other world that is going about its business on the same territory we are, albeit on a different schedule. After this pictorial realization of those responsible for the markings we've been looking at all day, the tracking process feels even more like one of discovery. "That's a female," Avila says as we look at a photo of a mountain lion. I ask how he can tell. "She's kind of skinny, and she has that long, beautiful neck, like a beautiful woman." Avila avers that he prefers cats to dogs and mountain lions to jaguar. I had taken him for more of a wolf guy.

Even among those who have strong allegiances to other animals, field biologists often have a favorite top carnivore. Wolves get praised for their highly sophisticated pack dynamics and their evident social sensitivity not just to each other but in relationship to *Homo sapiens,* and grizzly bears are lauded for their big old flat-out possession of their terrain. But cats by and large get the overall blue ribbon for success in and adaptability to the natural world. Part of this is due to their retractable claws, which allow them to grasp. Lacking this feature, the dog family has to hunt in packs or go for animals that are easy to catch and to kill by mouth. Cats' sense of smell is on a par with dogs' and far superior to that of humans; their eyesight has nearly double the visual acuity of ours. Their whiskers— *vibrissae,* "to vibrate"—help them figure out where they are in the dark and are never wider than their skull. Detached clavicle bones allow them to squeeze through openings as wide as their head. Jaguars kill in one fell swoop, often piercing the skull of their prey. Mountain lions are almost as big as jaguars, up to 250 pounds, but are emphatically beta to the jaguar alpha. While mountain lions asphyxiate, jaguars are known as "bone crushers." Just look at a photograph of a jaguar. That head is all jaw, and it looks like metal covered in fur.

All native cultures revere animal symbols but the jaguar likely tops this list as well, across continents and time. To the Mayans, the jaguar was on a par with priests and gods, and rituals around the animal were felt to cohere the order of nature itself. What scientists are discovering by delineating trophic cascades in the ecosystem is thus prefigured in an ancient cultural covenant between predation and creation. Avila has loaned me *Soul Among Lions,* by Harley Shaw, about which he comments that "being part biology and part hunting, this book gets it right, rather than focusing on the *genome* of the cougar, pah!" The author backs up to appreciate the German sense of *umwelt,* or the environment in its most liberal definition, including "the history of the whole universe and the makeup of each species," which he further elaborates are "a product of eons, physically, genetically, culturally . . . focusing all the evolutionary forces that molded it into the present and channeling them into an as yet unspecified result in the future." The big cats are an apex creation of the *umwelt.*

Traipsing around Rancho El Aribabi, there is more life apparent here than I have seen anywhere else in the Rockies, and more death. (The runner-up is Waterton Lakes in Alberta, where abound a plenitude and variety of animal tracks, scat, freshly gnawed bones, and up there, signs of grizzly and moose napping areas and wolf dens.) Signs of predation are exciting, because something went on here, life and death in one conjoined interaction, but the fact of it is also somewhat repellent to a sensibility (mine) that is quickly imagining pain, suffering, and blood. In this canyon where this fox took another step on its journey through the carbon cycle, I am reminded of a reminiscence by Peter Berg, who blogged on Planet Drum about Raymond Dasmann on the occasion of his death in 2003.[61] Dasmann was a highly influential biologist whose 1965 book *The Destruction of California* was one of the earliest calls to arms on the state of the environment; he was a colleague of Michael Soulé's at UC Santa Cruz, and Soulé calls him "a gentle man and a prophet." Berg recalls hiking with Dasmann in the Sierra Nevada foothills, and coming to a meadow in evident use by various predators as a place to kill, to eat, and to stash bones. As they walk along, Dasmann, never a big talker (the blog is titled "Ray Dasmann's Way to See"), begins to take off all his clothes. Berg and another man, walking among backbones, legs, skulls, antlers, feathers, and fur, are baffled, but Dasmann is their guru and they follow his cue, and pretty soon all three of them are naked. "Ray walked off a little way without any regard for us. His eyes were radiant. I discovered that I was going completely inside myself and sat down. We had walked into a great secret." After a timeless interval, the interlude was over. "We had gotten down to our basic species identity. Now it was right to get dressed and leave. We never spoke of the vision in the meadow again."

While the getting naked part seems to me a guy thing, the rawness of predation is compelling. One day we divide up. One group drives to a remote spot on a bumpy, unpaved road. When they come back, one of the professionals tells the rest of us about sighting an apparent jaguar kill. "Where else do you find a bunch of people who had a great day because they found a deer with its whole face bitten off [antlers still attached] and bones scattered in four parts below?"

BLOOD ON THE TRACKS

One morning we track and hike, along the way observing what's called "induced meandering" work being done on a creek, which more or less comes down to strategically placing rocks in the flow of the water to slow it down.[62] El Aribabi may be a vital, recovering ecosystem well on its way back to full health, but the waterways still show the deep incisions and erosion brought about by its cattle-grazed past. Typically a rancher trying to rectify the situation will build a dam in the stream or creek to trap sediment and give vegetation a place to take root. The trouble is, these eventually fail, collapsing when a weather event increases the velocity of the water. The collected sediment then hurtles downstream, pulling more soil with it as it goes, and you're worse off than if you'd done nothing at all. The progressive strategy demonstrated on this waterway involves rocks that are too small to do any damage if they get disrupted by the current. Braided water patterns fan out around an S-shaped placement of a series of rocks, making it look like Andy Goldsworthy was here. This method will take years to heal the streambeds, but it will work.

We eat lunch where some hunting cabins are under construction. It's hot. Everybody's relaxing. Avila is telling people about his relationship with Emil McCain, who was involved in the story of Macho B, a radio-collared jaguar that died shortly after it was captured in 2009. Since he has already told me most of this, I lie down on a low rock wall and shut my eyes. His voice is mellifluous, and occasionally punctuated by someone's question. I am almost dozing when the conversational murmur becomes distinctly emotional. I bolt upright. Avila smirks at me. "Get out your notebook," he advises.

The story under discussion is the life and death of Macho B, which plays out with the relentless surety of classic tragedy, and which these Arizona wildlife lovers have followed closely. The narrative trajectory begins in 1996, when Warner Glenn, a founder of the Malpai Border-lands Group, was out hunting for mountain lions with his hounds. Glenn is widely beloved and respected. The Malpai group is a progressive consortium of ranches where the southernmost tips of New Mexico and Arizona meet, and it advocates all the right ways to manage land, including controlled burns. At the same time, these guys have credibility with traditional ranchers.

Although the jaguar once ranged as far as Washington state, Nebraska, and Maryland, sometime in the last 15,000 to 100,000 years it lost its northernmost range, possibly to competition with a larger lion, *Panthera atrox,* that subsequently became extinct. Fossil records put jaguars in Florida 7,000 to 8,000 years ago. In *Wildlife in America,* Peter Matthiessen reports "Tygers" in North Carolina as late as 1737. John James Audubon described jaguar skins decorating various riding and shooting accoutrements in *Quadrupeds* and so on, and nineteenth-century travelogues include jaguar sightings in Monterey Bay redwood forests and the Mojave Desert. Jaguar persisted longer in Arizona and New Mexico, where they came under the deathly control of the Bureau of Biological Survey's predator eradication program. Arizona Game and Fish has records of thirty sightings it considers credible between 1901 and 1996. The jaguar was listed as endangered throughout its range outside the United States by the US Fish and Wildlife Service. Protection for the jaguar has been consistently faulty and it wasn't listed as endangered in the United States until the Center for Biological Diversity sued the Fish and Wildlife Service to require the listing, which the jaguar finally got in 1997.

When Warner Glenn sighted a jaguar, his first impulse was to take its picture, which he did. As Glenn put it, "Not only was it a fine trophy, but it was a predator that had a reputation for killing domestic livestock and it was a rather rare and 'macho' thing to say you had killed a jaguar. It was not illegal and there were even government hunters killing them occasionally." Six months later another hunter, Jack Childs, himself renowned for counting among his quarry the largest mountain lion ever shot, was out with his wife and his hounds in the Baboquivari Mountains when they bayed "the most magnificent animal we had ever seen" into the branches of an alligator juniper tree.

Both Glenn and Childs were moved by their experiences to instigate jaguar conservation. Glenn established a jaguar depredation fund at Malpai to compensate any rancher who might lose cattle to the big cat. Childs and his wife founded the Borderlands Jaguar Detection Project. With evidence of jaguar on its turf, the state's game and fish agencies joined up to create the ad hoc Arizona–New Mexico Jaguar Conservation Team (the Jag team), which convened academic biologists, state and federal wildlife personnel, NGOs, landowners, ranchers, you name it, and opened as many arms as wide as possible to welcome jaguar back to the Southwest. At least that was the idea.

Look Me in the Eye

The story of Macho B is sad not only for him, but also for Janay Brun, a young woman who was a volunteer on the detection project. It is a story that reflects very badly on the Arizona Department of Game and Fish, an agency that on other wildlife fronts is a leader in conservation efforts. The state of Arizona has completed an exemplary wildlife corridor mapping effort; only California has done the same. The official word on Macho B is that what happened to him was exceptional, a one-off resulting from the involvement of a rogue element, and in fact, that may be true to a point. But what happened to Brun afterward is another story, reflecting how conservation, and justice, are frequently sacrificed at the conjunction of culture and bureaucracy—not only for animals but for people.

I had to wait a few months before I was able to talk to Brun, for a reason that will become evident, and caught up with her after she had left Arizona to live with her parents in Pennsylvania for a while. "One day in fall 1999 I encountered a jaguar," Brun tells me. In her late twenties at the time, Brun was working as a waitress west of Tucson and was interested in wild cats. Hiking frequently in the Baboquivari range, on that fateful day she meandered with her small dogs up a trail that turned abruptly into a canyon. "It was about sunset. My dogs put their noses in the air. Fifty to seventy feet ahead of us was a boulder and the silhouette of a cat. The sun was setting—this all happened very quickly. I could see his eyes. He was looking at us. He jumped off the rock and started vocalizing, like a cough." (The jaguar roar is described as a low, chesty cough.) Brun's dogs chased the cat for about three seconds, then turned tail. "They were scared! After that, whenever they got a scent of lion they would do this sort of dance and head back to the truck. Whatever happens with 'I am predator, you are prey,' happened." The big cat then traveled down the trail. "We're standing across a small canyon from each other, and I'm listening to this vocalizing and thinking, 'This is a jaguar.'" She later came to realize she had encountered Macho B, who got his second-letter-in-the-alphabet name because a different male jaguar had been caught on camera earlier, Macho A.

Exchanging glances with a jaguar seems to have an impact on everyone who experiences it. Brun started to learn tracking in earnest. She moved away from the Baboquivari Mountains but returned to them frequently. Brun continued waiting tables and interned at the Buenos Aires National Wildlife Refuge. Five years after she began volunteering with the Borderlands Detection Project, she began to get paid. "I was a field tech," she says. "Mostly it's about cameras: changing the batteries, placing new cameras, taking the cards out, and entering the data into Excel spreadsheets." She went tracking several times with Sergio Avila. "I spent a lot of time in four or five places. I would follow tracks and get to know the animals, sometimes by a scar on the heel pad."

In 2004 Emil McCain joined the project and became Brun's supervisor. McCain had a long involvement with the jaguar world and something of a legendary status within it as a superior tracker and overall wilderness savant. Those who know him tell me McCain grew up in a counterculture world in rural Colorado, one of the least populated parts of the United States, and by all accounts he is an exemplary woodsman. Sergio Avila worked with McCain on a jaguar tracking project in Mexico in 2003. McCain was twenty-seven and Avila was thirty-one. "We were like two brothers with different mothers," Avila says, describing his excitement at spending time with a man who knew "everything, everything about the wilderness. I had everything to learn from him. We were two young machos in the outback tracking jaguars—it was a dream."

Avila and McCain had been hired to snare and radio-collar jaguar and mountain lions; radio-collaring animals is currently the ultimate way to track their movement, since it gives you GPS points in time. With the Mexico–United States border such a hot and perpetual issue, information about jaguar crossings would greatly bolster efforts to modify barriers so animals could get through. In Sonora with McCain, Avila snared a jaguar and came upon it alone. "You aren't supposed to do anything with an animal by yourself," Avila says. "I am supposed to wait for Emil to come join me. But the animal is going crazy in the snare. She's lunging at me. I thought I was going to die."

Wild animals do not like to be snared, or radio-collared, but jaguars take the whole ordeal very hard and are in serious danger of damaging if not killing themselves in trying to get free. They *really* cannot stand to be restrained. Though she was caught in the snare, the animal's forward thrust was intense. "In theory you don't run from a cat. I ran," Avila says. The jaguar of course was stopped short but Avila was beside himself. Eventually Avila drugged the cat with a dart. She was collared and released, and the two men celebrated with joy that night at the adventure and the capture. "We got drunk and talked to the stars," Avila says.

Two days later, headed to town to communicate with their supervisor, they started to load their cars. "We went out to the traps to disable them and there's a jaguar in one. We aren't prepared. It's a male and we put lots of drugs in him. He never woke up. The excitement of the first collar was totally destroyed. We brought the animal back with us. Emil wanted the skull. You're supposed to send dead captured animals to a special Fish and Wildlife location for a necropsy but Emil wanted to skin the animal." Avila tells me this turn of events put him "in emotional disorganization." He tried to talk McCain out of it. "But then I helped him. You can't do it alone." I ask him why he assented to McCain. "Emil is very charismatic, dominating. I couldn't go against him." Even those who might not think askance at skinning McCain today attest to his personal magnetism. Avila and McCain were, of course, fired for their actions and mediation was arranged with their employer, whom Avila says did not equip or supervise the two young men adequately. "I didn't want to be a biologist anymore," Avila recounts. "I'm seeing dead jaguars in front of me." The experience was a turning point for Avila, who today will not participate in radio-collaring any animal.

It is tempting to cast McCain as a coldhearted bounty seeker, but there is more nuance to take note of; he has after all dedicated his career to working for conservation organizations, often under fairly harsh conditions. Whether conservation provided a venue for McCain's devotion to jaguar or cover for his bloodlust is a matter of discernment; the answer, as Michael Soulé might say, is both. In some ways he is emblematic of our collective failure to truly protect animals we say we value for their own sake.

When McCain joined Jack Childs' Borderlands Jaguar Detection Project, he expanded the camera trapping project threefold beginning in 2004. Among 15,000 images of 25 wildlife species, they captured more than 70 photographs of jaguars and were able to identify one of them as a distinct individual, Macho B. He had a distinct rosette on his right side. Based on this feature Childs connected Macho B to his original 1996 sighting: "Our beautiful Baboquivari jaguar is still here ten years later!"

BLACK HEART, WHITE HUNTER

With the evidence of both Childs's and Brun's sightings in the area and the update of the camera trap photographs, it became clear that Macho B was alive and well in the Baboquivari Mountains. "All of a sudden, there were two jaguars in two states and they had endangered species status," recounts Brun. US Fish and Wildlife has jurisdiction over endangered species, but in the case of the jaguar, the agency deferred responsibility to the states, with the proviso that stakeholders across all categories should come together to steward the welfare of the animals. Thus, the "Jag team" was created. Under endangered species protocol, suitable habitat for the animals is directed to be identified and protected. Various snafus and confusions ensued about suitable jaguar habitat, and years after the animal was listed, there was still no habitat protected. The Center for Biological Diversity offered to complete the process of identifying suitable jaguar habitat in both states to facilitate the process, and the game and fish departments accepted. They prepared a report that has never been implemented.

Meanwhile, Jag team meetings proceeded. Brun attended some but felt they were a waste of time. They became generally known as jaguar conversation, not conservation. But that talk turned to the prospect of snaring and radio-collaring jaguar. The NGOs were uniformly against doing so; not only do many jaguars die in the process, but there was ample photographic evidence of jaguar, and nothing in particular had been done with that. The idea of risking the animals to keep better tabs on them made no sense. On the other side, agency personnel and Jack Childs were pro-collaring.

"The game and fish agencies really like to do this and it's true across the entire West," says Kieran Suckling, executive director of the Center for Biological Diversity. "They like to trap animals, relocate them, monitor them, much more than the feds. The feds use trapping and capture as a last resort." According to Brun, McCain had already been setting up snares at the camera trap sites, and both Childs and the agencies knew that.

But it was ostensibly on an Arizona Game and Fish (AZGF) project to snare mountain lions and black bear that McCain, who was employed part-time by the agency, captured Macho B. Once the jaguar had been documented in the area, he reopened deactivated snares and directed Brun to place female jaguar scat near them. "Basically I'm meeting Emil and his coworker [Thorry Smith] from AZGF and we're supposed to check cameras, and Emil is leaving town, so he's showing his coworker where the snares are." Brun had long been personally against snaring, and McCain was well aware of this. "I had asked McCain if he had permits for everything, including the scat, scat placement by a snare, and collaring Macho B," she said. "McCain said yes and Smith did not contradict him. I was getting a directive from my boss, who had assured me everything was permitted and thus legal."

On February 18, 2009, Thorry Smith and a coworker found and collared Macho B. They made note that he had a broken canine tooth. Within days the GPS collar, the signal of which was being transmitted to McCain in Europe, indicated Macho B was not moving. From Spain, McCain directed AZGF to search for the animal. When personnel found him, he was lethargic, his back leg atrophied ("black and felt like bubble wrap"). They brought him to the Phoenix Zoo, where he was examined, diagnosed with kidney failure, and euthanized. A "cosmetic" necropsy was performed, which preserves the hide for mounting but interferes with a forensic analysis of cause of death. (The later explanation for this is that the AZGF personnel who directed this kind of necropsy did not know there were different kinds of analysis to choose from.)

Janay Brun received word of Macho B's capture, collar, and death the way most people did, on YouTube and in the press, in which AZGF reported the jaguar had been accidentally captured. Since jaguar are an endangered species, capturing one without full agency protocols in place is against the law. Brun says, "I'm thinking, what happened? Accidental capture?" At this point Brun was not clear on exactly what had gone down and exactly how she had unwittingly participated in what to her was a total nightmare, the death of an animal she loved, that had inspired her for years.

Tony Davis, a reporter for the *Arizona Daily Star* who has thoroughly covered the saga of Macho B, published articles questioning the circumstances of the animal's death, with one expert opining that he was dehydrated and that euthanizing him was premature. Murk obfuscated confusion, and nobody took responsibility for anything. Brun, watching perplexed from the sidelines, decided to come forward with her story. Since AZGF appeared to have completely botched the handling of

Macho B and seemed to be trying to cover up the fact, and since Emil McCain was outright lying about the circumstances of the capture, she contacted Tony Davis. "I told him it was no accident. I was directed to put scat out to attract a jaguar." Immediately US Fish and Wildlife agents contacted her and she told them everything: "I handed everything over that has to do with the jaguar project, all the data and photographs. I had Emil's hard drive, leftover jaguar scat—I handed that over." To see for herself what Macho B had been through, Brun had visited the snare site and collected pieces of claw shavings from a tree he had evidently scratched trying to free himself. She handed these over, too.

McCain responded to Brun's confession by saying she was "unreliable, untrustworthy, and had drug cartel affiliation." AZGF, itself potentially liable for supporting the capture of an endangered species without a permit, in turn distanced itself from McCain and claimed he had acted without its knowledge. This, despite the fact that McCain was in constant communication with AZGF staff about the signals he was reading from the collar. "I hate to defend that bastard," says Brun, "but he was hung out to dry. He's a coward. He wouldn't have taken such a chance unless he had backup or even direction from AZGF."

AZGF conducted an internal investigation, interviewing employees under the auspices of the Garrity warning, which enjoins subjects to reveal everything, even illegality, with the proviso that they will enjoy total immunity from prosecution. Thorry Smith confessed and was simply fired. McCain got "use immunity" from the Arizona US Attorney and confessed; he got five years' probation. Of the involved parties, only Janay Brun was not in the employ of AZGF. Only Janay Brun, the whistleblower who brought this sad and tangled tale to some semblance of transparency, was not protected by the Garrity warning. Tony Davis let Brun know there was a question of proper permitting.

"That's the first inkling I had that there might be any legal implications," she says, but she didn't worry about that for herself. "I did what I was told to do. I didn't do anything wrong." After a year of meeting with the feds, she was told to get a lawyer. And they charged her with unlawfully taking an endangered species without a permit.

"Somebody had to go down for Macho B," she says. "I was the only person without power or immunity." It took approximately a year, but Brun's lawyer (paid for by her parents) succeeded in getting the charges against her dropped, calling them "absurd." "I ruined my life by coming forward," she tells me. For a year she lived in a border town in Arizona, enjoined by law not to leave the state. It is painful to contemplate her sense of betrayal, not only by McCain but by the state of Arizona and the federal government. And her powerlessness.

LEGACY

The jaguar elicits more outward reverence than does the cat's canid brethren the wolf, but this does not help the actual animal much. Management of top predators all over the West is vulnerable to political sacrifice, and here at the border dividing the US and Mexico, anti-immigration, drug trafficking, and homeland security issues pretty much trump wildlife considerations. In September 2010, the US Department of the Interior and the Department of Homeland Security agreed to fund nine environmental mitigation projects to address impacts resulting from the border wall. An expenditure of $771,000 was allocated to monitor the movement of jaguars in Arizona (University of Arizona researchers will implement this study), with the goal of helping to define and establish critical habitat for them. Senator John McCain objected to the use of these funds, citing "the uncertainty of the jaguar's existence in the United States at all."[63] He was reminded by the Department of the Interior that the presence of six individual jaguars has been confirmed in Arizona since 1986.[64]

Political maneuvering aside, what is missing from the discussion is the ecological implications of jaguar movement across the border. For many of us who are environmentally inclined, the freedom of this apex creation of the *umwelt* to reestablish its historic range is reason enough to safeguard its attempts to do so. Of course the moral imperative doesn't always hold sway. There are very practical reasons for ensuring jaguar movement. As asserted by Soulé, Estes, Terborgh, and others, an ecosystem without top predators suffers effects all down the food chain, the atmospheric carbon cycle, and the geological carbon cycle. The border has been called the biggest wildlife disaster in human history. Like all landscapes, this one depends on connection to keep it functioning; the wall is about as stark an interruption as can be imagined, unless a giant pair of scissors could be envisioned at the border, snipping away at the very threads of life.

As with the grizzly bear, the jaguar is an umbrella species; protect it, and you've protected many other species as well. Since 2007 Sky Island Alliance remote camera traps have captured at least four ocelots, predators a rung or two down from the bigger cat on the trophic scale, just 30 to 40 miles south of the border. The expectation is that as the climate changes, the natural dispersal activities of both jaguars and ocelots will be directed ever northward. Sergio Avila is not sanguine about official response to the ocelot evidence: "We're at the same turning point we were with jaguar fourteen years ago," he says. "We need to do it right this time."

CHAPTER 14

There Ought to Be a Law

"CORES," UNTRAMMELED EXPANSES OF WILDERNESS MINIMALLY IMPACTED by humans, have been an accepted focus of conservation at least since the 1964 Wilderness Act. The impetus for the act came from environmentalists concerned that when land is not expressly protected by law, it is vulnerable to being repurposed at the stroke of a pen. For example, the 1924 New Mexico Gila Wilderness was the first area so designated, but it was done by an administrative decree that was summarily altered to allow a road to bifurcate it, thus removing 132,000 acres from protection. Howard Zahniser of the Wilderness Society began efforts to establish the act in 1951 but was roundly opposed. The famed David Brower was a big supporter and in a 1956 Sierra Club bulletin declared, "Wilderness protection is paper thin, and the paper should be the best we can get—that upon which Congress prints its acts." The act was eventually passed stipulating that only Congress can designate wilderness areas, and only Congress can change them. The Wilderness Act established a national policy on what constitutes wilderness and how to protect it; its definition of wilderness as at least 5,000 acres with educational, scientific, or historic value, minimal human imprint, and ample recreational possibilities is an expressly anthropocentric vision that nowhere mentions biodiversity. But the Wilderness Act stands as a model for how to protect American land; 9.1 million acres were protected at its inception and today 107.5 million acres are protected.

Now that it is widely understood that to keep cores healthy, corridors need to connect them, the question is: How do we do that? First we have to define what exactly a corridor is. As mentioned earlier, the initial proposal of corridors as a conservation palliative met with some skepticism, questions about whether invasive species would be their biggest users, and whether the costs of creating them could be justified. The matter was essentially settled in favor of corridors in a 1998 paper in *Conservation Biology* by Reed Noss and Paul Beier: "Do Habitat Corridors Protect Connectivity?"[65] Noss, of course, is one of the earliest conservation biologists to actually implement corridor ecology. Beier is today its most prolific practitioner. A professor at Northern Arizona University and currently president of the Society of Conservation Biology, he is responsible for producing wildlife corridor maps for the entire states of California and Arizona, and wrote software that other people can use to design them. He has recently published a number of scientific articles proposing novel ways to assess the landscape in light of climate change. (Of course he had significant help from other researchers on all of the above.) In their paper Noss and Beier review thirty-two studies regarding the utility of corridors and conclude, "The evidence from well-designed studies suggest that corridors are valuable conservation tools. Those who would destroy the last remnants of natural connectivity should bear the burden of proving that corridor destruction will not harm target populations."

Nearly fifteen years following this assertion that corridors work, Beier cowrote another article in *Conservation Biology*: "Toward Best Practices for Developing Regional Connectivity Maps."[66] Observing that research has to date largely focused on fine-grained maps to produce linkage designs for small areas, Beier and colleagues enumerate seven steps "to coarsely map dozens to hundreds of linkages over a large area, such as a nation, province, or ecoregion." And in an update to that Wilderness Act language, they define "blocks to be mapped on the basis of a combination of naturalness, protection status, linear barriers, and habitat quality for selected species."

States are increasingly looking to identify land that connects big wild areas, keeping in mind where species are expected to move and to persist as the climate gets hotter. Josh Pollock, conservation director at Rocky Mountain Wild, is leading a project comprising several NGOs to counsel Colorado Parks and Wildlife in their land use decisions; he contracted with Healy Hamilton to make maps that help the agency "peer into the future and see what may happen to suitable conditions for wildlife." Pollock says Hamilton's maps are applicable in Colorado's zoning and statewide oil and gas permitting. "The agency has a big role in county land use planning review, so information on where corridors are now and how they might be affected by climate change in the future is really important to incorporate. They also get to look at oil and gas development plans. So instead of evaluating hundreds of single well permits, they will now be able to look at aggregate plans and see, oh, this whole well field will create a significant wildlife barrier."

You may notice that by connecting hundreds of linkages over a nation we are getting darn close to mapping the Humboldtian vision encompassing all nature's working: In addition, again, to massive computing power, this is made possible by those two acronyms I've been throwing around with impunity, GPS and GIS.

POSITIONS, PLEASE

GPS stands for "global positioning system," and its miracle originates in Ptolemy's conception and designation of latitude and longitude—the original coordinate system—nearly 2,000 years ago. Ptolemy was trying to flatten the globe, to provide measurement and orientation on a round surface communicated by way of a piece of paper, a map. The earth is a sphere, and spheres can be divided into 360 degrees. Latitude is north-to-south divisions measured against the imaginary circle around the earth known as the equator, and dividing it into hemispheres. Longitude measures east to west, with 0 designated at Greenwich, England, and progressing 180 degrees in both directions until they meet at the international date line.

In 1957 the Russians built the first satellite to orbit the earth, aka Sputnik. It used a radio transmitter to broadcast telemetry information, and more or less by accident, scientists at the Johns Hopkins University Applied Physics Lab discovered that the Doppler effect applied to the spacecraft. Remember Doppler? It's when you are standing on a sidewalk and you hear a fire engine siren, the sound increases as the truck approaches and subsides after it passes. If the scientists knew exactly where the satellite was up in the ether, they could determine their own precise location by listening in and measuring the satellite's radio-signal Doppler shift. The Department of Defense got on this right quick. Currently 24 satellites operated by the Department of Defense orbit 12,000 miles above the earth at 7,000 miles per hour. They pass over the same spot approximately every twenty-four hours, and they are positioned so that a GPS receiver can get signals from at least six of them at a time, from any location on earth.[67]

THREE-LETTER WORDS

It's easy enough to confuse the acronyms, but GIS stands for geographic information system, and that is a broad term for a new kind of map made using GPS data, with the capacity to simultaneously contain many ways of looking at that data. While robust computing power fuels GIS today, the concept behind it gets traced back to John Snow's 1854 map of a cholera outbreak in London, in which he used points to represent the locations of individual cases, thus studying its distribution, which led to the source of the outbreak, at a water pump, which he promptly disconnected. Today he would fix those locations by GPS but the idea is still the same. While mapping is qua conceptual, GIS allows for more and more nuanced and multiple concepts to cohere in one map.

If Lewis and Clark had had GPS capacity and GIS software, the map made from their travels for Thomas Jefferson would have been able to include version upon version of the terra incognita of the West, including soil and vegetation type and precise elevations. In addition to gathering information about what was there, it would include how it was used—they would have been able to fix where Indians lived and the quality of the landscape around them as they conducted precursors to our controlled burns. In fact, the first operational GIS was used in 1962 by a Canadian federal agency to map information about just these dimensions of its rural lands, including the baseline features of soil and water, but also noting forestry, agriculture, and recreational uses. As Lewis and Clark's map, in historian Bernard DeVoto's words, "satisfied desire and it created desire,"[68] the Canadian GIS map was meant to spur on more gung-ho land use.

MAPPING THE THREE C'S

Actually designing a corridor involves integrating the big three basic principles of conservation biology codified by Michael Soulé (and others, of course) and includes cores, and in Paul Beier's way of doing it, carnivores. (Beier became interested in connectivity when he realized the mountain lions he studied were becoming isolated in mountain ranges and were in danger of extinction.) So, to design a corridor you use a map of the area in question, and identify the blocks of wildlands you want to connect and what focal species are expected to move between them. Using a geometric or additive mean algorithm, you create habitat suitability models by combining GIS factors related to the habitat preferences of species. Then you divide the map of potential habitat for each species into patch sizes, those that can support a breeding pair and those that can support a breeding population. You will want to incorporate categories of species, including sensitive ones, such as large carnivores (as Beier says, "If they lose connectivity they will be gone"); habitat specialists, such as tree squirrels associated with oak woodlands; the least mobile species, such as salamanders, which don't move very far; and barrier-sensitive species, such as pronghorn, which just hate fences and roads. Finally you create a corridor model between the blocks for each species, select different-size corridors, and evaluate the maximum distances between patches and potential bottlenecks, using "general statistics on any vector or raster background dataset." Or you phone Paul Beier.

PROUD BUT NOT BRAGGING

Well, I am kind of asking Josh Avey to brag, because as habitat branch chief of Arizona Game and Fish (AZGF), he has presided over some of the most progressive connectivity initiatives in the country, much of the time with Paul Beier as mapping maestro. "'Connectivity' is a great buzzword," Avey says, "because connectivity serves as a public safety value, a genetic bridge, and an ecological adaptive management strategy for climate change." Avey counts AZGF's biggest successes along the preventing-roadkill lines, for which he shares credit with Arizona's transportation department. "Our biggest and loudest success to date is our oldest," and this is State Highway 260, along which elk "crosswalks" have been placed at critical junctures. Military-grade targeting software detects wildlife as it approaches the road and sets off flashing signs to notify motorists of oncoming hooves. Another success is US Highway 93—on YouTube you can watch bighorn sheep nonchalantly traversing an overpass built for them (there's a selection of footage—type in "Highway 93" and "Big-horn"), which Avey tells me they did a week before the overpass was actually open. When staff viewed remote camera footage showing this, "you should have heard the gasp," he says. US 93 is the road to Vegas, and it's also on the North American Free Trade Route and the Canada-Mexico Trade Corridor, designations that in themselves illustrate the competition from human interests those sheep, native to the Black Mountains, have to contend with on the landscape.

The designs Beier has assisted with not only connect up linkages within Arizona, but also extend out to surrounding states, because naturally, wildlife does not recognize state boundaries. A prototype of mapping tools that are busily being constructed in many places across the country is AZGF's online HabiMap. There you can pull up a map of Arizona and select features that interest you, such as "wildlife stressors," "species of economic and recreational importance," and "biotic communities"; the map will instantly show you where these are located. It's cool.

YOU'RE STANDING ON IT
In addition to identifying where animals are moving now, Beier proposes another metric by which to define corridors that he calls the "land facet approach." This identifies corridors by zeroing in on topographical and soil traits. "I came to that whole thought because I was designing corridors based on focal species. And I would get this question, 'How is this going to work with climate change?' And I had to say, 'I don't know.'" In his 2010 article "Use of Land Facets to Plan for Climate Change: Conserving the Arenas, Not the Actors," [69] Beier and his frequent colleague Brian Brost advocate designing corridors based on areas where high biodiversity occurs now, "recurring landscape units with uniform topographic and soil attributes," rather than based on "the temporary occupants" that live

there now. The best strategy is to conserve a variety of stages. Mountainous areas are good because they have so many landscape gradients; Beier says really the only areas where it may be hard to apply are extremely flat areas. Even so, since 1 foot in elevation can make a huge difference in water table and soil properties, it could work on these as well. "However, you would need super-super-precise elevation data" from remote-sensing technology that may not exist quite yet.

Arizona is 70 percent publicly owned, and much of that land is up for sale. The corridors Beier has designed are "agreements in principle," he explains. They have been designed to be included in future development, but there's absolutely no guarantee they will be, much less enforced even if they are. "It ain't over till the fat lady sings," says Beier, but he is optimistic that people want wildlife to stay around and will help make that possible. Really? I demur, what is going to motivate people to save wildlife? We will save them, Beier answers, "because we love them." GIS geeks usually just don't talk this way. "We should save them because they are beautiful," he says. "We have a collective guilt that we've extirpated so many species from so many ecosystems. We don't want to repeat those errors. Aesthetically, we value an ecosystem they are part of." Beier goes on: "We need to create corridors so these creatures can persist alongside us, so that people can feel they are good stewards of the land; there is a special function to each piece of land and we can take pride in being part of that. Instead of feeling, 'I live in a semidegraded landscape,' we can make sure we fulfill this landscape for the species who also live here. This helps create a sense of human place for human communities."

THE LONG HAUL

Kenyon Fields is inclined toward hedging his bets about human nature, and thus has his eyes on the prize of corridor legislation.[70] Fields is strategy director of the Wildlands Network and in addition to playing a central role in organizing the Western Landowner Network referenced earlier, he founded and continues to lead the Connectivity Policy Coalition. This is a group of policy and legislative representatives from most of the major national conservation organizations, as well as those from many of the same

NGOs that count themselves as part of the Spine. The group is working hard to get connectivity language sustained in proposed revisions to
Forest Service guidelines, and in President Barack Obama's America's
Great Outdoors initiative. With others, Fields nurtures the ambition to
establish a wildlife corridors act along the same lines as the Wilderness Act. "We should take our time developing it," he says. "We should
remember how long it took to get the Wilderness Act on the books"—
eight years—"and do it right." Fields wants to get wide buy-in from
members of Congress to establish a standardized, national mechanism
for protecting corridors. Because even with the progress his coalition has
made in articulating connectivity and providing concrete examples of
where it would do the most good, getting corridor language included in
guidelines is not enough. As with the Wilderness Act, we need a way for
citizens to petition for protection of corridors, and legislation that will
permanently safeguard them.

The Path of the Pronghorn

There is a prototype for actually safeguarding wildlife movement and that
is the Path of the Pronghorn, a 120-mile invariant (which means it never
changes) migration journey undertaken each year by a single group of
pronghorn antelope, *Antilocapra americana,* from Grand Teton National
Park to the Upper Green Valley in Wyoming. Forest Service rules pro-
hibit development and other impacts from impinging on it, and the way
this was accomplished provides a template for future action. First, start
with incredibly committed, idealistic people who love wildlife and are
willing to work very hard to protect it.

Many western states pose the same stark paradox. Home to some of
the world's most spectacular scenery and the wildlife that keep the view
healthy and vibrant, they also husband tremendous resources, the extraction of which often trumps all other concerns. Wyoming has an especially
schizophrenic profile. The first national park (Yellowstone, 1872), the first
national forest (the Shoshone, 1891), and the first national monument
(Devil's Tower, 1906) were all established in Wyoming. The state is proud
of its beauties. But when fracking technology and 3-D seismic surveys

made it possible to get at 40 trillion cubic feet of natural gas in the Jonah Field and the Pinedale Anticline Project, well—let's get fracking.

Joel Berger, author of *The Better to Eat You With: Fear in the Animal World* and a prominent Wildlife Conservation Society (WCS) biologist, came to the Upper Green River Valley to study predator-prey ecology. With his then wife, Kim Berger, also a WCS biologist, he began to notice a high uptick in the wildlife mortality around drilling activity in the area, the volume of which had tripled starting in the late 1990s. In 1994, 40 gas wells were approved for drilling in the Jonah Field; by 2006, there were 3,100. At the Pinedale Anticline, 4,399 additional wells were approved. As habitat gets converted to roads and well pads, the pronghorn are increasingly marginalized.

The yearly trek made by the antelope brings them just north of Jackson Hole—the town celebrates their arrival each year—and the animals are devoted to a specific circuit that gets them there and back. Not all antelope that reside in the Upper Green River Valley migrate. Why some animals do and others don't is not yet known by science. But this particular herd does, like clockwork, and they go to Grand Teton. Grand Teton typically gets tons of snow each winter, helping to make Jackson Hole a favorite destination for skiers, but the snow is too deep for pronghorn, who, unlike bison, for example, cannot dig down and find forage under it. If stranded there, unable to cross the road, the animals would face local extinction. While pronghorn are not endangered as a species, the Grand Teton herd migration corridor was headed down the same path to oblivion as six of eight historic pronghorn corridors in the greater Yellowstone ecosystem, all done in by development. The Green River corridor is a long and challenging one, and in the spring it takes the animals a month or more to traverse. (In the fall it takes just three days.) Any woman holding down a full-time job while pregnant may feel sisterhood with the does, who typically give birth upon completion of their springtime journey. *And* they have twins, which compose about 15 percent of their total body weight. Talk about dropping babies; the pronghorn fawns are ready within a few days to get going. It's survival chops like this that have helped this lineage stay viable so long.

THE LAST OF THEIR KIND

Antilocapra americana trace their roots to the Miocene (5 million to 26 million years ago); then a wide and diversified group, these dwindled to one species by the late Pleistocene (11,700 to 2.5 million years ago) and now are the last of their kin. They are the only large ungulate exclusively native (endemic) to the North American continent; their closest relatives are giraffes. Pronghorn coevolved with a now-extinct cheetah that caught them in a short dash. Avoiding its claws, they became what is now the second-fastest land animal on the earth (an African cheetah bests them), and they've been clocked at running more than 50 miles per hour. In response to that cheetah, they are equally incredible at sprinting as they are at distance running. In *Where the Wild Things Were,* author William Stolzenburg likens a moving herd to a "squadron of hovercraft." Their bodies are small but their insides are big: While a pronghorn front leg might be the width of your index finger, its windpipe is about the size of a vacuum hose, which brings oxygen to a commensurately large heart. Only hummingbirds and bats, in the vertebrate category, have higher oxygen uptake. Lance Armstrong, take note.

NIFTY KNIFFY

Radiocarbon-dated bones from along the path date back 6,000 years. The herd of 300 pronghorn in the Upper Green Valley has made the same annual migration for at least that amount of time, making it the longest land migration in the lower forty-eight. Taken with the majesty of this event, a piece of ancient evolution visibly in motion right among the gas drilling and the ranchettes, the Bergers had the idea to protect these animals under what they proposed would be the first American National Wildlife Corridor, joining Wyoming's other jewels in the crown of national protection firsts. There are numerous heroes in the story of the pronghorn but the real linchpin is the now retired Bridger-Teton National Forest supervisor, Kniffy Hamilton, to whom the Bergers presented their idea. Conversations between them started in 2002. Hamilton, as they say, took the ball and ran with it.

"I talked to congressional staffers," recalls Hamilton, because these national designations are made on the federal level, "but I couldn't get any interest from the senators and representatives from Wyoming to set aside public lands for that." So Hamilton set her sights closer to home. Wildlife responsibility is parsed out among state and federal agencies, and in addition to her own Forest Service provenance, Hamilton needed to get buy-in from other groups: Wyoming Game & Fish, Grand Teton National Park, the National Elk Refuge, and the Bureau of Land Management. The US Fish and Wildlife Service jumped on board right away. The BLM has pledged support but has been slow to implement any. The Bergers went to then Wyoming governor Dave Freudenthal, who "got the concept immediately," says Joel Berger. "He told us to show him agreement was gathering from the ground up. It was appropriate and that's what we did."

With Hamilton working the agency circuit, the Bergers and other activists set up meetings all along the path, presenting to ranchers, farmers, county commissioners—anyone and everyone who might have a stake in the use of this land. One of the cultural hurdles to conservation in the West is the suspicion held by private property owners that the federal government will grab up more land, and so it was very important to clarify that this was not the intention of the Path of the Pronghorn. Careful cultivation of grassroots support, together with the explicit delineation of the corridor's outlines, and tireless, cooperative effort, were critical to its eventual success, which was the 2008 Forest Plan Amendment establishing federal protection of the migration corridor. This means that land is managed with the pronghorn in mind. For example, this animal does not jump, so any fencing on the land needs to give them enough clearance to go under it. The pronghorn are not totally protected along this path. What became known as the "funnel" is a 110-yard-wide bottleneck along the route, and it connects public and private land. The Conservation Fund, leveraging monies from Acres for America, purchased an easement from the Carney Ranch Company to protect this swath. Acres for America is in turn a joint venture of Walmart and the US Fish and Wildlife Foundation. It doesn't take a village to protect a migration pathway, it takes a list of acronyms the length of your arm.

"The pronghorn is an easy one," says Rob Ament, who is senior conservationist with the Center for Large Landscape Conservation in Bozeman, Montana. Ament also works for the Western Transportation Institute as program manager for road ecology. "It's a single species, it's radio-collared. They use the same place year after year." The task to protect animal movement gets exponentially more difficult when less linear types of ecological functioning—such as the need for a top carnivore to disperse over large areas—are under consideration. Neither does connectivity locate itself to public lands—it crosses all boundaries. "We don't have ecological networks protected," says Ament. "Our big challenge is, how do we get a designation for those key, connecting landscapes?"

THE POWER OF AN IDEA

The success of the Path of the Pronghorn has subsequently rippled out to greater effect. Governor Freudenthal learned his conservation biology lesson from Joel and Kim Berger and he learned it very well. Made keenly aware that the development so many are hungry for is yet a dire threat to the wildlife many westerners are devoted to hunting, fishing, and observing, Freudenthal brought the concept of landscape connectivity to the Western Governors' Association (WGA), which represents nineteen western states and three Pacific islands. In 2008 the association passed a policy resolution called "Protecting Wildlife Migration Corridors and Crucial Wildlife in the West." It followed up with a Wildlife Habitat Council to implement its goals.

What this entity will succeed in accomplishing is a work in progress (Arizona's HabiMap project was partly funded by the WGA), but represents the first government-sanctioned acknowledgment of connectivity, and as such is a watershed. Hunting, fishing, bird watching, and hiking all bring in significant revenue. By a WGA report's tally, $40 billion is pumped into the nineteen states composing the organization per year by these activities. Another WGA habitat council report makes a grim equivalent calculation: "The US is now losing about 2 million acres of natural land per year, or 6,000 acres per day." Additionally, even as population growth is outpaced by habitat loss, people are building bigger houses, and "new cities in formerly remote areas . . . in crucial habitats, require roads, canals, energy infrastructure that fragment crucial habitats and sever wildlife corridors." As a result, "wildlife is in retreat."

The meeting at which this wildlife policy resolution was achieved had some strong conservation public relations going for it. Tom Brokaw, the former anchor for *NBC Nightly News* and an ardent conservationist, gave an impassioned opening address about the need to protect the wildlife we have left. Rick Ridgeway of the outdoor clothing and equipment company Patagonia told the governors the epic story of a wolverine, which like the pronghorn story owes its details and its accuracies to the magic of radio collars and GPS.[71]

Ridgeway told the western governors about the tracking of M3, "the biggest, snarliest, and most badass wolverine any of the biologists had ever encountered." He went on to tell them about how the signals from M3's radio collar tracked the animal leaving Montana, going north to Waterton in Canada, taking a 700-mile traipse through British Columbia, and heading back to Montana. This might sound like a good route for a wildflower tour in a camper, but M3 started in February, on foot, naturally, among other feats making a 10,466-foot ascent of Mount Cleveland, Glacier's highest peak. "Why?" posed Ridgeway. "Because it was there." Ridgeway reports thunderous applause after his presentation, including an epic hug from Freudenthal.

MY HOME IS FAR AWAY

In the winter of 2008, a young graduate student named Katie Moriarty from Oregon State University set up a camera trap in the snowy hills of Tahoe National Forest in California. She was hoping to get photographs of American marten for research on how forest management is affecting this small relative of the weasel. Moriarty affixed a motion-sensitive digital camera to a tree and trained it in the general direction of another one, to which she attached raw chicken just as the sun was setting. Once a week she checked for captured images of animals partaking of her protein bonanza. One day she got coyotes, mice, and spotted skunks. Over the course of a month, not a single marten went for the meat. One day

Moriarty caught an image that made her forget all about them, for the moment, anyway. She couldn't believe her eyes. She called in her advisers, who excitedly called in even more experts. What Moriarty visually captured hadn't been seen in California in nearly 100 years. One scientist who descended on the scene likened it to finding a "dodo bird—it's such a rare species." Moriarty had caught herself a wolverine.

Where had he come from, and how did he get to Tahoe? Despite the concerted efforts of twenty researchers scouring 150 square miles of Tahoe National Forest, none of them laid eyes on the wolverine, though Moriarty did get several more images of it. Dogs trained to track animals sniffed after hair, scat, and urine but turned up only coyote scat. Finally the scientists collected enough hair and wolverine scat around the baited trees to perform DNA analysis.

Because the wolverine has been absent so long from California, the main mission of the DNA analysis was to figure out what lineage this newcomer hailed from. The historical framework for the question was provided by the work of Joseph Grinnell, famed naturalist and vertebrate taxonomist from the University of California–Berkeley. In 1937 Grinnell published research indicating that by 1893 the wolverine population in the state was restricted to high-elevation alpine habitats in the southern Sierra Nevada. The last one spotted in California hearkens back to the 1920s. Mike Schwartz, the geneticist at the Rocky Mountain Research Station in Missoula, obtained DNA from nine wolverine specimens in the taxonomical collections of the Smithsonian Institution and the University of California's Museum of Vertebrate Zoology. These specimens had been collected between 1891 and 1922, and comparing them with DNA sequences from the new wolverine could lead to the rough outline of a genealogy for this creature. It was not expected to have a California lineage (and it doesn't), but would perhaps be revealed as a captive release or an escapee—people are known to trap and harbor all manner of wild animal. What the DNA did show astounded everyone.

Schwartz's DNA analysis did not reveal a California lineage, or even a more likely one from Canada. Based on genetic similarities, the Tahoe wolverine in fact most closely resembles those in the Sawtooth

Mountains of Idaho. This is an area that Doug Copeland, a Forest Service biologist and head of the Glacier Wolverine Project, knows well. "This Tahoe wolverine looks like a Sawtooth wolverine—but not like the Sawtooth wolverine of today. He looks like a Sawtooth wolverine from ten years ago. The Sawtooth wolverine today looks more like the ones in Glacier." To translate into a possible scenario, an original wolverine from the Sawtooth Mountains migrated to California within the past ten years to establish a new territory. Meanwhile, a wolverine from Glacier headed down to Idaho. Moriarty's wolverine, which has since been photographed in the general vicinity, corroborated by DNA analysis, traveled over 600 miles to stake this new ground.

THE FEDS

The state is not the only level of jurisdiction thinking hard about connectivity. Before he died unexpectedly in 2010, Sam Hamilton, then director of the Fish and Wildlife Service, established Landscape Conservation Cooperatives (LCCs) defined by ecoregion across the nation and even our borders, to promote landscape connectivity and interjurisdictional cooperation. Hamilton was building on the success of conservation efforts to protect migratory birds across North America; he expanded the model to include multiple species. Department of Interior Secretary Ken Salazar is sustaining the forward momentum of LCCs. "I've never seen a message that is so consistent coming from the top," says Yvette Converse, who as director of the Great Northern LCC presides over connections between federal, state, and tribal organizations as well as nonprofits (including Y2Y), half in British Columbia and half in the United States. "It's clear that there's a big picture going on here." Converse credits NGOs with pushing the connectivity message behind all this through to the agency level. "It's the Rob Aments and the Gary Tabors who have gotten us here," she says.[72] "And *The Theory of Island Biogeography*." Both LCC and WGA databases include Wildlands Network designs originally created by the Spine of the Continent partners.

Kenyon Fields is not all that sanguine about the WGA or the LCCs, and like many other conservation soldiers who've seen more than a few battles, his is a "we'll see" attitude. "The real task," he says, "is to move the ball beyond sunny policy rhetoric and vagaries to action on the ground." Paul Beier calls LCCs a "great initiative" but worries they "may limit themselves to helping managers describe and think about connectivity without going the last step" to actually conserving and managing the lands. Both the LCCs and the WGA are offering up connectivity as something good to do if you want to do it. This doesn't strike Fields as adequate; he's not alone in thinking there that the question of saving nature is not multiple choice.

Part III

Congratulations, You've Won Climate Change

CHAPTER 15

Picka Pika

THE TERM "ECOLOGY," CREDITED TO ZOOLOGIST ERNST HAECKEL IN the late 1860s, reflects the cheerful ordering by which science continued to divide up and grapple with the bewildering whole of nature as more of it was discovered and studied. "Eco" means house or habitation, and "-ology" means study, or discourse.[73] Discussion about this house of nature includes such concepts as "assemblages," "distributions," and "communities." Charles Elton in his 1927 book *Animal Ecology* (still a good read) asserted that what's going on in nature is a densely meshing dynamism of interaction among a series of moving targets. While he did his own bit of diagramming, giving us the food pyramid, Elton perceived the hierarchical relationships among plants and animals to function as much in a holistic as a linear way.

Elton's insights went far beyond the diagrammatic reduction connoted even by the circular image of a web. Ecosystems are not something that can be isolated and described in two or even three dimensions; the term refers to the way all living and nonliving elements in a given area relate to each other, over time. An ecosystem is equally microcosmic as macrocosmic. For example, a rotting log is an ecosystem in which energy is flowing through growth and decomposition, predation and reproduction, as microbes, fungi, bugs, birds, plants, and animals partake in nature's ongoing rave. A hunk of wood that is left over from a fire takes its place in a long time frame of cyclical disturbance events that shape the forest over hundreds and thousands of years. Take a piece of the scene, any piece, and you could trace the evolutionary history of that particular interaction, let's just say between a flower and its pollinator, and then the relationship to that flower and all its big, long family tree and ditto for the bird or the bee or whoever is trucking its pollen around as part of its own life history. To return to Paul Ehrlich's metaphor about removing rivets from an airplane, taking out single pieces of nature may not immediately cause the whole system to collapse, but doing so always has ramifications and effects on other species.

TIMING IS EVERYTHING

We all feel overscheduled and at certain points in our life, perhaps prodded by a "biological clock." But it is nature's way to unfold with regularity. The dynamism of all biological interactions are only roughly predictable, but there is a big pattern in most of North America and it is seasonal. First there is the circadian clock by which life-forms tick along. Circadian is from Latin (*circa*, about; *dies*, day) and this twenty-four-hour cycle allows organisms to sync up with the length of daylight, an accurate proxy for the time of year. Grizzlies and other hibernators also possess an inner "circannual" clock orienting them to the passage of a single year. Plants green up, bloom, and die in concert with the onset of frost and the first snowmelt. Animals that depend on those plants wake up to eat them if that's their routine, or travel somewhere else to find them. Phenology—from the Greek *phaino*, to show, and again *logos*—concerns itself with regular biological events, such as flowering and hibernation, and how they are connected to the climate. And here's where things are getting messed up.

To give you a brief refresher on climate change, it's making things hotter, and if we take as our starting point photosynthesis, here's how. The green-pigmented chlorophyll in plant leaves absorbs light from the sun, metabolizing it with the aid of CO_2 and water drawn in through stomata ("little mouths"), which are pores on the underside of the leaf. The resulting sugars feed the plant and help make the fruits, nuts, and leaves that the next level of the food chain dines out on. That's the eating part; it's called "resynthesis," and it goes on during the day, when the sun is out. At night, respiration (which has been occurring all day as well) keeps on going, releasing the sugars created by photosynthesis for use in the plant's metabolism and also releasing some CO_2 into the atmosphere. Overall, plants take in more CO_2 than they release, and in making use of it, they break the molecule apart, releasing the oxygen and keeping (most of) the carbon. By their own "breathing," or respiration, they allow us to breathe as well.[74] And the carbon they keep, or "sequester," is what they use to build themselves. When you eat a salad, you are eating sequestered carbon and sending it on the next leg of its journey.

It is perfectly natural to have CO_2 in the atmosphere; it's the very substance of what's being captured, stored, transferred, released, and recaptured. Photosynthesis provides plant life with the roots, stems, trunks, and leaves that in their very structure hold or sequester carbon. CO_2 is biochemical energy. The climate issue now is that burning fossil fuels is putting more of it into the atmosphere faster than a balancing amount can be sequestered in the plants, trees, and in the soil itself. Too much CO_2 in the atmosphere creates the "greenhouse effect," which causes changes in the climate that we're not happy about.

In what has been by and large a stable climate regime up to now, sunlight has come on down to warm the ground and the oceans. The earth's warmed surface holds some of that heat and releases some of it back in the form of infrared radiation, which is invisible to us. This infrared radiation, or light, would keep going straight up and out of our atmosphere, taking all that warmth with it, were it not for the gases (most important, CO_2) that hold it in. Without them the earth would be way too cold for us to live on. Ergo, the guardian gases act like the glass in a greenhouse, letting in sunlight and retaining some of it. So now we have too much CO_2 in the atmosphere, and it's holding in too much warmth.

THE FEELING IS MUTUAL

As the seasons get torqued by warmer weather coming earlier in the year, the cues that schedule animal behavior are changing. Yellow-bellied marmots studied for thirty-five years at the Rocky Mountain Biological Lab in Crested Butte are coming out of hibernation an average of twenty-three days earlier than historically, and this affects what plants they eat.[75] Scientists identify an increased "asynchrony" in predator-prey and insect-plant systems due to this warming, but the disconnect has further consequences, as this insect-plant dynamic also interacts with the predator-prey dynamic. Consider the fungus pine blister rust, wreaking destruction on whitebark pine forests in the West because the mountain pine beetle that carries the disease is taking big advantage of warmer temperatures. Altering its life cycle, the mountain pine beetle now takes one year to produce a generation, rather than the previous two. This results in big populations spreading more pine blister rust. The whitebark pine have also languished because fire suppression has allowed Douglas fir to grow up big and tall, shading them out. So what happens when you lose white-bark pine, aside from missing its aesthetic on the landscape?

Whitebark pine has a mutualistic relationship with Clark's nut-cracker, named for William Clark of that most famous western expedition. The Corps of Discovery took it for a woodpecker, but it is in fact a corvid, and the Clark's nutcracker performs loud vocalizations that do its crow lineage proud. The term "mutualism," mentioned earlier, means the species evolved together, through interactions that do both parties good. Whitebark pinecones don't open naturally, like most other pinecones do, but are ripped apart exclusively by Clark's nutcrackers, which feed on some seeds and cache the rest for later. On the Galapagos Islands, those famous multiple species of finches each have different styles of beak evolved to perform a specific function, but the Clark's nutcracker has a beak that combines most of them. The bird pounds into the cone as if with a hammer or a chisel. It plucks the seeds out and stores them in a pouch under its tongue. Once it has pocketed roughly eighty seeds, the nutcracker finds a place to "locate" them, then uses its bill like a hoe, swiping the ground to make a trench as a gardener does to plant seeds. It coughs up the seeds one by one, placing three to five seeds at each location, and covers them with soil. In a year of heavy seed production, a Clark's nutcracker can bury nearly 100,000 seeds; it remembers exactly where by using landmarks, for up to nine months, and comes back to eat up at least some of them. This bird is capable of planting an entire forest in its lifetime. The whitebark pine needs Clark's nutcrackers to continue its lineage, and the bird needs the tree. Although the Clark's nutcracker can eat other seeds, they don't have the same density of nutrients as the whitebark pine's and are more easily gotten at; thus, there's much more competition from other birds and small mammals for them. It's really like the whitebark pine saves itself up especially for the Clark's nutcracker.

The nutcracker goes for the pine nuts beginning in mid-August, when they are ripe, which is just when grizzly bears start losing interest in everything but eating, and prefer to eat whitebark pine nuts above all else. The whitebark pine nuts are high in fat and protein, and the bear is now in a stage of "hyperphagia," anticipating hibernation. The bears raid the birds' caches and gobble the nuts. When grizzlies in Yellowstone don't get enough to eat from the whitebark pine nuts, they venture closer to humans, which is dangerous to both bears and people. There's a correlation between low whitebark pine nut years and higher grizzly mortalities. In deciding to put the grizzly back on the Endangered Species List in 2009, from which it had been removed for two years, Judge Donald Molloy cited the decline in whitebark pine as one reason for doing so. To reprise our theme: Everything is connected.

DON'T SHOOT

Chris Ray didn't so much inherit her now twenty-three-year-old pika project from Mike Gilpin as relieve him of its burden. Mike Gilpin just isn't too keen on the persistent attention to detail required by field study, and Chris Ray, who is a research associate in the Department of Ecology & Evolutionary Biology at the University of Colorado–Boulder, excels at it. Not that the study site is difficult—on this normally 5-mile hike up to Emerald Lake in Hyalite Canyon, near Bozeman, Montana, this summer 2 more miles are added by the closing of a Forest Service road, while a new parking lot is constructed at the trailhead. And not that the study subject poses more than the usual difficulties—pika are small rabbit relatives that live here in talus slopes, which are big spills of rock deposited by glacial ripping and roaring. The talus is hard to hike over, if you are me (not Ray). Pikas are saucy little bunnies, and one of the main things they do is cache "haypiles" in the rocks. That means they race around with flowers in their mouths much of the time. And when they aren't mowing down vegetation and stuffing it into their winter hoard, they sit on the rocks looking darn cute, or yelling at you. Their calls have been described as "cheeps," and the juveniles do sound like that, but the adults make much longer, louder declarations that remind me of the squealing honk of a clown horn.

The fact that Gilpin was a bit short on the details became clear to Ray when she joined him at the outset of his field study of pika at Emerald Lake. "He asked the class in San Diego if anyone wanted to work with him on this metapopulation project," Ray says. "So I volunteered. He said, 'Can you bring a gun?' Now, I'm a twenty-something student and he's a famous professor, so I say, 'I guess so.'" (Ray actually tried to check her father's rifle in her luggage at the San Jose airport; needless to say, it was confiscated.) "Mike wanted to do a 'disturbance experiment,'" she tells me. "He thought he would shoot out all the pika on a talus slope, and then see if it got recolonized. The trouble was, neither of us could shoot." By the time they got out onto the talus, Ray mustered up the moxie to suggest to the revered man that they try another tack. "I said, 'Mike, we'll shoot and miss. The pika won't come out again for another two hours. We will have no way of knowing if we got them anyway.'" So no pikas were harmed in the initiating of this study.

When they started, neither Gilpin nor Ray could have anticipated that pika would become the poster child for climate change, which the species has, partly through the efforts of the Center for Biological Diversity to get them on the Endangered Species List. Recently the North America Congress for Conservation Biology designated "Stony the pika" as its mascot, noting that since pika are largely alpine animals, extremely sensitive to high temperatures, and are poor dispersers, they are "a candidate indicator species for responses to global climate change."[76] The congress acknowledges that while the pika listing has been denied (thus far) due to local abundance and widespread distribution, "some historic pika populations have gone locally extinct within the past century, most likely due to climatic influences," and this warrants further study. What is now supported in spirit by Gilpin, who provides Ray and her crews with the respite of showers and beds midway through her two-week field season each summer, has been for the past twenty-one years Ray's study "to evaluate evidence for competing hypotheses about the nature and mechanics of contemporary range shift in a species noted for its sensitivity to climate."

In some ways, because they are so limited to a particular part of the ecosystem, and don't disperse all that much, pika are not addressed directly by Spine of the Continent efforts to create linked landscapes. On the other hand, in their noted "sensitivity to climate" and habituation to microclimates, and their evident suffering at the forward march of climate change, pika are a species by which we can better understand that ever-so important dimension of connectivity, the connection between biological systems (pika), earth systems (the mountain itself), and meteorological systems (climate). Also, science has a way of peeling back layers and revealing surprising truths. While many have written the end of the story for pika by pointing upward and finding nowhere for them to go, Chris Ray has in the back of her mind another idea. She wonders if what makes pika so sensitive and evidently vulnerable will wind up being their salvation. "Pikas are so good at finding the microclimate they need that they may avoid climate change altogether," she says. That of course also depends on our protecting the mountain ecosystems that provide so much heterogeneity, or pockets of difference, which of course have to stay connected to each other to persist.

MARKING THE TERRAIN

When Ray took over the study, her father, a surveyor, helped her set up two stations in the Hyalite Canyon from which he used a theodolite (which measures horizontal and vertical lines using a rotating telescope) to establish transects. "We didn't have radios available for the project in those days," Ray remembers. "So I ran along the canyon with mirrors. We signaled to each other with flags on a stick." The transects were marked with sprayed white dots on the talus, which are still there. "Now of course I use GPS," Ray says, "which is more convenient, but less accurate." The vertical walls of the canyons can interfere with the satellite signals.

At Emerald Lake, located in a box canyon at about 9,500 feet, she collects data about pika presence and absence at 100 control points in a study area that is overall 2 kilometers by 3 kilometers. Several years ago she added a comparison site in Colorado. She also tracks temperature throughout the year using "iButton" data loggers dispersed around the talus. Using four different ear positions and five colors of tags, Ray ear-tags pika annually—this summer she tagged 45—thus recognizing their individuality, by which she can keep track of their mortality. To date she has tagged and tracked 625 unique pika; she has observed some individuals as many as nine years in a row. This year she documented a very high mortality rate in Colorado. Ray surmises that the late snowmelt caused many pika to starve to death, since they weren't able to forage on their usual schedule. Pika typically colonize one talus slope per breeding pair, but the coexisting male and female aren't known to have much to do with each other. This year Ray is intrigued by unusually prevalent signs that the males are actually provisioning haypiles for the females. Nursing offspring can delay female haypiling, and it's possible the males are helping out.

BEAUTY AND THE BEAST

You might guess from the name "Emerald Lake" that this is a beautiful spot, and you would be right. The lake itself is indeed a small jewel, and in mid-August 2011, when I join Ray, the relatively late snowmelt here, along with the elevation, has resulted in an extended wildflower season. One afternoon I walk along the roaring Hyalite Creek through mobs of wildflowers that reach my chin. The scene is bucolic but also intense, all this color, this profusion of form. There are successive rain showers, and gusty winds come and go, one waterfall after another hurtles downstream, and the psychedelic greenery blows around, shaking off water. It feels crazy that I am witnessing this alone. I want to step up on a rock and testify.

It is *not* such fun, for me, to hike up the talus slopes. These are intermittent gullies making gray stripes down the otherwise evergreen-covered rises around Hyalite Canyon, which is named for a mineral in the opal family that appears on some of the slabby boulders, glistening like hard water drops in the sun. Ray is gone from her tent at the campsite before 6:30 each morning, carrying equipment to the talus slopes, leaving her husband, Jeff Van Lanen, and her almost-four-year-old son, Max, asleep. By 7:30 her two young research assistants head out after her, armed with radios and more equipment. They call in to Ray and she gives them GPS points for her location. The first morning I head out with them, it takes us a full hour to reach her. Once we start ascending the talus, I fall behind these two fit youngsters, but it's no cakewalk for them, either, I can tell. The rocks are piled up on each other and unsteady. The angle is steep. They are braver about their footing, but they both fall, and the thing about youth is, they don't care. I am rather obsessed with the distinct possibility of breaking my leg.

THE LIFE OF A FIELD BIOLOGIST MOM

Van Lanen and Max bring us lunch in the talus fields. I am still exhausted from getting here, and marvel in awe as the two young research assistants head off with Van Lanen, who is an ice climber and all-around mountaineer, for what they describe as a bit of downtime. The three of them ascend the nearly vertical face of the canyon. Ray transfers data from the iButtons to the laptop, which reads them directly through a cable. She is also able to instantly compare this year's data to last year's. Max is very articulate and relational, and chatting with him I almost forget he is a child, except that he keeps steering the conversation back to superheroes. I follow Max's directives back and forth between a rotten tree stump and a fallen log; in this childhood interval—the likes of which the experts would heartily approve—we ascribe superhero personalities to chunks of wood, small pinecones, and bark, and purpose them in a drama that unfolds real-time from Max's mind. Periodically I look up at the three hikers, tiny dots on a rock face, who look like they are being moved by an unseen hand on Valium. Later I think myself very clever to go back to the campsite with Max and Van Lanen, correctly assuming that with this small child along, a less precipitous path will be chosen. But it's still incredibly steep, and going down is harder than going up. Max cheers me along, "Slow and steady, Mary Ellen! Easy does it!" When we hit a dirt trail he releases his father's hand and takes mine. We are rather stretched between two gullies and I say, "Max, is this comfortable for you?" "Yes, Mary Ellen, my hand is very comfortable in yours."

BUT IT WAS TOO HOT

Pika spend all summer "making hay while the sun shines," because they don't hibernate. They live off their haypiles, in the talus, under the snow, all winter, and when the snow melts, they come out and start all over again. These little bunnies take the Goldilocks syndrome very far, with finely tuned sensitivity to hot and cold. While other animals have natural thermoregulatory responses to temperature fluctuations, the pika have to deal with these behaviorally. Because they don't hibernate, they need a very insulating fur coat, which is good in winter, but in summer it becomes a problem, because they can't get rid of heat. To help deal with the winter chill, the resting body temperature of a pika is near its lethal maximum, which is what makes them intolerant to summer heat. Pika have to be out working hard all summer to collect enough food to last them all winter, and during the hottest part of summer days they take refuge in the spaces under the rocks in the talus.

Ray calls the talus a "rocky carapace," making a skeletal analogy. Thus, the actual rocks of the mountainside provide for the pika what a turtle's shell does for the reptile, including protection from predators and climate. The talus itself is a rock-ice formation, which evinces the chimney, or stack effect. Warmer air is more buoyant than cold and it rises. The air spaces and the angle of the talus create a flue by which the temperature below the rocks stays colder, and ice forming there melts more slowly, providing water more gradually into the warmer months when aboveground ice has already melted, flowed, and evaporated away. This water feature of the talus is going to mean more to us as well—as the glaciers recede, we will count more on what is essentially a storage capacity to mete out water. In the summer, pika need the cool provided by the talus, and in the winter they need the blanket of snow to insulate and keep them relatively warm.

As Ray describes it, there's a "one-two punch" that takes pika out, and that is chronically high summer temperatures and severe, cold winters with no snow. "That's the hypothesis to beat."

CLIMATE CHANGE ALSO RISES

In the six years since it was published, Camille Parmesan's paper "Ecological and Evolutionary Responses to Recent Climate Change"[77] has been cited in other people's papers 1,198 times.[78] Parmesan is a professor of integrative biology, and with the other members of the 2007 Intergovernmental Panel on Climate Change, a recipient of the Nobel Prize. Somebody else do the math, please, but Parmesan would seem to be keeping pace with MacArthur and Wilson in the matter of influencing her peers (their "Theory of Island Biogeography" paper has been cited 9,506 times in forty-five years). One of Parmesan's assertions in her highly influential paper is that "range-restricted species, particularly polar and mountaintop species, show severe range contractions and have been the first groups in which entire species have gone extinct due to climate change."

Species extinction is the primary focus of the Center for Biological Diversity (CBD), a pugnacious NGO devoted to enjoining the federal government to protect species and their habitats under the Endangered Species Act. The US Fish and Wildlife Service (FWS) is the agency that administers the Endangered Species Act for species occurring in the terrestrial realm, and the National Oceanic and Atmospheric Administration (NOAA) for those in the aquatic; they share responsibility when a species bridges both worlds. There is a state petition for a listing and a federal listing. The federal listing is better known to the general public, but the states can grant protection more quickly. While there is a candidate selection process by which both agencies can nominate species for protection, species get nominated for listing mostly by NGOs that litigate to make FWS consider their cases. They are leveraging a dispensation in the law that says citizens can invoke it.

The idea that a species can be listed and thus protected because of climate change is new, and controversial. In 2007, CBD petitioned both the

State of California and the FWS to list the pika. They have been denied by FWS but are still battling at the state level. As of this writing in late 2011, Shaye Wolf, who is the PhD biologist in CBD's climate change program, feels that the entire species should be listed but that a single subspecies of pika, disappearing as we speak from the Great Basin, has the best chance to eventually win this protection. One of the interesting things about this saga is the way science and politics have mixed it up over the pika listing. What is often an impasse between the two in this instance coheres into something of an unholy alliance.

Chris Ray contributed analyses that were used in support of the petition, but she doesn't feel all that hot about the Endangered Species Act (ESA). "The act isn't strong enough to enforce any action against climate change," Ray tells me. She is echoing what many conservationists in this era worry about, which is that right-wing anti-ESA sentiment will be empowered by extending the law where it has only begun to be applied, into the future of climate change. "On the other hand," she concedes, "I find zero evidence that we can do anything for them except turn the climate around. These animals respond strongly to climate. Nothing but climate change can wipe out this species."

"There's a disconnect," says Wolf. "Many scientists who are doing studies on individual species don't understand the ESA and how it operates." Greg Loarie, the Earthjustice attorney trying the pika cases on behalf of the CBD, says, "Some scientists are convinced that if species are listed it will provoke a bunch of red tape that will restrain their work." Both Wolf and Loarie point out that lockdown on a species is not the outcome of a listing. Rather, a considered, step-by-step analysis of what it needs to recover is instigated. Scientists persist in feeling the Endangered Species List takes something away from them, although as Loarie says, "Once the northern spotted owl was listed, a whole lot more money got poured into studying it."

ORWELLIAN

"I'm sorry you have to read this," Shaye Wolf says to me. While slogging through a thirty-four-page document with the catchy title "Endangered and Threatened Wildlife and Plants; 12-Month Finding on a Petition to List the American Pika as Threatened or Endangered," I console myself with 62 percent cacao chocolate and frequent brain baths in "Politics and the English Language." The FWS finding states on page 7 that "climate change is a potential threat to the long-term survival of the American pika. Thermal and precipitation regime modifications may cause direct adverse effects to individuals or populations. Climate change has the potential to contribute to the loss of and change in pika habitat." And on page 9 that "the biology of the American pika makes the species a useful indicator of changing climatic conditions and useful to test extinction theory." On page 10 the finding notes "the disappearance of populations at relatively lower elevations and hotter sites ... and loss ... from habitats that do not maintain adequate snowpacks," and acknowledges on page 11 "that there is evidence that eastern Sierra Nevada and Great Basin pikas may be responding to recent climate change."

But then the finding seems to change its tune. On page 15: "We do not anticipate the species to be adversely affected on a range-wide basis by increased summer temperatures. . . . This determination, paired with the fact there is a significant amount of habitat not at risk from climate change, prevents the species from being threatened or endangered from climate change." How did we suddenly get from grim observation to this ameliorating shrug? What is "significant habitat not at risk from climate change"? This whole earth is at risk from climate change.

As Orwell says of similarly convulsive and opaque stringing-together of words, "The writer either has a meaning and cannot express it, or he inadvertently says something else, or he is almost indifferent as to whether his words mean anything or not." None of this verbal dillydallying was, in the end, used to buttress the FWS's decision to turn down the petition. Instead, it dismissed the climate modeling CBD had provided to illustrate how no matter the situation the pika may or may not be in right now, their future is bleak. CBD provided papers from three sets of scientists who projected higher temperatures and shrinking ranges for pika through 2100. The Fish and Wildlife Service response was that they could use climate projections that go only through 2050.[79]

The FWS finding buckles with internal contradictions, but there is no way to lay the blame for that on a single author. Patches of it are clear and persuasive. Patches of it are admirable historical overviews of pika biology; all the pika bases are covered here. But as with any listing decision, the final product is something of a black box. Clearly multiple hands wrote, edited, and re-edited this document. It is a palimpsest. In fact, there is a distinct sense in this document that originally the narrative direction was going somewhere different from where it ended up.

BROTHERS IN ARMS

Disillusionment is not something you want to see on Scott Loarie's face. Loarie is a postdoc at the Carnegie Institute for Global Studies, and yes, Greg Loarie's brother. They are both young men in their thirties, both extremely well-spoken, both earnest. They're not afraid to bridge the science-policy divide by representing both sides in one family, and applying their separate expertise to the same issue. They do the right thing because it should be done! What did their parents feed them? The answer is: a steady diet of nature. The Loarie brothers grew up in a rural part of Northern California's wine country and, in Greg's words, "spent most of our time messing around by the Russian River."

Scott Loarie is, as Henry James would say, one upon whom nothing is lost. He pretty much sees what has to be done and does it. After attending meetings where senior scientists were hashing out the question of how fast climate change is moving, Loarie decided to actually answer the question. The numbers he came up with matched those produced by Phil Duffy, a physicist at Climate Central, a Palo Alto think tank. Their subsequent collaboration resulted in a paper titled "The Velocity of Climate Change,"[80] which among other things indicates mountainous regions will be refugia for species as the beast advances. On the issue of the pika, Loarie took note of the questions around climate science and went twelve ways from Sunday to tighten every potential loophole in the statistics and modeling business to show without question where pika are disappearing. "What's cool, what's novel about what he did, is that he partitioned uncertainty in the extinctions process explicitly, and quantitatively," says

Erik Beever, a research ecologist for the US Geological Survey in the Northern Rocky Mountain Science Center, and a frequent collaborator of Chris Ray's. The idea that the FWS could simply throw all his work away because it extended fifty years past their (arbitrary) cutoff point would seem to issue from someplace separate from common sense.

As I muddle along in the pika world, seeing puzzlement and disappointment in the faces of Greg and Scott Loarie and Shaye Wolf, hearing from Chris Ray that FWS had used a "sleight of hand" to deny the listing, and hearing some other off-the-record grumblings from various participants, I put the whole thing up to, perhaps, a difficult suite of personalities. I hear about an old-time pika scientist who did experiments on pikas in the 1970s to gauge their heat tolerance. He kept pika aboveground in cages, giving them water and food but not allowing them to run into the talus when the sun got hot. That's how we know that pika die at 78 degrees Fahrenheit—because they died. Perhaps this scientist thinks he wouldn't be able to do that kind of experiment if the species was listed. Shaye Wolf had remarked to me that one reason the historic listing of the polar bear's threatened status due to climate change succeeded was that all the scientists involved were on the same page.

Gary Frazer, assistant director of endangered species for FWS, tells me that "we're dealing with a threat that is different than anything we've dealt with before. Changes in atmosphere, precipitation patterns, temperatures, and they result from many sources of greenhouse gas emissions. The effects are global. The relationship between a particular emitter and the effect on the species—the causal connection is difficult to make. We can't make it now." Okay . . . I get that . . . but you listed the polar bear. And anyway, this is not the rationale posited for denying the pika listing.

PIKA IN PERIL

In February 2011 I attend a pika consortium in Riverdale, California. Much of the discussion devolves around streamlining a way to collect pika pellets to better quantify presence-absence data. There is also discussion about the best way to anesthetize pika, which have a habit of dying when you look at them cross-eyed.

An affable white-haired man runs around the conference room distributing papers. "No one asks for these, no one cites these!" he says. "Take them, read them!" He turns out to be Andrew Smith, who is the senior statesman of pika. "This is so great," he says. "Forty years ago I had nobody to talk with about pika." Smith has been studying pika longer than anyone else, and is active in conservation efforts to halt mass extermination of Tibetan pika in Asia. There are researchers here whose work he approves and others whose work he disapproves; Smith is asked by journals to peer-review virtually every pika paper submitted, and so he wields enormous power over their careers. When it is his turn to present, Smith puts forth "a plea. We have to get the science right. Don't title your papers 'Pika in Peril.' That's value-laden. Use 'Pika Population Study' instead." Chris Ray drily remarks that the study he's referencing got funding "because pika are in peril."

"Another plea. There is a photograph of a pika at the California Academy of Sciences. The caption says the animal dies when the temperature reaches 78 degrees. The general public now thinks all pika die when the temperature reaches 78! But that's based on my study, as you know, and anybody who reads it knows I placed pika in cages and didn't let them move. The public does not know this!"

Despite the mundanity around hammering out things like pellet transects, there is an urgency and tension in the room all day, partly due to the submerged personal tensions, but also due to the general awareness that however any of these people feel about the Endangered Species Act, most of them are working on studies that are finding pika declines. Near the end of the day Shaye Wolf speaks, and asks in her clear and passionate way that those present support the efforts of the Center for Biological Diversity to get the pika listed.

Chris Ray comments that "Shaye is asking us to look into the future. We're having difficulty agreeing about what's happening now. But it's a good guess that pika will be negatively affected by climate changes." Another participant comments that "it's not just about temperature, but about changes in predators, parasites, disease, community. We don't understand ecology well enough to predict it."

As the meeting concludes, Andrew Smith beckons me. "I have things to tell you," he says. We chat. "How could you fry those bunnies?" I ask him. He makes a very sad face. "Oh God, it was the '70s. We didn't know what we were doing. I would never do that again."

Then Smith tells me that the FWS contacted him to comment on the petition to list the pika. "I said, 'You bet I want to comment.' But I was in Tibet and I couldn't do it in their time frame. So they waited for me. I missed the deadline, so my comments are not in the public record, but they heard me." Scales drop from my eyes. "I hate the Center for Biological Diversity," he says. "I used to support them. But this, this is nonsense. There are pika all over the place." I say, "But that doesn't mean there always will be." "I believe in climate change," Smith asserts. "It's real. But if you promote bad science around it, you hand the naysayers ammunition. It's difficult for me to figure out how to engage."

"Did you see that guy?" Smith asks me. "The one on the screen?" That would be Scott Loarie, who had Skyped into the gathering. "His brother is the Earthjustice lawyer on this, so I'm totally outflanked." Interesting that Smith is finding politics at play in other people's actions when he has just confessed to plying them himself. I say, "I think those two are trying to save nature." "Oh, I know," Smith says. "I guess so." "Do you have trouble with the computer modeling?" I ask. "Yes!" he says.

In his response to the pika petition, Smith emphasizes that the disappearing pika populations are "peripheral to the main body distribution of the American pika," and that pika are more adaptable than is generally understood. He slams Loarie's work but according to different terms than those upon which it was written: namely that it "cites no papers concerning the biology of the species and fails to list any of the restrictive assumptions of the climate-envelope model utilized. It is hard to know what to make of this analysis, but it would be in error to put too much emphasis on a document of this nature." Addressing a similar analysis, he says, "It is difficult to examine these climate-envelope models with regard to the American pika as they do not incorporate the actual temperature that pikas experience, nor incorporate any of the biology of the species."

I can just feel a whole bunch of biologists wincing as I type those words. In fact, of course, the computer models do incorporate the biology of the species. Their starting point and center point are exactly what Smith says they ignore, the actual temperature that pikas experience. They model this temperature getting hotter. While yes, pika may find refugia for a time, at a certain point there will be no refugia. The coolness in the talus will be warmer. There is a lot of noise around what Smith is saying but essentially he is refusing the future scenario, and he handed the FWS a respected scientist's excuse to refuse it, too.

GENERATION GAP

Of consequence to conservation today is the divide between the older generation and the younger in the matter of computer modeling. Even Jim Estes, who was originally trained as a statistician, tells me that at a certain point he gave up trying to keep pace with the advances in computer software and statistical programming. "All these kids know GIS," he says. "They come out of graduate school with tremendous abilities to model." He is at least open to it and appreciates its powers. Many senior scientists embrace modeling as the way to do their work now but draw the line at future projections. "Smoke and mirrors! Smoke and mirrors!" more than one senior biologist calls it.

The whole idea that we have to look into the future if there is to be a palatable one meets with tremendous resistance. Some of it, of course, is from older scientists who deny that a new methodology has emerged. They have built careers and reputations on certain ways of seeing things, and they still need funding, too. Questions around future climate modeling are fair enough, and scientists all over the world are sweating out better and better ways to quantify the unknown. As John Isanhart, the lead FWS biologist on the pika petition, puts it, "Only God knows where species will live in the future." Isanhart praises Scott Loarie's work to me, even as he agrees with the decision to exclude its conclusions from the finding. "Scott did a probabilistic risk assessment. I really like it. Is it good for management decisions? We aren't there yet."

Woman Warrior

When I ask Kassie Siegel about the pika, her demeanor changes. We have talked for about an hour, and she has with consistent ebullience batted away all the usual caveats people level against the Endangered Species Act as applied to climate change. Siegel heads the Climate Law Institute of CBD and is widely credited with getting the polar bear listed as endangered due to climate change. She is also credited with helping the nascent realm of climate law develop into something meaningful. Upon her being named one of California's ten most influential lawyers in 2010, Patrick Parenteau, professor at Vermont Law School, put it this way: "If I was facing extinction, I'd want Kassie Siegel as my lawyer."

With patience Siegel explains to me that naysayers claim "'you can't trace the path of a carbon molecule to the death of a polar bear, so we aren't going to do it.' And we say, 'Yes, you do.' Dioxin is a molecule, like mercury, and it can be traced. You can measure it like you measure mercury in a fish. There's no reason for treating greenhouse gases any differently." About the ESA she says, "It's the world's most successful biodiversity protection statute. Ninety-nine percent of the species on it have not gone extinct. Many others have. ESA has led to designated habitat and recovery plans. It has massively elevated conservation. It is an overwhelming success. It works; it's powerful, and that's why it's controversial.

"The pika is a really sad story," she says quietly. "I hope that as a society we can turn things around and still live in a world where we have pika. But I'm afraid pika will be a cautionary tale."

CHAPTER 16

Eyes in the Sky

WALKING THROUGH ANY QUARTER OF CALIFORNIA'S SILICON VALLEY, the term "climate change" feels like an oxymoron. It's early March, the temperature is 74 degrees, and humidity is 21 percent. Last week every day was precisely the same temperature, and the Internet-published forecast going forward is one happy sun after another. I'm at Moffett Field, home to NASA's Ames Research Station, located between Sunnyvale and Mountain View, and both purviews indicated by the names of these places are plausible. There is no one around.

Moffett Field was built in 1933 and its buildings look like long dormitories. At this former naval facility, NASA took provenance in 1958 when Congress passed the National Aeronautics and Space Act. One of the world's most powerful computers, Pleiades, is located here, but the fusty campus feel of the place belies this. I'm going to talk to Rama Nemani, director of NASA's Ecological Forecasting Lab, and the master of this particular universe, which feels more and more like an alternative to the one I'm used to.

I enter the building where Nemani works; it appears to be deserted. I walk down low, silent halls, take a staircase or two up to another floor. More empty rooms. I hear masculine murmurings and coughs but see not a soul. It's like a scene out of Michael Soulé's favorite book, *The Disappearance*. When I find Nemani he is sitting with settled intensity in a moderately sized office in front of two unremarkable-looking computer screens. There is some sort of marking between his eyebrows at the top of his nose; I can't tell whether it's a patch of eyebrow or a shadow or a birthmark or what. I think, "Okay, here's where some force field comes shooting out of that place in his head and pins me to the wall." He turns out to be a nice guy.

One of the constant themes of this book is the distribution of species, the concept of which spurred on Darwin to figure out natural selection, and the drill-down of which led to MacArthur and Wilson's theory of island biogeography. Evolutionary biologists such as Michael Soulé and Mike Gilpin applied population viability analysis to the problem of figuring out the level of extinction risk for particular species. The species-area relationship, which broadly indicates there are more species in larger areas, is now also under the scrutiny of one of the most sophisticated technologies mankind has yet devised: remotely sensed data from aircraft and satellites modeled using gargantuan computing power.

Remote sensing sounds like something you do to prevent stubbing your toe in the dark. But in the context of ecological application, it basically refers to aircraft or satellite detection of electromagnetic energy. Land cover and land use are measured mostly by passive sensors roaming the skies that register visible, near-, and middle-infrared and thermal infrared radiation much the way a camera captures light to make an image. Active sensors, including light detection and ranging (LIDAR) sensors, emit pulses of radiation and read the returned signal to outline the physical properties of the objects it is trained on.

Remote sensing is used to identify habitat types, such as forests or grasslands, the density of species living in which is inferred. As Nemani tells me, "Anything that happens on the surface of the earth has a signature that we can use a sensor to detect—but 'biodiversity' is something we cannot directly express. We can define features of biodiversity as equal to so much light coming off the ground, but we are looking at manifestations of the process, not the process itself." But remotely sensed imagery is hugely useful to conservation biology. It delineates land-cover changes, such as deforestation at scales ranging from local to continental, and using the species-area curve, it allows biodiversity loss to be quantified. The remotely sensed imagery provides the area part of the curve.

THE GREEN PULSE

Nemani is the chief architect of NASA's Terrestrial Observation and Prediction System, or TOPS, which can basically keep daily tabs on what's happening on the earth. TOPS combines ground, aircraft, and satellite sensor data with weather, climate, and applications models. For example, TOPS provides the California wine industry with sea surface temperature projections for six to twelve months, helping management adjust planting and harvest times accordingly. Early in the growing season, remotely sensed data about canopy cover can even guide vintners about pruning schedules. In the annals of "connectivity," TOPS observes and models the relationship between Earth's physical systems, such as weather, and Earth's biological systems, such as growing grapes.

Satellite remote sensing as practiced by NASA is definitely big-picture, but technology is increasingly allowing it to be useful at smaller and smaller scales. "When you talk about continental scale, Mary Ellen, and that's what Soulé and company are talking about, managing at the scale of the continent, you have to keep tabs on it," Woody Turner tells me. Turner manages the Biodiversity and Ecological Forecasting programs at NASA headquarters. He oversees the agency's basic research and its applications to use satellite-derived information to "understand the relationship of biodiversity to climate, landscape change, and ecosystem function"; he is the administrative side and Nemani is the technical side of this effort.

"When I first started asking land managers what NASA could do for them," Turner remarks, "some said, 'Help me see this building or that parking lot.'" He says that federal land-management agencies, such as the US Fish and Wildlife Service and the National Park Service, used to be largely concerned only with protecting lands under their jurisdiction, but climate change has gotten everyone to think about the bigger picture. "In the last four to five years we've seen a huge change of attitude; everyone's concerned about connectivity, about how their place on the map connects with other agencies' places. Climate change is leading us to focus on the matrix, those lands surrounding the parks and refuges, along with the broader airshed and watershed." Observations at vastly different scales are starting to match up.

In March 2011 Nemani unveiled NASA Earth Exchange, or NEX, again a mind-boggle of a platform, principally designed by Nemani's team in Mountain View. NEX makes the vast computing power of Pleiades, and many of the models developed for use on it, available to the public at large.[81] Describing it as a scientific social-networking portal, Nemani says NEX "engages more people to connect the dots. It is a place where you can go and have access to all the data, and all the models developed across disciplines, so you don't have to solve them all over again." As an example of the efficiency and power of NEX, Nemani tells the story of two big droughts that occurred in the Amazon rain forest within ten years. "This is unheard of," he remarks. "You don't put the terms 'rain forest' and 'drought' together." The first one occurred in 2005, and "it took one and a half years to analyze data about it collected from three major sources. The second one occurred in 2010, and using NEX, we analyzed the data in one month."

Not only does NEX act like Hercules with data, but since it is equally available, it will streamline efforts to cope with climate change across the board. "So before NEX, San Francisco hires a consultant to analyze how the water scenario will change in the next fifty years. And LA hires one and Fresno hires one, and there's no sharing. It's all duplicative." NEX will save people the trouble of reinventing the wheel. Since NEX can provide both huge, macroscopic views of what's going on and can equally provide information down to the exact rate of evaporation or how much photosynthesis is going on within a particular field, it is an amazing tool for not only revealing where nature's connections are most vital, but where they are most stressed, and it allows monitoring these on a daily basis.

"What Rama did," Turner explicates, "is set up a computational framework that allows people to bring in environmental data from different scales—ground-based rain gauges, satellites—to integrate these data and plug them into models." Pleiades provides the power to do this; statistically the more data you have, the more opportunity there is to get something right. In terms of ecological forecasting, Turner says, "We're lost without the connection between space and ground. We are looking to connect information about ground-based species, their populations and distributions, with meteorological and other information."

Turner says that surprisingly, it is the relative paucity of biological data that constrains NASA's ability to do ecological forecasting. "In the early days I used to think, gee, we've only had satellites up since the '60s and '70s. We have only one generation of data, which isn't much, and that's kind of embarrassing because these biologists have been collecting data for years and years. Come to find there aren't that many longtime series of biological information out there." To measure climate change effects, you need to track where a species has lived over time. Relatively few museum collections include specimens taken from the same place at progressive dates, "so you can know for sure who lived where when. You can then say, 'Wow, these mice live much farther upslope than they did fifty years ago, and that corresponds to a change in temperature of X degrees.'"[82]

Despite Nemani's caveat that he is looking at manifestations of nature and not at the process itself, in one way of defining it he is looking at the essence of creation. "The common theme in all this," he tells me, "is sunlight. The sunlight falls on the earth. It is absorbed; it instigates photosynthesis, crops, the forest, the basic mechanism of life. The sensors collect sunlight coming down and then reflecting back to another satellite. That's how we tell how dense the forest is, or whether it is burning or not. It's largely based on radiation from the sun going back." There is sunlight, and then there is greenness. "If you don't have rain, you don't have greenness. Without green, you have no soil cover. Then you get erosion. We have this one measure, the green cover of the planet over the last thirty years. We can tell so much from that, how much deforestation has occurred, how much crop production decreased and increased where and when, how the plants and the landscapes are interacting." Nemani provides a different perspective on the same thing thousands of scientists are studying on the ground—but what a view.

One fan of the practical, on-the-ground uses of NASA's remote-sensing and modeling capacities is John Gross, climate change ecologist in the Inventory and Monitoring division of the National Park System. Of all the federal agencies, the National Park Service is perhaps the most sensitive to what climate change is doing to its job description, which is based on some pretty firm boundaries that are shifting as we speak. "We have so many problems within our fences," Gross comments, "but climate change has shown this is all a moving target." He tells me that, for example, recent big floods in Yosemite prompted the question of whether this is the new normal. "The floods washed out some of our campgrounds, bridges, and culverts. We built our culverts for 100-year floods. If we need to prepare for 10-year floods, maybe we need to put in bigger pipes. We probably need to change the timing of our prescribed burns. At a Yosemite lodge they were within two weeks of running out of water during a prolonged drought. Climate models predict fire season starting a month earlier. This has a really big impact on fire crews and could literally double the effect of fires."

Getting objective measurements and projections from an outside agency such as NASA provides individual park managers with modeling power they couldn't possibly generate on their own. "Rama did some model projections including snowmelt and runoff, which showed that 80 percent of the effects of climate change could be seen in the next thirty years," Gross says. "This tells us this is not something that's going to happen after I'm dead and gone. It's on the agenda now." In addition to increased flooding, there will be increased fire. No national park has boundaries drawn according to ecosystem definitions, and as climate change and habitat fragmentation advance, this is becoming more of a problem. Most parks are embedded in larger systems or overlap several. Gross and colleagues have been refining a "park-area-centered ecosystems" monitoring program and using TOPS to keep tabs on them. Using phenology (again, the cycle by which plants grow, bloom, and die back) as a leading indicator, park managers will be able to extrapolate animal movements on a daily basis. From leaf area it can actually provide daily measurements having to do with water, including evaporation, transpiration, stream flow, and soil water, and likewise having to do with the carbon cycle, including net photosynthesis, plant growth, and nutrient uptake and mineralization.

CHAPTER 17

Welcome Home

SUMMER'S LEASE HATH ALL TOO SHORT A DATE, PARTICULARLY IF YOU are relocating a family of beaver, and by August 1 Sherri Tippie has captured only Dad and the kids. "I'm not forgetting about Mama," says Tippie, stopping at a gas station outside Denver, Colorado, not only to fuel up but also to get bags of ice and Butterfingers. In the hours since Steve Reddy and another volunteer helped Tippie collect a third beaver kit from Sand Creek that morning, Tippie has circled back around and around again to the nagging fact that in several consecutive live-trapping forays, the matriarch of the family she is pursuing has eluded capture. Tippie opens the hatch of her small SUV and invites other travelers to come look while she pokes holes in the bags of ice and places them on top of a transport cage. "The water will drip down on them, keep them cool, remind them of home," Tippie explains to a woman in a powder-blue tracksuit. The woman is excited. "Can you wait here a sec?" She wants her husband and daughter to come look. "They've never seen live beavers before," she says. I hadn't either, until this morning, when I also got to hold one of the kits in my arms.

Sherri Tippie is a beaver celebrity. She has been written up in newspapers and featured on the Discovery Channel. People for whom she has relocated beaver include the Japanese musician Kitaro, whose photograph in Tippie's collection is signed with affection. Mary O'Brien asked her to write a thirty-page guide called *Working with Beaver for Better Habitat Naturally!* "Tippie is pure gold," says O'Brien. "I edited her pamphlet—mostly just took out about a thousand exclamation points." Tippie's pamphlet is not a lesson in biodiversity, but a how-to manual. Chapter 4 is titled "Let's Do Lunch: How to Protect Trees from Beaver" (wrap the trees loosely with wire). Chapter 5 is "Go with the Flow: Beaver Deceivers, Double Filter Systems & Castor Masters." With the right equipment and the right attitude, it is really not so hard to live with beaver. O'Brien has also had Tippie train field biologists in handling the animals. Partly what Tippie does is remind them that their study subject is sentient, has its own point of view, and should be respected.

"I used to feel so insecure and sometimes still do, you know," she confides to me. "I didn't go to college. I'm a hairdresser. I would talk to these biologists at the agencies and I was just in awe." In a wire transport cage in the back of Tippie's car, Daddy beaver looks with seeming equanimity back at the gas station gawkers. Piled up one on top of each other and huddled next to him are his three kits. They are not so sure. "Poor babies!" croons Tippie. "Can you imagine? What on earth? You're living in a creek and suddenly you're sitting in a cage, in a *car?*" Addressing what has by now become a small crowd of onlookers, Tippie explains that she is relocating these beaver from a municipal waterway where they are not wanted, to a rural idyll where they are eagerly awaited. "Don't worry, little ones," Tippie continues. "I'm taking you to a beautiful place, clean water, good food, the works."

The season for relocating beaver in Colorado is Memorial Day through Labor Day. Most beaver kits are born in May, and received wisdom provides that by two months old they can be moved. Tippie disagrees. She waits until July to trap beaver, and she insists on keeping the nuclear unit together. Tippie does agree with the Labor Day cutoff, giving the beaver enough time to establish a lodge before winter sets in. She's sincerely worried that since the matriarch of this family broke a trap and got away, she won't fall for the ruse again until next summer. The way Tippie explains it, the adult female is the brains of the beaver operation, and directs the building of their lodges and dams. "The males are like Homer Simpson," she says fondly. "'Dood-de-doot, what's this good smell? I think I'll eat it.' Click, you've trapped him. You see the dads hanging out with the kits while Mom is at work. Beaver are monogamous. Dad is going to be mighty lonely unless I get Mom, too. I'm *really* worried about this."

Sherri Tippie first took beaver matters into her own hands about twenty-eight years ago. One afternoon, while scrubbing her kitchen floor and tuned in to the television news, she heard that a nearby municipality had just hired a trapper to kill a beaver that was cutting down trees on a golf course. "I thought, oh *no!* These beaver are going to be killed for doing what beaver are supposed to do." Admittedly, the sight of felled aspen first thing in the morning might get kind of tiresome if you are managing a golf course and need to both remove the trees and replace them.

"But you don't have to kill the beaver!" she says. Tippie called the trapper directly and told him he could capture and move the animal; she had seen evidence of this on *National Geographic*. The trapper responded that every time he had tried to live-trap a beaver, it had drowned. Recounting this sort of thing incites Tippie to snorting derision. Tippie is tall and supremely feminine. She lives with and cares for her ailing mother ("Mama says if it was between her and the beaver, she don't know what would become of her"). For many years her regular job has been cutting prisoners' hair in the Aurora County Men's Jailhouse. Before this gig she was an Arthur Murray dancer. "Oh, I used to wear a bikini when I went in and started trapping beavers," she tells me. "I was having a great time. I was thinner then and, you know, pretty." Tippie has light blue eyes and big cheekbones—she is still pretty. Her bright red hair is a cue that her attitude is likewise tangy, and her language veers between the soothing dulcet tones she uses with animals and something a lot saltier. "I mean, motherf***er! You can't take the time to figure out how to trap one of God's precious animals and move it without *killing* it? Who the *f*** are *you?*"

As has happened with some frequency over her beaver-relocating career, Tippie eventually won over the trapper to her point of view. Fine, he said, relenting. Go ahead and trap the beaver yourself.

"But Mary Ellen," she explains to me, as we are driving to St. Malo's Catholic Retreat Center about two hours away, at the edge of Rocky Mountain National Park, "you know how people can, you know, set you up for failure? I smelled it." The Colorado Division of Wildlife loaned her two brand-new traps, still in their boxes. "They didn't give me any instructions for putting them together, or for operating them." Feeling the heat of their smirking obstruction, Tippie phoned the local newspaper. A reporter accompanied her and documented Tippie hauling the fifty-pound beaver into her arms and putting it in the backseat of her car. "I didn't know any better," she says about that. "My first 150 or so, I picked them right up. I put one arm under their butts. I was belly to belly with them and a nose in my face." Now she uses a smaller carrier to get beaver to their next destination; she drove that first beaver to Rocky Mountain National Park, which had given her permission to deposit it there. All told, Tippie has relocated more than 1,000 beaver since she got started.

One of Tippie's steadiest clients is Mike Earnest, maintenance supervisor with the City of Aurora, just outside Denver. It is Earnest who has directed us to the family of beaver in Sand Creek that are (mostly) now in the transport cage in Tippie's car. Earnest's division is storm water: "We do general maintenance, trash and debris, clear out household stuff people dump in the drainage channels. Aurora has four basins—we're mostly working with smaller creeks and channels. We're semiarid. The South Platte River is one of our largest but back east it would be considered a stream." Ruefully, Earnest tells me that Aurora provides excellent habitat for beaver—wide channels and open space, few predators (though there are coyote and fox around), and plenty of willow and cottonwood.

"This is my personal opinion," he tells me. "I'm very pro-beaver. Especially on the large opens." As beaver boosters will, Earnest enumerates their beneficial effect on our aquatic systems—their dams protect against floods; water retained by them is stilled, and thus dirt and mud can settle out. "The waterfowl and the fish come in," he says. "All this and the creation of calmer, cleaner water." The exigencies of civic life intrude. "Since we're in the storm-water line of work, we have to abide by federal government rules. We have to remove blockages from our creeks—it's a FEMA requirement. We have to maintain our channels to a minimally acceptable level. Our drainage system is rated accordingly, and that system is used to calculate flood insurance.

"Beaver are also a problem for us because we have so few trees along our drainage channel," he adds. "When they chew them down, people get alarmed. We had a call from a woman who thought kids were chopping down trees with axes. She thought there was vandalism going on."

So when Earnest hears of beaver in his waterways, he calls Tippie. "We pay her a set fee per beaver, and mileage. She finds the home for the beaver. Often it's ranchers who want them." Earnest is very fond of Tippie and laughs just thinking about her. "Have you seen her put her little attractant on her wrists, her eau de cologne?" Indeed I have. Tippie has concocted her own special mixture of beaver bait, made with castoreum she buys at conventional hunting and trapping stores. She has also been known to put beaver pee on her wrists. Suffice it to say Tom Ford might follow Tippie's lead, but the rest of us will stick to Flowerbomb.

The week before I joined her, Tippie and Reddy had visited Sand Creek several times, in one night getting Dad and two of the kits. Tippie sets her traps around 3 p.m. and is religious about revisiting them as early as possible the next day. "Some trappers leave their traps for days," she says, shaking her head. "Can you imagine leaving a poor frightened animal in a trap like that?" The night before I arrived in Denver, she had set her traps and was watching television with her mother at 9 p.m. News of a flash flood came across the screen and Tippie leaped into action. Reddy met her at Sand Creek and they waded back into it, in the dark, in the rain, to pull out the traps they had set earlier in the evening. "The lucky thing was, we had actually caught a beaver!" she tells me. "If the flood had hit while we were in the water, we would have been dead along with the beaver." The only time Tippie has lost a beaver was during a flash flood; her trap was submerged in the rapidly risen water and the beaver drowned. She's not about to let that happen again.

In pursuit of the rest of the family, we approach Sand Creek very simply, by wading down into its cloudy waters fully dressed at 7 a.m. on a hot July morning. The water reaches my collarbone, and I marvel at Tippie's navigation of the creek's uneven bottom, making her way through tangles of vines and branches lacing the waters. Several of the traps that morning are empty, and then we hit pay dirt with the little one destined for a family reunion. It is absolutely adorable, like a warm stuffed animal.

Joining the two kits she had already trapped, and their father, this almost complete beaver family is destined for St. Malo's Catholic Retreat Center in Estes, Colorado. St. Malo's sits on 160 acres just to the north of Rocky Mountain National Park and is lush and beautiful. "I don't know how she thought to contact me," she says of Sandy Harem, director of the John Paul II Adventure Institute, a summer program for Christian kids. "Sandy told me about a meadow on the property that they wanted to restore to full health. The Forest Service had told her to burn the meadow, but she wanted to try beaver instead. There had been beaver on the property in the past, so I was intrigued and thought it would work."

We arrive at St. Malo's, recognizing the entrance to the place by a tiny, picturesque stone chapel standing sentinel; we are greeted by a small crowd. The beavers are here! The beavers are here! After the heat and concrete of Denver and Aurora, the place is an idyll. Cameras are brandished. The wildlife manager of St. Malo's is fetched to take Tippie's trapping permit. Harem directs a group of kids on the younger side of adolescence to come watch. Keeping track of the effects the beaver will have on the ecosystem will become part of the camp curriculum. The kids have painted Harry Potter–style glasses on their faces and already look the part of wilderness nerds.

The stream here is a Platonic ideal, audible even above the chattering crowd, mesmerizingly clear, a stark contrast to the muddy slog of Sand Creek in which we waded not five hours earlier. When the trap is opened, Big Daddy Beaver quickly slips into the current; as he swims away, the beaver's pelt looks like another burbling surge of water. The first kit makes a break for it: good-bye and good luck. The second kit enters the water . . . and comes back out again. Tippie scoops it up. "It's cold, love, but you'll get used to it," she says. Under her breath she admits she knows the baby just wanted to say a formal good-bye. "I love you, too," she says, and puts it back in the water.

Harem takes Tippie, Steve Reddy, and me to lunch. The restaurant is cute as can be, nestled on a steep hillside like a tree house, and the food in front of the other patrons looks homemade. A waitress promptly takes our order. And then we wait. Harem tells us more about her John Paul

II adventure camp and about the Creatio program with which it is allied. The conversation thus takes a heavy-duty turn into hard-core Christianity, and since Tippie was pretty vocal on the trip about her disdain for organized religion, I start to worry. Our food hasn't come (ultimately we waited an hour for it, but it was good when it arrived). We're hungry and now we have God in the mix. Reddy puts his head down on his arms.

It's a fallen world, especially on an empty stomach. Tippie looks like she might blow. Then she collects herself and says, "I'm okay with anybody's beliefs, as long as they don't hurt anybody else. And my main view is that we all have to work together to heal this world. I think we should worship what really gives us life." Reddy sits up again, and our sandwiches arrive.

A year and a half later, in November 2011, St. Malo's retreat center burned. The little stone chapel was spared, and so was the lodge completed just months after the beavers were relocated there. Ricardo Simmons, director of Creatio, wrote me, "Everybody was OK, but pretty much most property was lost. St. Malo is temporarily closed, not sure it will be rebuilt. Last I saw the beavers were fine, their lodge seems to be going on. I guess now they will have greater peace and silence to be themselves."

TREK WEST

"This is a very crooked spine," someone says, laughing. I'm looking over the shoulders of a bunch of conservation professionals at a Spine of the Continent meeting in Tuscon, Arizona, in March 2012. They have gathered to plot out the route by which John Davis will physically traverse the spine in 2013, a journey the public is heartily invited to join at various junctures. Kurt Menke, Wildlands Network's GIS specialist and map-maker exemplar, has provided five big, detailed maps representing chunks of the spine from Mexico to Canada. The NGO representatives from each region are sketching out the route by which Davis will traverse their landscapes; they are discussing where he will be able to hike, where he'd be better off traveling by bicycle, and where he will utilize a lightweight, portable boat and travel by water. As I move among the five huddled groups, I'm struck by the similarity of the sight to what I imagine the first Wildlands meetings must have looked like, with opinions and magic markers flying over dense topographical depictions of the continent. Yet how very far we have come; Menke will take these five maps and in three hours synthesize their squiggles, making a single, glossy map of Davis's eventual journey, comprised of 3,975 miles of human-powered travel ("That's nothing!" says Davis). Intervals where he will need to be shuttled across inhospitable terrain by air or by car add up to 1,500 additional miles. Going over the map the next day, Davis calls it "a work of art. This is a great story we're starting to tell."

"I wanted to ground-truth the lessons of conservation biology," Davis explains, "to look and see evidence of what my teachers have been teaching me." John Davis is in his late forties, but he looks younger. He's boyishly handsome and, as one might guess, incredibly fit. He also eats like a teenager, which is amusing to watch. Davis and his mother, Mary Bird Davis, were on the original slate of folks starting up the Wildlands Project. Mary died in 2011; in her honor, Davis traveled the eastern seaboard that year, bringing attention to conservation issues along the way. He had a hard time keeping his weight up—the biking portion of the trip totaled approximately 4,000 miles; he hiked 2,000 and logged an additional 1,000 miles paddling. Davis himself has been active with Wildlands for twenty-five years. He was once a grants officer for the Foundation for Deep Ecology and editor of *Wild Earth* journal.

At this meeting Wildlands Network executive director Margo McKnight enjoins the participants to please, please, please start utilizing social networking sites to spread the word about Davis and his journey, called "Trek West." Although Wildlands Network must raise funds to adequately support Davis next year, McKnight points out that all told, "he's an incredibly cheap conservation strategy—runs on coffee and peanut butter." McKnight further points out that Davis's effort is, yes, similar to other heroic endurance feats, but it is also very different. "This isn't just about one man's journey," she says. "This is about connecting all our journeys—it is a huge, collective effort."

His East Coast trek made Davis "painfully aware of the challenges big animals face in just trying to get around. I saw hundreds if not thousands of dead animals along the road." Another observation concerns waterways: "The best hope for reconnecting the land is to buffer the riparian zones. Waterways are the arteries of the land, and taking care of them is the first step in knitting the landscape back together. A properly protected river offers great recreational opportunities, and habitat not only for aquatic animals but for other mammals, which are likely to follow rivers when they disperse."

Davis remarks that on his East Coast journey, "the most difficult lesson I learned is that all the terrific grassroots organization efforts—the land trusts, the advocacy groups, and even some great regional connectivity efforts—are totally inadequate. Every grassroots effort I came across is worthy and vital, but they have to come together somehow. We are not achieving connectivity on a continental scale, and we have to." Trek West is an opportunity for all of us to join the effort, by connecting with Davis and Wildlands Network via social media, and by joining him on his journey. Check it out on the Wildlands Network website (www.twp.org).

Before the meeting concludes, Kim Crumbo leads a champagne toast for Michael Soulé, who has been helping to hammer out how Davis will travel across Colorado. "The sole reason many of us are here is Michael Soulé, our stalwart. I first heard him speak in 1988 in Estes Park, Colorado. It was a spectacular event." Crumbo reflects on his own evolution: "I had acquired a number of skills as a Navy SEAL that were totally inappropriate for conservation," he says, laughing, and adds that he has learned a great deal from Soulé. "Michael is both a brave heart and a tender heart, which is something I aspire to. I'm proud to call him a friend. He's the father of conservation biology, but a lot more."

Soulé is taken by surprise and clearly moved. McKnight has put together a slide presentation in honor of him, and introducing it she says, "When I first heard Michael talk, I thought, of course, this is what we should be doing. Small conservation efforts should work together to get large conservation done. 'All you need is love,' is what he said, too!" Someone else calls out, "He also said he was the *mother* of conservation biology." "I was getting in touch with my inner feminine at the time," Soulé says, and we all raise a glass. "We wouldn't be doing Trek West without you, Michael," McKnight concludes. "We all love you. So cheers."

BE HERE NOW

Homo sapiens have gotten awfully good at analyzing nature. We are able to grapple with millions if not billions of pieces of data and assemble them into patterns that tell us (partly) how nature operates. But as we have refined our comprehension of how nature coheres, we have become even better at breaking nature apart. Whether it is God or some other entity that makes it, or even if creation makes itself, we have become the great unmakers. It is entirely within our powers to become as the people profiled in this book, cocreators of a healthy nature that respect and safeguard its processes.

Biogeography has been about understanding and appreciating place, as characterized by its climate, topography, vegetation, plants, and animals. Biogeography also encompasses the history of *Homo sapiens*. It is incumbent upon each of us to stop and appreciate where we live and who lives nearby—perhaps traversing the geography on a different schedule. And then to ask, how can I help my cotravelers keep on keeping on?

If you don't feel like traversing hundreds of miles under your own steam, tracking jaguar, or hauling beaver around, don't worry; you can still make a difference in connectivity conservation. Habitat is found everywhere. Even my urban deck qualifies as habitat because hummingbirds stop regularly to dine on a passionflower vine. Fire escapes and window sills can usually support a flowerpot or two; almost every kind of plant performs some sort of contributing function to the other life-forms around—bugs and birds, for example. All plants help clean the air, moderate temperatures, and sequester carbon.

If you have a garden or a lawn, your contribution is that much larger. Native plants evolved with soil, temperature, and precipitation patterns of an area, and it is best to plant them. San Francisco was originally sand dunes, but the climate is mediterranean, so plants suited to that climate do well there. Depending on where you live, it may take a bit of research to figure out what "native" means for your ecosystem. Connectivity starts with understanding where you are located, what "home" is, and that is not just your address.

Every once in a while a coyote from the Presidio National Park is spotted near my house, stalking miniature poodles, no doubt. This reminds me that living with carnivores in the 'hood is rather unnerving. Likewise a raccoon in your garbage is a pest, as is a beaver intent on flooding your backyard. Instead of having these critters killed outright, which is sometimes necessary, take the time to phone animal control, and figure out ways to minimize further unfortunate encounters. There are NGOs all over this country devoted to a piece of nature or a natural process or an environmental issue. As sociologist Doug Bevington shows, local grassroots activities have the most reliable impact. If you don't have the time to go out and pick up litter or help recuperate a creek yourself, even small donations to these groups go a long way.

The most important element in connectivity conservation is the land itself: habitat. Support open-space programs that help create conservation easements around development. If you are in a position to contribute to one, land trusts protect big swaths of nature into perpetuity—perhaps there is no greater gift to posterity. As much land as we can possibly safeguard from development is the way we want to go; where that is not possible, mindful placement of infrastructure to accommodate wildlife is the next best option. The thing to remember is that it is not just people and our buildings and roads using the landscape, and even when we don't notice plants and animals, we depend on them.

Only connect.

Endnotes

Chapter 1

1   The Montana Blackfeet are part of the Blackfoot Confederacy, which is completed by three more related nations in Alberta, Canada. The Blackfeet creation story has Old Man creating the first woman, her son, and a multitude of animals out of the earth, the same ground upon which Blackfeet generations have trod ever since.

2   Fox also found this reference to the Rocky Mountains in Washington Irving's *Adventures of Captain Bonneville,* in which if not the letter of the phrase, certainly the majesty of its context is conveyed, probably from the vantage of Mount Bonneville, Wyoming: "Here a scene burst upon the view of Captain Bonneville, that for a time astonished and overwhelmed him with its immensity. He stood, in fact, upon that dividing ridge which Indians regard as the crest of the world; and on each side of which, the landscape may be said to decline to the two cardinal oceans of the globe. Whichever way he turned his eye, it was confounded by the vastness and variety of objects. Beneath him, the Rocky Mountains seemed to open all their secret recesses: deep, solemn valleys; treasured lakes; dreary passes; rugged defiles, and foaming torrents; while beyond their savage precincts, the eye was lost in an almost immeasurable landscape, stretching on every side a dim and hazy distance, like the expanse of a summer sea."

3   I owe the term "American corridor" to Franz Schultz, a German photojournalist who is also really good at coming up with names. His book about the northernmost part of the SOC effort is called *Freedom to Roam,* which became the name of an NGO sponsored by the outdoor clothing company Patagonia.

4   Y2Y and Wildlands Network have common origins, formed at the same time and according to the same principles. Harvey Locke, who founded Y2Y, in an MOU between the organizations credits Wildlands Network as the impetus for applying large landscape connectivity principles to the Yellowstone-to-Yukon landscape.

5   Clevinger, Anthony, et al. "Highway 3: Transportation Mitigation for Wildlife and Connectivity in the Crown of the Continent Ecosystem," Final Report. 2010. Costs of carnivore mortality are not included in the study.

6   Quammen's *The Song of the Dodo* follows with equal parts charm and thoroughness the subject of island extinction and conservation all around the world, concluding more or less at the point where Michael Soulé has established the Wildlands Project to achieve physical connectivity on the ground. Interestingly, the book barely touches on climate change, which tells us that it wasn't quite on the radar even as

recently as 1996, when the book was published, its pressures not yet brought to bear on the science or the conservation.

7   Nature as mesh has also been taken up by cultural critics including Timothy Morton and Slavoj Zizek.

8   Joseph Epes Brown, *The Spiritual Legacy of the American Indian* (Bloomington, IN: World Wisdom, Inc., 2007).

Chapter 2

9   According to Michael Soulé, the seven deadly sins have pagan roots, but the concept was greatly amplified and embraced by Christianity, beginning with Pope Gregory in the sixth century.

10 The narrator of F. Scott Fitzgerald's emblematic novel *The Great Gatsby* calls his tale "a Western story." The electric fire of naive civilization telegraphing at its conclusion keeps consumer excitements burning. Leopold's counterforce in nature dies.

11 Merriam's list doesn't work everywhere, but it does in the Rockies: at the top, the arctic alpine zone grows lichen and grass; next comes the spruce forest of the Hudsonian zone; then the Canadian fir forest; followed by a transitional zone of open woodlands and ponderosa pine; next is the Upper Sonoran Desert of chaparral and sagebrush; and finally, the Lower Sonoran or hot desert. These life zones are roughly discernable down the Spine of the Continent and are one way to describe it. In 1947 Leslie Holdridge added his own diagram to the concept, dividing life zones by mean annual biotemperature; annual precipitation; and the rate of evapotranspiration. All of which is highly relevant given climate change.

Chapter 3

12 Janet Browne, *Charles Darwin: The Power of Place* (New York: Knopf, 2002).

13 Most of us, I would hazard to guess, not only have sympathy for Isabel Archer in this novel but consider her its heroine, the winner of the book, based on her admirable morality and mature acceptance of life. However, on purely evolutionary terms, she is the hands-down loser of the story. Her potential to reproduce is totally co-opted by Gilbert and company, and so are her other resources. She doesn't get to pass on her genes. The novel is a biological tragedy.

14 You can check out the maps for yourself: http://persquaremile.com/2011/01/03/the-map-that-started-it-all.

15 *Science* 326, no. 5956 (November 20, 2009): 1067–1068.

Chapter 4

16 Ayala was a famous student of the even more famous Theodosius Dobzhansky, one of the titans of evolutionary biology, who famously coined the phrase "Nothing in biology makes sense without evolution." Dobzhansky was a geneticist integral to the modern synthesis, which reconciled Darwin with genetics.

Chapter 5

17 Thomas Lovejoy is the chief advisor on all things to do with biodiversity to the World Bank and the UN, and his work has been among the most important in hashing all this stuff out.

18 Curt Meine, Michael Soulé, and Reed Noss, "A Mission-Driven Discipline: The Growth of Conservation Biology," *Conservation Biology* 20, no. 3 (2006): 631–651.

Chapter 6

19 See www.barcodeoflife.org.

20 Janet Browne, *The Secular Ark* (New Haven, CT: Yale University Press, 1983).

21 Aaron Sachs, *The Humboldt Current: Nineteenth-Century Exploration and the Roots of American Environmentalism* (New York: Viking, 2006).

22 Bill Moyers, *The Language of Life: A Festival of Poets* (New York: Doubleday, 1995).

23 Drengson is associate editor of *The Selected Works of Arne Naess* (Sausalito, CA: Foundation for Deep Ecology, 2005).

Chapter 7

24 With Foreman, Wolke is the author of *The Big Outside: A Descriptive Inventory of Big Wilderness Areas of the United States* (New York: Harmony Books, 1989, 1992). It is still a very useful synthesis that includes not only what you will find in the wilderness areas of the title, but what used to live there as well, and what kinds of pressure to develop they are under.

25 Peacock has a main-stage role in the wilderness conservation drama of the past forty years; he reflects on Abbey's death in counterpoint with memories from service in Vietnam in *Walking It Off: A Veteran's Chronicle of War and Wilderness* (Cheney, WA: Ewu Press, 2005). Peacock's masterwork is *Grizzly Years*.

26 E. O. Wilson and E. O. Willis, "Applied Biogeography," in *Ecology and Evolution of Communities*, ed. Jared Diamond and M. L. Cody (Cambridge, MA: Harvard University Press, 1975), 522–534.

27 Reed F. Noss, "Corridors in Real Landscapes: A Reply to Simberloff and Cox," *Conservation Biology* 1, no. 2 (August 1987): 159–164.

28   Wilderness watchers find it ironic that dissent and proud advocacy begat the Nature Conservancy, which now places itself resolutely outside any friction zones. This is good or bad depending on your point of view. The apolitical stance of TNC allows its practitioners to get along with politicians and landowners who otherwise might not sit down with them.

29   NatureServe is an NGO that collects biodiversity data from conservation and natural heritage efforts all around the world, making it widely available; it also develops mapping and software applications for purposing that data in on-the-ground projects: www.natureserve.org.

30   Doug Tompkins Foundation for Deep Ecology funded the Wildlands Project for many years.

31   www.nature.org/ourscience/ourscientists/conservation-science-at-the-nature-conservancy-sanjayan.xml.

32   Henry Nash Smith, *Virgin Land* (Cambridge, MA: Harvard University Press, 2007).

Chapter 8
33   John Hollenhorst, "Central Utah's Pando, World's Largest Living Thing, Is Threatened, Scientists Say," *Deseret News,* October 7, 2010.

34   Aldo Leopold, *Round River* (New York: Oxford University Press, 1993).

35   Subway travelers at the Astor Place stop on the 1-2-3 line in Manhattan: Check out the beaver tile, which honors John Jacob. Astor was arguably the most astute and successful of all fur traders and wisely got out of the business in 1834; plowing his fortune into New York real estate, he became one of the wealthiest men in the world, and provides another example of how the US financial establishment owes its underpinnings to the beaver.

36   Southern Utah has perhaps the "darkest" night sky anywhere in the United States. Our human penchant for electricity is literally wiping out our view of the night sky. This also hugely affects the activities of many animals and plants that are attuned to the diurnal/nocturnal cycle.

37   Denise Burschsted, et al. "The River Discontinuum: Applying Beaver Modifications to Baseline Conditions for Restoration of Forested Headwaters," *BioScience,* 60, no. 11 (December 2010) 908–922.

38   The Freedom of Information Act provides the public with access to government documents, unless they qualify as restricted; while FOIA provides that the burden of disclosure should fall on the government, in the case of making written requests year after year for the same thing, certainly the burden in this case fell on O'Brien. It was good of the Forest Service to start saving her the trouble.

39 See www.geostrategis.com/p_beavers-longestdam.htm.

40 Mark Buckley, et al., "The Economic Value of Beaver Ecosystem Services: Escalante River Basin, Utah," Portland, Oregon, ECONorthwest, February 2011.

41 More than fifty years old, Trout Unlimited is an NGO devoted to healthy North American fisheries, and much of its work is on connecting protected, pristine habitat with restored habitat downstream.

Chapter 9

42 Daniel B. Botkin and Edward A. Keller, *Environmental Science* (Hoboken, NJ: John Wiley & Sons, 2009).

43 Archer House, 1959.

44 David E. Brown and Neil B. Carmody, eds., *Aldo Leopold's Wilderness: Selected Early Writings by the Author of* A Sand County Almanac (Harrisburg, PA: Stackpole Books, 1990).

45 Joseph Grinnell and Tracy Storer, "Animal Life as an Asset of National Parks," *Science,* 44, no.1133 (September 15, 1916): 375–380.

46 Carol Raish and Alice M. McSweeney, "Economic, Social, and Cultural Aspects of Livestock Ranching on the Espanola and Canjilon Ranger Districts of the Santa Fe and Carson National Forests: A Pilot Study," US Department of Agriculture, General Technical Report RMRS-GTR-113, 2003.

47 Mark Salvo, *Western Wildlife Under Hoof: Public Lands Livestock Grazing Threatens Iconic Species* (Santa Fe: Wild Earth Guardians, 2009).

Chapter 10

48 At the nearby Rocky Mountain Biological Lab in Crested Butte, Colorado, UC Berkeley professor John Harte presided for more than twenty years over one of the longest running climate-change experiments in the nation. He simply set up a grid of heaters on a hillside and ran them continuously. (Other researchers have recently taken over the project.) The plots underneath the heaters are responding to the heaters' varying temperatures. Wildflowers in the plots that replicate projected higher temperatures due to climate change are disappearing. In their place: sagebrush. Gonna be kind of a downer for the "Wildflower Capital of the West" when they're all gone.

49 Nelson Hairston, Frederick E. Smith, and Lawrence B. Slobodkin, "Community Structure, Population Control and Competition," *American Naturalist* 94, no. 879 (November–December 1960): 421–425.

Chapter 11

50 From "In Memoriam," completed by Alfred Lord Tennyson in 1849, a decade before Darwin's opus, *On the Origin of Species*, appeared. Art so often lays out the shoes science will step into.

51 John Terborgh, "Why We Must Bring Back the Wolf," *New York Review of Books,* July 15, 2010.

52 *Endless Forms Most Beautiful,* Carroll's book about evo-devo, is a fun, accessible read on the subject.

53 Permittees, to remind you, have bought permits from the Bureau of Land Management and the Forest Service to graze livestock on public lands. To qualify, you have to verify ownership of a base property to which the public land is accessible. Possessing the permit allows a rancher to graze more cows.

Chapter 12

54 Bob Barbee, "Barbee Retrospective," *Yellowstone Science* 13, no. 1 (Winter 2005): 5.

55 Joel S. Brown et al., "The Ecology of Fear: Optimal Foraging, Game Theory, and Trophic Interactions," *Journal of Mammalogy* 80, no. 2 (May 1999): 385–399.

56 *Philosophical Transactions of the Royal Society,* February 2, 2011.

57 Anthony D. Barnosky, et al., "Has the Earth's sixth mass extinction already arrived?" *Nature* 471 (March 3, 2011): 51.

Chapter 13

58 James A. Estes, et al. *Science,* 333, no. 6040 (July 15, 2011): 301–306.

59 Based on the work of UC Berkeley researcher Justin Brashares. Check out *National Geographic*'s "Strange Days of Planet Earth" on Youtube: www.youtube.com/watch?v=HijeLfI9Uwo. Uploaded by StrangeDaysAction on August 18, 2008.

60 This is one of the only mountains in the United States named for a woman, Sarah Lemmon, a botanist, who reportedly was the first white woman to scale its heights, in 1881. Lemmon also goes down in history for getting the poppy designated California's state flower.

61 Peter Berg, who died in 2011 at age seventy-three, was an activist who predicted that environmentalism as a movement had its day in the 1970s with the passage of the Clean Air and Water Acts and will not come again. He promoted "ecoregionalism" as a way forward: advocating that individuals identify strongly with the place where they live, understand its natural resources, and work to restore them. With the actor Peter Coyote he founded the Diggers, an anarchist improv group, in

the 1960s. In the annals of nature quotations he deserves a special place for this one: "We didn't play it for the Big Time. We didn't play it for the Small Time. We played it for Real Time."

62 Induced meandering was largely developed by Dave Rosgen, www.wildland hydrology.com. *Let the Water Do the Work* by Bill Zeedyk and Van Clothier, a how-to guide on the subject, is available through the Quivira Coalition.

63 Susan M. Collins and Senator John McCain to The Honorable Ken Salazar, US Department of the Interior, and The Honorable Janet Napolitano, US Department of Homeland Security, memorandum, 13 December 2011.

64 Assistant Secretary Rhea Suh, US Department of the Interior, to The Honorable John McCain, US Senate, memorandum, 29 February 2012.

Chapter 14

65 Vol. 12, no. 6 (December 1998): 1241–1252.

66 Vol. 25, no. 5 (October 2011): 879–892.

67 While what you see on Google Earth is derived from satellites, it is not real-time imagery, but collated images taken over the past several years. Google Earth started as a commercial software program called Earth Viewer, originally developed by Keyhole Inc. Keyhole was the code name for a secret surveillance satellite, so the developers were being funny.

68 Bernard DeVoto, ed., *The Journals of Lewis and Clark*. New York: Houghton Mifflin, 1953.

69 *Conservation Biology* 24, no. 3 (June 2010): 701–710.

70 A Wildlife Corridor Conservation bill was proposed by Representative Rush Holt, D-NJ, 2010; it didn't make it out of the House. Since it included no enforcement mechanism, Fields doesn't think it's the right bill anyway.

71 Ridgeway was speaking on behalf of Freedom to Roam, Patagonia's connectivity initiative, which has since been incorporated into the World Wildlife Fund. Ridgeway's initial impetus to support connectivity came directly from a conversation with Michael Soulé.

72 The mention of Tabor, a longtime soldier in conservation, gives me the excuse to quote Mary Oliver, without whom no book about nature could really be complete. This from his e-mail template: "What is it you plan to do with your one wild and precious life?"

Chapter 15

73 Going further into it, "-ology" is derived from *logos* meaning "word." "Logos" in the Gospel of John is Christ, the member of the Trinity "through which all things are made." If by inherited language alone, we are back to a numinous foundation for the givens of science. Ecology, indeed, is that which through all life-forms are made.

74 The process so deep at the heart of our physical life has the same place in our cultural lives as well; Adam and Eve would be golems without "inspiration"; "the breath of life" is Christ in the New Testament; *prana*, or breath, is the ancient Ayurvedic life force, and Qi the comparable Chinese formulation. See, everything's connected.

75 Arpat Ozgul, et al., "Coupled dynamics of body mass and population growth in response to environmental change." *Nature* 466, no. 7305 (July 22, 2010): 482–485.

76 "Indicator" or "sentinel" species for climate change is more accurate than the term often used in the general press, which calls pika the "canary in the coal mine." (This has also been said of polar bears.) When canaries sent into mines died for lack of oxygen, the miners knew not to follow and suffer the same fate. By the time the pikas die off, there will be nowhere for us to go.

77 *Annual Review of Ecology, Evolution, and Systematics* 37 (2006): 637–669.

78 Parmesan's 2003 paper, coauthored with Gary Yohe, has been cited 2,408 times. "A Globally Coherent Fingerprint of Climate Change Impacts Across Natural Systems," *Nature* 421 (January 2003) 37–42.

79 NOAA, by contrast, accepted climate projections through 2100 in evaluating the status of two Arctic seals. Shaye Wolf quotes NOAA's decisions stating that projections through the end of the twenty-first century "currently form the most widely available version of the best available data about future conditions."

80 Loarie et al. *Nature 462 (*December 31, 2009):1052–1055.

Chapter 16

81 See https://c3.nasa.gov/nex.

Chapter 17

82 One notable example of a long-time series study is the Grinnell Resurvey Project of the Museum of Vertebrate Zoology at UC Berkeley. More than one hundred years ago, Joseph Grinnell accomplished a massive inventory of California flora and fauna, taking meticulous notes (which you can peruse at http://mvz.berkeley.edu/Grinnell). Contemporary scientists have gone over the same ground. Comparisons of the current and historic data have yielded rich observations. One prominent publication about the survey is "Impact of a century of climate change on small-mammal communities in Yosemite National Park, USA," Craig Moritz et al. *Science* 322, no. 5899 (10 October 2008): 261–264.

Bibliography

Abbey, Edward. *Desert Solitaire*. New York: Ballantine Books, 1968.

Ackerly, David, et al. "The Geography of Climate Change: Implications for Conservation Biogeography," *Diversity and Distributions*, 2010.

Adams, Jonathan. *The Future of the Wild: Radical Conservation for a Crowded World*. Boston: Beacon Press, 2006.

Ambrose, Stephen E. *Undaunted Courage*. New York: Simon & Schuster, 1996.

Asma, Stephen T. *Stuffed Animals and Pickled Heads*. Oxford, England: Oxford University Press, 2001.

Attenborough, David. *The Life of Mammals*. London, England: BBC Books, 2002.

Barnosky, Anthony D. *Heatstroke: Nature in an Age of Global Warming*. Washington, D.C.: Island Press, 2009.

Beckman, Jon P., Anthony P. Clevenger, Marcel P. Huijser, and Jodi A. Hilty. *Safe Passages: Highways, Wildlife, and Habitat Connectivity*. Washington, D.C.: Island Press, 2010.

Beever, Erik, et al. "Testing Alternative Models of Climate-Mediated Extirpations," *Ecological Applications*, 2010.

Beier, Paul, and Reed Noss. "Do Habitat Corridors Provide Connectivity?" *Conservation Biology*, December 1998.

Beier, Paul, et al. "Toward Best Practices for Developing Regional Connectivity Maps," *Conservation Biology*, October 2011.

Berger, Joel. *The Better to Eat You With: Fear in the Animal World*. Chicago: Chicago University Press, 2008.

Bevington, Douglas. *The Rebirth of Environmentalism: Grassroots Activism from the Spotted Owl to the Polar Bear*. Washington, DC: Island Press, 2009.

Blunt, Wilfred. *Linnaeus: The Compleat Naturalist*. Princeton, N.J.: Princeton University Press, 2001.

Brewer, Jo. *Butterflies*. New York: Harry N. Abrams, 1976.

Brown, Joseph Epes. *The Spiritual Legacy of the American Indian*. Bloomington, IN: World Wisdom, Inc., 2007.

Browne, Janet. *Charles Darwin: The Power of Place*. New York: Knopf, 2002.

———. *Charles Darwin: Voyaging*. New York: Knopf, 1995.

———. *The Secular Ark: Studies in the History of Biogeography*. New Haven, CT: Yale University Press, 1983.

Burns, Ken, and Dayton Duncan. *The National Parks: America's Best Idea*. New York: Knopf, 2009.

Cannon, Susan. *Science in Culture*. New York: Neale Watson Academic Publications, Inc., 1978.

Carroll, Sean B. *Endless Forms Most Beautiful: The New Science of Evo Devo and the Making of the Animal Kingdom*. New York: Norton, 2005.

Carrol, Sean B. *Remarkable Creatures*. New York: Houghton Mifflin Company, 2009.

Chadwick, Douglas. *True Grizz*. San Francisco: Sierra Club Books, 2003.

———. *The Wolverine Way*. Ventura, CA: Patagonia, 2010.

Charlesworth, Brian & Deborah. *Evolution: A Very Short Introduction*. Oxford, England: Oxford University Press, 2003.

Childs, Jack L., and Mary Childs. *Ambushed on the Jaguar Trail*. Tuscon: Rio Nuevo, 2008.

Chittendon, Hiram Martin. *The American Fur Trade of the Far West*. New York: Rufus Rockwell Wilson, Inc., 1935.

Chronic, Halka. *Roadside Geology of Utah*. Missoula, MT: Mountain Press Publishing Co., 1990.

Climate Central and Sally Ride Science. *Twenty Questions and Answers About Climate Change*. San Diego: Sally Ride Science, 2010.

Cody, Martin L., and Jared M Diamond, eds. *Ecology and Evolution of Communities*. Cambridge, MA: Harvard University Press, 1975.

Colbert, Edwin H. *Wandering Lands and Animals*. New York: E.P. Dutton, 1973.

Collinge, Sharon K. *Ecology of Fragmented Landscapes*. Baltimore, MD: The Johns Hopkins University Press, 2009.

Cronon, William. *Changes in the Land*. New York: Hill and Wang, 2003.

Cronon, William, editor. *Uncommon Ground: Toward Reinventing Nature*. New York: W.W. Norton, 1995.

Crooks, Kevin R., and M. Sanjayan. *Connectivity Conservation*. New York: Cambridge University Press, 2006.

Dary, David A. *The Buffalo Book: The Full Saga of the American Animal*. Athens, OH: Ohio University Press, 1989.

Dasmann, Raymond F. *Called by the Wild*. Berkeley, CA: University of California Press, 2002.

Davis, Wade. *Grand Canyon: River at Risk*. San Rafael, CA.: Earth Aware Editions, 2008.

Dawson, Terence P., et al. "Beyond Predictions: Biodiversity Conservation in a Changing Climate," *Science*, April 1, 2011.

DeMers, Michael N. *GIS for Dummies*. Hoboken, NJ: Wiley Publishing Inc., 2009.

De Panafieu, Jean-Baptiste. *Evolution*. New York: Seven Stories Press, 2007.

DeVoto, Bernard. *The Journals of Lewis and Clark*. New York: Houghton Mifflin, 1953.

Dolin, Eric Jay. *Fur, Fortune, and Empire: The Epic History of the Fur Trade in America*. New York: Norton, 2010.

The Economist. "The Anthropocene: A Man-Made World." London: May 26, 2011.

Ehrlich, Paul, and Anne Ehrlich. *The Population Bomb*. New York: Touchstone Books, 1991.

Eisenberg, Cristina. *The Wolf's Tooth: Keystone Predators, Trophic Cascades, and Biodiversity*. Washington, D.C.: Island Press, 2010.

Elbroch, Mark. *Mammal Tracks & Sign: A Guide to North American Specie*s. Mechanicsburg, PA: Stackpole Books, 2003.

Elton, Charles. *Animal Ecology*. Chicago: University of Chicago Press, 2001.

Fagan, Brian. *Elixer: A History of Water and Humankind*. New York: Bloomsbury Press, 2011.

Flannery, Tim. *The Eternal Frontier*. New York: Atlantic Monthly Press: 2001.

———. *The Weather Makers: How Man is Changing the Climate and What it Means for Life on Earth*. New York: Grove Press, 2005.

Foreman, Dave. *Confessions of an Eco-Warrior*. New York: Crown, 1991.

Forman, Richard T. T. "Some General Principles of Landscape and Regional Ecology," *Landscape Ecology*, 1995.

Frankel, O. H., and Michael Soulé. *Conservation and Evolution*. Cambridge, England: Cambridge University Press, 1981.

Fraser, Caroline. *Rewilding the World: Dispatches from the Conservation Revolution*. New York: Metropolitan Books, 2009.

Gibson, James Jerome. *The Perception of the Visual World*. Boston, MA: Houghton Mifflin. 1950.

Gilbert-Norton, Lynne, et al. "A Meta-Analytic Review of Corridor Effectiveness," *Conservation Biology*, October 2009.

Goldstein, Natalie. *Earth Almanac: An Annual Geophysical Review of the State of the Planet*. Phoenix, AZ: The Oryx Press, 2000.

Grayson, Donald K. "A Brief History of Great Basin Pikas," *Journal of Biogeography*, 2005.

Gross, John E., Andrew J. Hansen, Scott J. Goetz, David M. Theobald, Forrest M. Melton, Nathan B. Piekielek, and Rama R. Nemani. "Remote Sensing for Inventory Monitoring of the U.S. National Parks." *Remote Sensing of Protected Areas*. Boca Raton, FL: Taylor & Francis, 2011.

Groves, Craig R. *Drafting a Conservation Blueprint*. Washington, D.C.: The Island Press, 2003.

Gunter, Michael M. Jr. *Building the Next Ark: How NGOs Work to Protect Biodiversity*. Hanover, NH: Dartmouth College Press, 2004.

Haidt, Jonathan. *The Happiness Hypothesis*. New York: Basic Books, 2006.

Hanscom, Greg. "Visionaries or Dreamers?" *High Country News*, April 26, 1999.

Hanson, James A. *When Skins Were Money: A History of the Fur Trade*. Chadron, NE: Museum of the Fur Trade, 2005.

Hart, Donna, and Robert W. Sussman. *Man the Hunted*. New York: Westview Press, 2005.

Hashimoto, Hirofumi, et al. "Monitoring and Forecasting Climate Impacts on Ecosystem Dynamics in Protected Areas Using the Terrestrial Observation and Prediction System (TOPS)." *Remote Sensing of Environment*, 2009.

Heller, Nicole E., and Erika S. Zavaleta. "Biodiversity Management in the Face of Climate Change: A Review of 22 Years of Recommendations," *Biological Conservation*, 2009.

Henig, Robin Marantz. *The Monk in the Garden: The Lost and Found Genius of Gregor Mendel, the Father of Genetics*. New York: Houghton Mifflin, 2000.

Heuer, Karsten. *Walking the Big Wild*. Seattle: The Mountaineers Books, 2004.

Hilfiker, Earl L. *Beavers: Water, Wildlife and History*. Interlaken, NY: Windswept Press, 1991.

Hood, Glynnis. *The Beaver Manifesto*. Surrey, BC, Canada: Rocky Mountain Books, 2011.

Horning, Ned, et al. *Remote Sensing for Ecology and Conservation*. New York: Oxford University Press, 2010.

Hudson, Wendy E., editor. *Landscape Linkages and Biodiversity*. Washington, D.C.: Island Press, 1991.

Huggett, Richard John. *Fundamentals of Biogeography*. New York: Routledge, 1998.

Isbell, Lynne A. *The Fruit, the Tree, and the Serpent: Why We See So Well*. Cambridge: Harvard University Press, 2009.

Jablonka, Eva, and Marion J. Lamb. *Evolution in Four Dimensions*. Cambridge: Massachusetts Institute of Technology Press, 2005.

Janick, Jules. *Gregor Mendel*. Classic Papers in Horticultural Science, 1989.

Jones, Christine. "The Back Forty Down Under: Adapting Farming to Climate Variability," *The Quivira Coalition*, February 2010.

Jones, Lisa. "The Buckshot Bodhisattva," *Tricycle*, Winter 2003.

Judson, Olivia. *Dr. Tatiana's Sex Advice to All Creation*. New York: Henry Holt & Co., 2002.

Kashian, Daniel M., William H. Romme, and Claudia M. Regan. "Reconciling Divergent Interpretations of Quaking Aspen Decline on the Northern Colorado Front Range." *Ecological Applications*, 2007.

Kauffman, Matthew J. et al. "Are Wolves Saving Yellowstone's Aspen? A Landscape-level Test of a Behaviorally Mediated Trophic Cascade," *Ecology*, 2010.

Krech, Shephard (ed). *Indians, Animals, and the Fur Trade*. Athens, GA: University of Georgia Press, 1981.

Lavender, David. *The Rockies*. Lincoln: University of Nebraska Press, 2003.

Lawing, A. Michelle, and P. David Polly. "Pleistocene Climate, Phylogeny, and Climate Envelope Models: An Integrative Approach to Better Understand Species' Response to Climate Change," *PloS One*, December 2, 2011.

Lecointre, Guillaume, and Herve Le Guyader. *The Tree of Life: A Phylogenetic Classification*. Cambridge, MA: Harvard University Press, 2006.

Leopold, Luna. *Water: A Primer*. San Francisco: W. H. Freeman and Company, 1974.

Leopold, Luna B. *A View from the River*. Cambridge, MA: Harvard University Press, 1994.

Lewin, Roger. *Patterns in Evolution: the New Molecular View*. New York: Scientific American Library, 1997.

Lomolino, Mark V., Brett R. Riddle, and James H. Brown. *Biogeography*. Sunderland, MA: Sinauer Associates, 2006.

Lopez, Barry. *Of Wolves and Men*. New York: Scribner's, 1978.

MacArthur, Robert H. *Geographical Ecology*. Princeton, NJ: Princeton University Press: 1972.

MacEachren, Alan M. *How Maps Work: Representation, Visualization, and Design*. New York: Guilford Press, 1995.

MacGillivray, W. *The Travels and Researches of Alexander von Humboldt*. London, England: T. Nelson and Sons, 1832.

MacShane, Thomas O., and Michael P. Wells. *Getting Biodiversity Projects to Work: Towards More Effective Conservation and Development*. New York: Columbia University Press, 2004.

Mahler, Richard. *The Jaguar's Shadow: Searching for a Mythic Cat*. New Haven: Yale University Press, 2009.

Martin, Calvin. *Keepers of the Game*. Berkeley, CA: University of California Press, 1978.

Mattheissen, Peter. *Wildlife in America*. New York: Viking Penguin, 1987.

McNamee, Thomas. *The Grizzly Bear*. New York: Lyons & Burford, 1997.

———. *The Return of the Wolf to Yellowstone*. New York: Henry Holt & Co. 1997.

Mech, David L., and Luigi Boitani, eds. *Wolves: Behavior, Ecology, and Conservation*. Chicago: University of Chicago Press, 2003.

Meine, Curt D. *Aldo Leopold: His Life and Work*. Madison, WI: University of Wisconsin Press, 1991.

Meine, Curt D. *Correction Lines: Essays on Land, Leopold, and Conservation*. Washington, D.C.: Island Press, 2004.

Meine, Curt, Michael Soulé, and Reed F. Noss. "'A Mission-Driven Discipline': The Growth of Conservation Biology." *Conservation Biology*, 2006.

Mills, Enos. *In Beaver World*. Boston: Houghton Mifflin Company, 1913.

Mills, L. Scott. *Conservation of Wildlife Populations: Demography, Genetics, and Management*. Malden, MA: Blackwell Publishing, 2007.

Montgomery, David R. *Dirt: Erosion of Civilizations*. Berkeley: University of California Press, 2007.

Morelli, Toni Lyn, and Susan Carr. "A Review of the Potential Effects of Climate Change on Quaking Aspen (*Populus tremuloides*) in the Western United States and a New Tool for Surveying Sudden Aspen Decline." Gen. Tech. Rep. PSW-GTR-235. Albany, CA: U.S. Department of Agriculture, Forest Service, Pacific Southwest Research Station, 2011.

Morgan, Susan. *A History of the Wildlands Project*. Dissertation. The Union Institute, 1998.

Muller-Schwarze, Dietland. *The Beaver*. Ithaca, NY: Cornell University Press, 2003.

Naiman, Robert. J. , et al. eds. *The Freshwater Imperative: A Research Agenda*. Washington, D.C.: Island Press, 1995.

Nelson, Michael P., and Baird J. Callicott, eds. *The Great New Wilderness Debate*. Athens, GA: University of Georgia Press, 1998.

Nemani, R., et al. "Collaborative Supercomputing for Global Climate Change Science," *Eos*, March 2011.

Neme, Laurel A. *Animal Investigators*. New York: Scribner, 2009.

Newman, Peter C. *Caesars of the Wilderness*. Volume 11. New York: Viking, 1987.

———. *Company of Adventurers*. Volume I. New York: Viking, 1985.

Nijhuis, Michelle. "The Ghosts of Yosemite," *High Country News*, October 17, 2005.

———. "In the Great Basin, Scientists Track Global Warming," *High Country News*, October 17, 2005.

———. "Prodigal Dogs," *High Country News*, February 13, 2010.

Niklas, Karl J. *The Evolutionary Biology of Plants*. Chicago: University of Chicago Press, 1997.

Noss, Reed. "Corridors in Real Landscapes: A Reply to Simberloff and Cox," *Conservation Biology*, August 1987.

Odum, Eugene P., and Gary W. Barrett. *Fundamentals of Ecology*. Belmont, CA: Brooks/Cole, 2005.

Outwater, Alice. *Water: A Natural History*, New York: Basic Books, 1996.

Padian, Kevin. "Darwin's Enduring Legacy." *Nature*, February 2008.

Parmesan, Camille, and Gary Yohe. "A Globally Coherent Fingerprint of Climate Change Impacts Across Natural Systems," *Nature*, January 2, 2003.

Patterson, Colin. *Evolution*. Ithaca, NY: Cornell University Press, 1978.

Paul, Rodman W. *The Far West and the Great Plains in Transition, 1859-1900*. New York: Harper & Row, 1988.

Peacock, Doug. *Grizzly Years: In Search of the American Wilderness*. New York: Holt, 1996.

Peacock, Doug, and Andrea Peacock. *In the Presence of Grizzlies*. Guilford, CT: Lyons Press, 2009.

Pearson, E. S. *Studies in the History of Statistics and Probability*. New York: Macmillan, 1970.

Prest, John. *The Garden of Eden: The Botanic Garden and the Re-Creation of Paradise*. New Haven, CT: Yale University Press, 1981.

Quammen, David. *Monster of God: The Man-Eating Predator in the Jungle of History and the Mind*. New York: Norton, 2003.

———. *The Song of the Dodo*. New York: Scribner, 1996.

Randin, Christophe F. et al. "Climate Change and Plant Distribution: Local Models Predict High-Elevation Persistence," *Global Change Biology*, 2009.

Raup, David M. *Extinction: Bad Genes or Bad Luck?* New York: W.W. Norton, 1991.

Reisner, Marc. *Cadillac Desert: The American West and Its Disappearing Water.* New York: Viking, 1986.

Rees, Tony. *The Arc of the Medicine Line.* Lincoln: University of Nebraska Press. 2007.

Rhodes, Richard. *The Audubon Reader.* New York: Knopf, 2006.

Richter, Daniel K. *Facing East from Indian Country.* Cambridge, MA: Harvard University Press, 2001.

Rinella, Steven. *American Buffalo: In Search of a Lost Icon.* New York: Spiegel & Grau, 2008.

Robinson, Michael J. *Predatory Bureaucracy: the Extermination of Wolves and the Transformation of the West.* Boulder, CO: University Press of Colorado, 2005.

Root, Terry L. et al. "Fingerprints of Global Warming on Wild Animals and Plants," *Nature,* January 2, 2003.

Rothenberg, David. *Why Birds Sing.* New York: Basic Books, 2005.

Russell, Andy. *Grizzly Country.* New York: Lyons & Burford, 1967.

Sachs, Aaron. *The Humboldt Current: Nineteenth Century Exploration and the Roots of American Environmentalism.* New York: Viking, 2006.

Schneider, Stephen H., and Terry Root, eds. *Wildlife Responses to Climate Change: North American Case Studies.* Washington, D.C.: Island Press, 2002.

Schultz, Florian. *Freedom to Roam.* Seattle: Mountaineers Books, 2005.

Shaw, Harley. *Soul Among Lions: The Cougar as Peaceful Adversary.* Tucson: University of Arizona Press, 2000.

Shephard, Paul, and Barry Sanders. *The Sacred Paw: The Bear in Nature, Myth, and Literature.* New York: Viking, 1985.

Short, Lester L. *The Lives of Birds.* New York: Henry Holt, 1993.

Shubin, Neil. *Your Inner Fish.* New York: Pantheon, 2008.

Silverton, Jonathan. *Demons in Eden: The Paradox of Plant Diversity.* Chicago: University of Chicago Press, 2005.

Simberloff, Daniel, and James Cox. "Consequences and Costs of Conservation Corridors," *Conservation Biology,* May 1987.

Simberloff, Daniel, et al. "Movement Corridors: Conservation Bargains or Poor Investments?" *Conservation Biology,* December 1992.

Skinner, Brian J., et al. *The Blue Planet: An Introduction to Earth System Science.* New York: John Wiley & Sons, Inc., 1999.

Soulé, Michael, ed. *Conservation Biology: The Science and Scarcity of Diversity.* Sunderland, MA: Sinauer Associates, Inc., 1986.

Soulé, Michael, and Bruce Wilcox. *Conservation Biology: An Evolutionary-Ecological Perspective.* Sunderland, MA: Sinauer Associates, 1980.

Soulé, Michael, and Daniel Simberloff. "What Do Genetics and Ecology Tell Us About the Design of Nature Reserves?" *Biological Conservation,* 1986.

Soulé, Michael, and Gary Lease, eds. *Reinventing Nature? Responses to Postmodern Deconstruction.* Washington, DC: Island Press, 1995.

Soulé, Michael, and Gordon H. Orians, eds. *Conservation Biology: Research Priorities for the Next Decade.* Washington, D.C.: Island Press, 2000.

Soulé, Michael, and John Terborgh, eds. *Continental Conservation: Scientific Foundations of Regional Reserve Networks.* Washington, D.C.: Island Press, 1999.

Stegner, Wallace. *Beyond the Hundredth Meridian.* New York: Penguin, 1953.

Stein, Mark. *How the States Got Their Shape*. New York: Harper, 2008.

Steinberg, Ted. D*own to Earth: Nature's Role in American History*. New York: Oxford University Press, 2009.

Steinhart, Peter. *The Company of Wolves*. New York: Knopf, 1995.

Stolzenburg, William. *Rat Island: Predators in Paradise—And the World's Greatest Wildlife Rescue*. New York: Bloomsbury, 2011.

Stolzenburg, William. *Where the Wild Things Were*. New York: Bloomsbury, 2008.

Taylor, Alan. *American Colonies*. New York: Viking Penguin, 2001.

Tingley, Morgan W., and Steven R. Beissinger. "Detecting Range Shifts from Historical Species Occurrences: New Perspectives on Old Data," *Trends in Ecology and Evolution*, August 14, 2009.

Waring, Gwendolyn L. *A Natural History of the Intermountain West*. Salt Lake City: University of Utah Press, 2011.

Weiner, Jonathan. *The Beak of the Finch: A Story of Evolution in Our Time*. New York: Knopf, 1994.

Westergaard, Harald. *Contributions to the History of Statistics*. New York: Agathon Press, 1968.

White, Courtney. *Revolution on the Range*. Washington, D.C.: Island Press, 2008.

Wilcox, R. Turner. *The Mode in Hats and Headdress*. New York: Scribner's, 1945.

Wilensky-Landford, Brook. *Paradise Lust: Searching for the Garden of Eden*. New York: Grove Press, 2011.

Wilson, Edward O. *The Diversity of Life*. Cambridge, MA: Harvard University Press, 1992.

Wilson, Edward O., ed. *From So Simple A Beginning: The Four Great Books of Charles Darwin*. New York: Norton, 2006.

Wilson, Edward O., and Robert MacArthur. *The Theory of Island Biogeography*. Princeton: Princeton University Press, 2001.

Worster, Donald. *Rivers of Empire: Water, Aridity, and the Growth of the American West*. New York: Oxford University Press, 1992.

INDEX

A

Abbey, Edward, 24, 73–74
Acres for America, 205
adaptation, 36, 44, 57
agriculture, 118
Akcakaya, H. Resit, 58–59
Allen's Rule, 66
alternative stable state, 51
Ament, Rob, 206
American National Wildlife Corridor, 204
America's Great Outdoors initiative, 82, 202
animal movement, 14–15
Arizona Game and Fish (AZGF), 186, 190–93, 199–200
aspen, 93–96, 138, 163
Avey, Josh, 199–200
Avila, Sergio, 175–94
Ayala, Francisco, 49–50

B

Babbitt, Bruce, 27–28, 164
balance of nature, 126
Barbee, Bob, 164
Barnosky, Anthony, 171–72
basins of attraction, 173
Bateson, William, 155
BC Highway 3, 8, 11–12, 14, 15
bears, 3–18, 182
beaver, 91–117, 139, 238–44
   dams, 107, 108–9, 113–14
Beever, Erik, 227
Beier, Paul, 196, 199, 200–201, 210
Belly River Valley, 3, 8, 9
Berg, Peter, 183,
Berger, Joel and Kim, 203, 204, 206
Bergmann's Rule, 66
Beschta, Bob, 162–64
Bevington, Douglas, 73–74, 248
big cats, 182–83

biodiversity, 79, 178, 200–201
Biodiversity and Ecological
   Forecasting programs, 234
biogeography, 21, 30, 33, 38, 40, 59–60, 65, 66, 247
biological bridge, 57
Biological Conservation (Ehrenfeld), 52
bioregions, 79
biotic conveyor belt, 11–12
bison, 119–21, 139
Blackfeet, 9
border, Mexico-U.S., 175–94
botanical arithmetic, 68
Brost, Brian, 200–201
Brown, Joel, 164–66
Browne, Janet, 67–68
Brun, Janay, 186–94
buffalo. *See* bison
Buffon, Comte de, 65–66
Bureau of Land Management (BLM), 27, 138, 205
Burke, Kelly, 27–28

C

Cadillac Desert (Reisner), 91–92
cameras, remote, 181–82, 189
Campbell, John Lennon, 137, 143, 153, 154–55, 157, 158
carbon, 132, 134–35
Carnegie Institute for Global Studies, 226
Carson, Rachel, 41
Catlin, Jim, 22, 27, 122, 128–29
cattle grazing, 105–6, 111–12, 117, 118–35. *See also* ranching
Center for Biological Diversity, 81, 190, 223, 228, 229
Center for Large Landscape
   Conservation, 206
Changes in the Land (Cronon), 85
Childs, Jack, 186, 189, 190

Citizen Science program, 176
climate change, 4–5, 68–69
  affect on species, 59
  and cattle grazing, 118
  and connectivity, 199, 234
  and Endangered Species Act, 231
  future trends, 96
  how fast it's moving, 226–27
  and landscape, 196
  overview, 214–15
  and pika, 218–31
  and snowmelt, 11
Climate Law Institute, 231
coevolution, 104
Coffin, Pat, 116
collective impact, 26
Colorado Plateau, 19, 24–29, 92
competitive exclusion, principle of, 49
Concho water snakes, 58
connectivity, 5, 77, 82, 83, 219, 234
  and climate change, 199, 234
  conservation, 13, 247, 248
  landscape, 206, 209–10
Connectivity Conservation (Crooks), 62
Connectivity Policy Coalition, 82,
  201–2
conservation
  connectivity, 13, 247, 248
  and hunting, 153
  three C's, 5
Conservation and Evolution (Frankel),
  43, 44
conservation biology, 19–22, 62, 199
  beginnings of, 52–53
  what it is, 82–83
Conservation Biology (Soulé), 44, 52, 62
Conservation Fund, 205
Conservation of Wildlife Populations
  (Mills), 62
Continental Conservation (Soulé), 80
Converse, Yvette, 209
Copeland, Doug, 209
cores, 195

cores, carnivores, corridors paradigm,
  5, 80, 151, 199
corridor conference, 78–79
Corridor Ecology (Merenlender), 61
corridors, 77, 195–96, 197, 200–202
cottonwood trees, 163–64
cows. *See* cattle grazing
coyotes, 124, 143, 148
Cronon, William, 85
Crooks, Kevin, 62, 82–83
crossing structures, animal, 14–15, 200
Crown of the Continent ecoregion, 9
Crumbo, Kim, 23–24, 25, 246
Crutzen, Paul, 170
Curtis, John T., 40

D

Darwin, Charles, 30–34, 35, 64, 68,
  132–33
Dasmann, Raymond, 183–84
Davis, John, 74, 244–46
Davis, Tony, 191–92
deconstructionist alternative, 86
deep ecology, 71, 79, 84
demographic impact, 57
Diamond, Jared, 20, 47–50, 52
dirt. *See* soil
Dirt (Montgomery), 132
Disappearance, The (Wylie), 45–47
diversity
  genetic, 37, 38, 43
  habitat, 48
DNA, 35, 68, 133, 156, 158, 208
drilling, natural gas, 203
Duffy, Phil, 226

E

Earnest, Mike, 241–42
Earth First!, 72–75
Ecological Forecasting Lab, 232–37
ecology, 213
  corridor, 196
  of fear, 164–66

geographical, 39
and wolves in Yellowstone, 165
ecoregionalism, 254n61
ecosystems, 153, 173–74, 213–14
without top predators, 193–94
Eden, 65, 86
Ehrlich, Paul, 16, 52, 53, 74, 104, 142
Eisenberg, Cristina, 136–48, 149
elk, 149–50, 154, 163–64
endangered species, 41, 174, 190, 224
Endangered Species Act, 41, 223, 231
Endangered Species List, 14–15, 58, 129, 218
epochs, geological, 170–71
equilibrium theory, 38–40, 48
erosion, 10, 11, 32, 130–31, 133
Estes, Jim, 137, 143, 145–46, 153, 172–74, 230
Evans, Carol, 116
evolution, 30, 37
evolutionary development (evo-devo), 155
extinction, 17, 19, 39, 42, 50, 53, 58, 171–73
acceleration of, 64
species, 223–24

F

fate maps, 156–57
feedback loop, 58
Fields, Kenyon, 82, 140–41, 201–2, 209–10
fire, 139
First Nations. *See* indigenous cultures
Fish and Wildlife Service, U. S. (FWS), 82, 223, 227
food chain, 15–16, 193–94
forecasting, ecological, 235–36. *See also* modeling, computer
Foreman, Dave, 23, 72–75, 75–76, 177
Forest Plan Amendment, 205
Forest Service, U. S., 27, 72–73, 82, 123
foundational species, 95

Foundation for Deep Ecology, 79
fracking, 202–3
fragmentation, habitat, 16, 19–22, 40, 57
Fragmented Forest, The (Harris), 78
Francis, Wendy, 12, 15
Frankel, Otto, 42–43
Frazer, Gary, 227
Freudenthal, Dave, 205, 206
fur trade, 91, 99–103

G

gap analysis, 79
Garrity warning, 192
gel electrophoresis, 36, 38
genetic diversity, 37, 38, 43
genetics, 35, 56, 62, 64, 68, 155–56
Gilbert, G. K., 25
Gilpin, Mike, 49–50, 53–59, 217–18, 233
GIS (geographic information systems), 198
Glenn, Warner, 185–86
Global Biodiversity Information Facility (GBIF), 69
Gloger's Rule, 66
GPS (global positioning system), 197–98
Grand Canyon Trust, 22, 92–93
Grand Canyon Wildlands Project, 27–28
grazing. *See* cattle grazing
green-world hypothesis, 144–45
Grinnell, Joseph, 125, 208
grizzlies, 3–18
Gross, John, 236–37

H

HabiMap, 200
habitat
connecting separated, 77
damage from poor cattle grazing, 129
destruction of, 42

diversity, 48
fragmentation, 16, 19–22
loss of, 64
safeguarding diversity of, 48
suitability, 199
types of, 233
Haidt, Jonathan, 152
Hamilton, Healy, 4–5, 69, 142,
    196–97
Hamilton, Kniffy, 204–6
Hamilton, Sam, 209
Harem, Sandy, 243–44
Harris, Larry, 78
heredity, 35–36
Herring, Hal, 149–51, 154, 158
hibernation, 17–18, 215–16
High Lonesome Ranch, 136–48
highways and roads, 8, 11–12, 14, 15,
    200
Hilgard, E. W., 66
hot spots, 79, 178
Hox genes, 156, 157, 158
Humboldt, Alexander von, 66–68
hunting, 125–26, 136–48, 149–51,
    153, 169

I

impact, 57–58
inbreeding depression, 20, 44, 55, 57
indicator species, 218
indigenous peoples, 11, 17, 98–100, 121
induced meandering, 184
insect-plant dynamic, 216–17
International Conference on
    Conservation Biology, 52, 53
International Migratory Bird Treaty, 179
International Union for Conservation
    of Nature Red List Standards, 58
International Union for the
    Conservation of Nature and
    Natural Reserves, 41
Isanhart, John, 230
Isbell, Lynne A., 181

island biogeographical theory, 56,
    59–60, 61, 233
islands, 31–32, 40, 47

J

jaguars, 179, 182–83, 185–94

K

Kauffman, Boone, 135
keystone species, 109, 120

L

Lamberton, Jessica, 175
land facet approach, 200–201
landmass, stranded, 47–48
landscape connectivity, 206, 209–10
Landscape Conservation
    Cooperatives, 82, 209–10
land trusts, 248
land use planning, 197
Larsen, Eric, 163
law, environmental, 41, 55
Leopold, Aldo, 25–26, 77, 124–25
Lewis and Clark expedition, 102–3
life zones, 28
Linnaeus, Carl, 64–65
livestock. See cattle grazing
lizards, 30–40, 42
Loarie, Greg, 224
Loarie, Scott, 226–27, 229, 230
Lopez, Barry, 166–67
Lovejoy, Thomas, 20, 52
Lyell, Charles, 31, 130–31, 170

M

MacArthur, Robert, 38–40, 47
Macho B, 185–86, 187, 189–93
maps and mapping, 9, 22–23, 39–40,
    196–97, 199
McCain, Emil, 187–93
McInnis, Scott, 159–61
McKnight, Margo, 245
McMayon, Shirl, 112–15
Mendel, Gregor, 35–36

Menke, Kurt, 142, 244, 245
Merenlender, Adina, 61, 62–63
mesopredators, 147–48
metapopulation theory, 56
migration, 202–4
Miistakis Institute, 14
Mills, Scott, 61–62, 82–83
minimum viable populations, 44, 51, 55, 56–57, 58, 233
mining, 23, 115–16
Mobley, Megan, 40
modeling, computer, 4–5, 49–50, 58, 69, 199, 230, 237
Monkey Wrench Gang, The (Abbey), 73–74
Montgomery, David, 132
moral ecology, 20–21
Moriarty, Katie, 207–9
Muir, John, 20, 122–23
mutualism, 216–17
Myer, Norman, 79

N

Naess, Arne, 70–71, 79, 84
NASA Ecological Forecasting Lab, 82, 232–37
National Forest Management Act, 41, 55
national forest system, 123
National Heritage Network, 79
National Oceanic and Atmospheric Administration (NOAA), 223
national parks, 59–60
National Park Service, 82, 236–37
Native Americans. *See* indigenous peoples
natural gas, 203
natural selection, 30, 32–33, 37, 140
Nature Conservancy (TNC), 78, 84
nature preserves, 44, 47–48, 51
NatureServe, 79
Nemani, Rama, 232–37
Newmark, William, 59–60

NEX (NASA Earth Exchange), 234–35
Noah's ark, 21, 65–66
Noss, Reed, 52, 77, 78–79, 81, 196

O

O'Brien, Mary, 22, 91–117, 238
open-space programs, 248
otters, 146
Outwater, Alice, 108
overgrazing, 111–12, 129
Owens, Richard, 155, 158

P

Paine, Robert, 144–45
Pando Clone, 94–95
Parmesan, Camille, 223
Path of the Pronghorn, 202–3, 206–7
permittees, 254n53
photosynthesis, 214–15
pika, 213–31
Pimm, Stuart, 20
Pinchot, Gifford, 123
Pollock, Josh, 196–97
population, human, 53, 152
population genetics, 156–58
population viability, 44, 51, 55, 56–57, 58, 233
Porter, Joshua, 104–5
Powell, John Wesley, 10–11, 91–92
prairie dogs, 57–58
predators and prey, 16, 123–26, 141, 144–45, 146, 147–48, 151, 158, 163, 164–66, 174, 183–84, 203, 216
Predatory Bureaucracy (Robinson), 122
prescribed burns, 139
prescriptive grazing, 117
private lands, 85, 141
pronghorn, 202–6
proximal problems, 152
public land, 27, 118, 140, 201

Q

Quammen, David, 16, 62

R

radio collars, 12, 188, 189, 190
railroads, 122
ranching, 116, 118–19, 121–22, 126, 127, 128–29, 153. *See also* cattle grazing
RARE II, 72–73, 177
Ray, Chris, 217–31
Rebirth of Environmentalism, The (Bevington), 73–74
recovery zones, 13
Reddy, Steve, 238, 242
Regional Connectivity Maps, 196
Reisner, Marc, 91–92
religion, 21, 65, 86–87
remote sensing, 233–37
rewilding, 26
Rewilding North America (Foreman), 74
Richter, Daniel, 40
Ripple, Bill, 162–64
Rivers of Empire (Worster), 92
roadkill, 13–15
Robinson, Michael, 122, 128
Robles, Carlos, 175–76
Rocky Mountains, 9–10
Rocky Mountain Wild, 196
rotational grazing, 117, 135

S

Salawasser, Hal, 55, 56
Salazar, Kenneth, 82, 209
salvation biology, 86–87
Sanjayan, M., 53, 62, 82, 83–84
Sarawak Law, 31
Schwartz, Mike, 208
Scott, Mike, 79
seasons, 215–16
Servheen, Chris, 14–15
seven deadly sins, 20, 84–85, 152–53, 250n9
Shaffer, Mark, 56–57
Shelford, Victor, 77–78
Shubin, Neil, 158
Siegel, Kassie, 231

Simberloff, Dan, 20, 48–51, 77
Sky Islands, 175, 177–78, 194
SLOSS debate, 48–49, 50
Smith, Andrew, 228–36
Smith, Doug, 167–69
Smith, Thorry, 190–91, 192
snaring, 190–91
snowmelt, 11
Society for Conservation Biology, 52, 61, 196
software, modeling, 58
soil, 130–33
Sonoran Joint Venture, 179
Soulé, Michael, 19–22, 24, 29, 30, 38, 246
    character of, 54
    and conservation biology, 52, 199
    and evil, 124
    four processes of nature, 85–86
    Gilpin's observations about, 53–59
    humanism of, 84
    and hunting, 136–48, 151
    and population viability analysis, 233
    publications, 41–42, 44, 56, 62, 80
    and rewilding, 74
    seven deadly sins, 20, 84–85, 152–53
    SLOSS debate, 50
    students of, 62
    study of lizards, 33–36, 39, 42–47
    and systematics, 63–64, 69–70
    taxonomy, 63, 69–70
    and trophic cascades, 140, 147–48
    and wolves, 143, 167
    and Zen Buddhism, 47, 62–63, 70
species, 31
    demographics, 61
    distribution modeling, 4–5
    distribution of, 69, 233
    extinction, 223–24
    identifying, 64
    indicator, 218
    loss, 16
    policy decisions about, 59

species problem, 64
State of Observed Species report, 63–64
Stevens, Larry, 28
Stolzenburg, William, 204
Suckling, Keiran, 81, 190
survival time scale, 44
systematics, 63–64, 69–70

T

talus, 217, 220, 222, 230
taxonomy, 63, 69–70
Terborgh, John, 20, 52, 80, 146–47, 151
Terrestrial Observation and Prediction Systems (TOPS), 233–34
Three Forests Coalition, 92–93
Tippie, Sherri, 22, 238–44
Tompkins, Doug, 79
tracking, animal, 150, 175–94
Trek West, 244–46
trophic cascades, 125–26, 137, 139, 140, 143–48, 164, 172–73, 183
Turner, Woody, 234, 235–36
turnover, 39

U

umbrella species, 16, 194
Utah, 92–117

V

Vacariu, Kim, 23–24, 26, 75
Vahldiek, Paul, 136–48
Viable Populations for Conservation (Soulé), 56
vision mapping, 80–81

W

Wallace, Alfred Russel, 30–34, 37, 64
Water (Outwater), 108
water cycle, 162–63
waterways, 92, 108, 184, 245–46
Watt, Rob, 3–18

Western Governors' Association (WGA), 82, 206
Western Landowner Network, 142, 201
Western Transportation Institute, 206
wetlands, 108–9
Where the Wild Things Were (Stolzenburg), 204
Wick, John, 134–35
Wilcox, Bruce, 44, 52
Wilderness Act, 41, 195
Wildlands Network, 9, 22–23, 84, 140, 177, 201, 245, 246. *See also* Wildlands Project
Wildlands Project, 79–81, 245. *See also* Wildlands Network
Wildlife Conservation Society (WCS), 203
Wildlife Corridor Conservation bill, 255n70
Wildlife Habitat Council, 206
Wild Utah Project, 22, 122
willows, 110, 112–15
Wilson, E. O., 20, 38–40, 47, 52, 77
Wolf, Shaye, 224–25, 227, 228
Wolf's Tooth, The (Eisenberg), 136, 140
wolverines, 207, 208–9
wolves, 123–26, 143–45, 150, 151, 162–74, 182
  and elk, 164–66
  as predators, 168–69
  in Yellowstone, 163–64, 167–68, 173
worms, 132–33
Worster, Donald, 92
Wylie, Philip, 45–47
Wyoming, 202–4

Y

Yellowstone National Park, 162–64, 167–68, 173
Yellowstone to Yukon Conservation Initiative (Y2Y), 12, 15

ACKNOWLEDGMENTS

THE IDEA FOR THIS BOOK CAME TO ME IN THE PRESENCE OF HEALY Hamilton, and I'm surely not the first or the last to be hugely inspired by her gift for communicating how nature works and what it needs. The appearances of Kenyon Fields in these pages are far less than his outsize patience and generosity with me deserve. Cristina Eisenberg consistently shared her knowledge and experience with me. Although the research trip I went on with Wendy Moore and Rick Brusca in Arizona landed on the proverbial cutting-room floor, I'm grateful for their insights, especially into the Sky Island region. (Also, they run a highly civilized field study, and that's fun). Matt Wagner of Freedom to Roam has been a great confederate and also helped me make important contacts.

General context for many specialties was provided to me by Lance and April Craighead, Connie Millar, John Weaver, Diana Hadley, and Kim Vicariu. Michael Robinson's book *Predatory Bureaucracy* deserves special mention, as do my conversations with Robinson, which helped me begin to understand the cultural imprints on western cattle-grazing practices. Courtney White of the Quivira Coalition added much depth to my impressions. David Johns shared with me wisdom gleaned from decades of involvement in conservation. UC Berkeley professors John Harte, David Ackerly, Anthony Barnosky, and Steve Bessinger allowed me to sit almost quietly (furiously typing) in their graduate seminar on climate change and biodiversity—if the world can be saved, these guys and their super-intelligent, turbo-motivated students will have a big part in doing it.

It is my privilege to enjoy consistent mentoring over the years from Peter Wiley, Roy Eisenhart, Matthew Lore, and Eric Himmel. My agent, Eleanor Jackson, is one of the world's great readers, a great advocate, and a valued friend. Good friends supported my field adventures in various ways; thanks to Eve Niquette, Diane Foug, Brigitte Sandquist, Erica Newman, Jean Wildberg, Ann Van Balen, and Marvin Morgenstein.

Thanks to Holly Rubino, Antoinette Smith, Meredith Dias, Tracy Salcedo-Chourre, Sue Murray, Kathleen Rocheleau, Melissa Haendel, Michael Macrone, and Irene Ray (Chris Ray's mom!) for careful reading and feedback. An Alicia Patterson Foundation fellowship provided essential financial support, and a bucolic stay at the Mesa Refuge was a blessing; thank you, kind philanthropists.

Cella Mitchell, the Wallace Stegner Environmental Librarian at the San Francisco Public Library, dug up some really useful books and materials for me, and her enthusiasm for the subject kept me buoyed in general. Most of the printed materials I relied on for research—books and journal articles—came to me one way or another through the San Francisco library system. As of this writing, Governor Jerry Brown is proposing to cut all state funding to California's public libraries; as federal funding levels are set by the measure of state monies, this would deal a double death blow to a library system that today exemplifies "connectivity." Most of the books I sourced came through Link+, a service the library provides by connecting users to library catalogs in a big geographical area. These budget cuts would sharply curtail Link+ and make important research inaccessible to most. As nature needs connection to persist, so does our intellectual life depend on connection to our historical repository of knowledge—which is in the library!

Deepest gratitude to the multitude of field assistants, volunteers, and everybody else working in conservation on planes both esoteric and mundane, many of whom I have been lucky enough to meet on this journey. They are doing the right thing. Finally, my husband Richard and children Eva and Nick made the book possible, and for me, necessary.